Asian Megatrends

Asian Megatrends

Rajiv Biswas

palgrave
macmillan

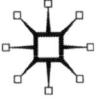

First published 2016 by
PALGRAVE MACMILLAN

Palgrave Macmillan in the UK is an imprint of Macmillan Publishers Limited, registered in England, company number 785998, of Houndmills, Basingstoke, Hampshire RG21 6XS.

Palgrave Macmillan in the US is a division of St Martin's Press LLC, 175 Fifth Avenue, New York, NY 10010.

Palgrave Macmillan is the global academic imprint of the above companies and has companies and representatives throughout the world.

Palgrave® and Macmillan® are registered trademarks in the United States, the United Kingdom, Europe and other countries.

ISBN: 978–1–137–44188–1

This book is printed on paper suitable for recycling and made from fully managed and sustained forest sources. Logging, pulping and manufacturing processes are expected to conform to the environmental regulations of the country of origin.

A catalogue record for this book is available from the British Library.

Library of Congress Cataloging-in-Publication Data.

Biswas, Rajiv, author.
　　Asian megatrends / Rajiv Biswas.
　　　　pages cm
　　Includes bibliographical references and index.
　　ISBN 978–1–137–44188–1
　　1. Asia – Economic conditions – 21st century. 2. Economic development – Asia – 21st century. 3. Economic forecasting – Asia. I. Title.
HC412B5467 2016
330.95—dc23   2015025948

Contents

List of Figures

List of Tables

Preface

The emerging markets risk landscape

I learnt about emerging markets risk at the sharp end, caught in a war. Bullets slammed into walls next to me and fighter jets flew overhead, strafing and rocketing artillery positions in the woods nearby. At night, the sky above the inner city glowed an ugly orange-red from the flames of the burning buildings, as fierce fighting raged and artillery shelling continued intermittently.

After some days of intense fighting a ceasefire was declared. I met a neighbour who was returning home from his militia unit, still wearing his heavily stained military uniform and helmet. Normally he was a tough, confident man, but he looked devastated by his experience. He explained that his unit had been decimated in the fighting, with heavy casualties and few survivors. The talk turned to the gruesome atrocities being committed by the enemy forces, and what would happen when they occupied our area. Fortunately that never transpired. Many years later I am glad to say we shared happier times, snorkelling, spear-fishing and enjoying beachside barbeques with his family.

Sadly there are few happy endings amidst the turbulence of conflict that still afflicts many developing countries. The lives of millions are destroyed by wars, famine and genocide. Seventy years after World War Two ended and the Bretton Woods system was established, many developing countries are still ravaged by recent conflict. Syria, Iraq, Ukraine, Bosnia, Libya, Nigeria, Yemen, Georgia, Lebanon, Somalia and Afghanistan are among these nations, but the list is very long.

At the end of World War Two, much of the Asia-Pacific, Africa and the Middle East were still under European colonial rule. During the next two decades, many of these European colonies obtained their independence, either by bitter revolutionary conflict, as in the Indonesian fight for independence against their Dutch colonial rulers, or by relatively peaceful transition of government, as in Malaya.

Although most of the world's colonies that existed in 1945 won their independence over the next twenty years, few of these nations have managed to achieve either developed country status or stable governments.

The Middle East is ablaze in a sea of conflict and political turmoil, with civil wars currently raging in Iraq, Libya, Syria and Yemen. Egypt, one of the world's largest emerging markets, has also been through tremendous political upheaval since the Arab Spring. The economies of these nations have been wrecked by the effects of protracted conflict.

Several years ago when the situation in Yemen was deteriorating politically but it was still not a conflict zone, I was asked if I would consider undertaking a consultancy project to help with economic development planning for Yemen. I was assured that the political situation was safe enough to live in the country while conducting the project. I had in my briefcase at this meeting the same day's newspaper stating that the US State Department had just issued an advisory recommending its citizens to leave Yemen. While I could figure out the political risk outlook for myself and declined the offer on the spot, I also could not see much purpose in doing a strategic development plan for a nation on the verge of collapsing into civil war. Sadly the situation in Yemen has continued to deteriorate ever since then and my political assessment of the outlook for Yemen unfortunately proved to be quite right. In this case, my life depended on making the right political risk assessment.

Yet several decades ago when I lived in Aden, it was so peaceful that I would walk all around the inner city at any time of day or night without any concern about my personal safety. Indeed it was so tranquil that we would drive to the BP Beach Club in Little Aden at weekends to swim and have lunch at their excellent restaurant, and we would even drive there at night to watch movies being screened in the club. Another favorite pastime was to go to the open air cinema in the Crater district of Aden, relaxing in the evening weather after the blazing afternoon heat, sitting amongst the very friendly and good-natured Yemeni families also enjoying the cool night air.

Much of Sub-Saharan Africa has also fared poorly since independence, with many nations still mired in abject poverty. Economic development has been held back by the effects of political instability and conflict, such as the devastating civil wars that took place in Somalia, Sierra Leone and Rwanda. Nigeria, Africa's largest economy, has been destabilized by Boko Haram, an Islamic fundamentalist extremist group that is waging a civil war against the Nigerian government. Kenya has also suffered from attacks by Al Shabaab, an Islamic militant group linked to Al Qaeda, including recent attacks on the Westgate shopping mall in Nairobi and the slaughter of university students at the Garissa University College campus. These attacks have disrupted Kenya's tourism industry, which has long been a vital part of the economy.

Having lived in the Horn of Africa in both Somalia and Ethiopia, I have witnessed the tremendous natural beauty of both nations; if durable peace and stability returned to the Horn of Africa, international tourism could play a very important role in driving future economic development. While living in Addis Ababa, I sometimes went on camping trips to the Awash River and the Rift Valley lakes, occasionally going on hikes through the rugged bush terrain. I also visited other wonderful sites in Ethiopia, including the spectacular Blue Nile Falls near Bahar Dar, and excavations of one of the Queen of Sheba's palaces. Recently I was serendipitously reunited with my two best friends from my school in Addis Ababa, Ralph Dubisch and Ed Fortenberry, both Californians, and we shared many fond memories about our various experiences in Ethiopia.

In Somalia, the undeveloped coastline near Mogadishu was also fascinating, and our regular weekend hunting trips usually yielded a rich bounty of wild game, including deer, warthogs, guinea fowl, partridge and even duck. This was no aristocratic pastime but an essential source of food, and was the only way to get fresh, reliable meat. There were no supermarkets and the open air meat markets in Mogadishu had unrefrigerated meat lying out in the open air that had been decaying in the hot tropical weather for an unknown length of time. The Indian Ocean was teeming with plentiful large fish, but there were also enough prowling sharks to keep the risks evenly balanced for both sides when spearfishing.

With political stability and the development of local tourism infrastructure, international tourism could again become a very important growth engine for the East African region, as the rugged natural beauty of the East African rift valleys, the beautiful Indian Ocean coastline and spectacular sites such as the Blue Nile Falls would be a major attraction for international tourists.

The failure of many developing countries to achieve political stability and sustained economic development has generated increasing shock waves for the developed world. The advanced economies face large inflows of illegal refugees fleeing political unrest and poverty, escalating terrorism threats from terror groups thriving in climates of failed governance, and the growing threat of transnational organized crime groups exploiting weak governance in many emerging markets.

Against this relatively bleak political and economic landscape in developing countries, the Asia-Pacific stands out as a region that has made tremendous progress in advancing living standards and improving political stability during the past 50 years.

With around 60 per cent of the world's population living in Asia, the prospects for the Asia-Pacific region in the long-term will play a very important role in determining the overall progress of economic development globally. However, the key structural trends that have driven the rapid growth of Asian economies are now going through significant change. The megatrends that will shape the Asian political and economic landscape over the next thirty years will therefore be crucial to the future economic development of Asia as well as the global economy.

I would like to acknowledge the help and advice of friends and colleagues who have been positive influences during my many years of work on Asian emerging markets.

I would first like to acknowledge the research help of Danika Biswas for this book, which is much appreciated.

I would also like to particularly thank Zbyszko Tabernacki, Elisabeth Waelbroeck-Rocha, Tan Sri Dato Michael Yeoh, Ambassador Pradap Pibulsonggram, Indrajit Coomaraswamy, Professor Joergen Oerstroem Moeller, Frank Jurgen-Richter, Dr Tim Huxley, Vivek Tulpule and Paul Morris for their great helpfulness over the years. I would also like to thank Professor Chris Alden, Dr Alvaro Mendez and Dr Yury Bikbaev of the London School of Economics for encouraging my research on Asian development finance. Special thanks are also due to Heng Qian in Beijing and Yong Ngee Ng in Singapore. I am also most appreciative of the advice and guidance from the editorial team at Palgrave Macmillan.

The views and opinions expressed in this book are entirely my own, based on a lifetime of observing the Asia-Pacific and other emerging markets, and should not be attributed in any way to any organization I have worked for or been associated with, whether public or private, or to any other person.

Introduction

Beyond the East Asian Miracle

Asia's economic ascendancy

The economic ascent of East Asia since the end of World War Two has transformed the Asia-Pacific economic landscape, lifting hundreds of millions of Asians out of poverty. The rapid economic development of war-ravaged economies such as Japan and South Korea within a few decades has been remarkable.

In the Office of the Government of Hyogo Prefecture in the city of Kobe in Japan where I used to work, there was a large aerial photo on display in the entrance of the main building showing Kobe at the end of World War Two. It showed that Kobe had been absolutely flattened by US Air Force bombing. Most of Japan's other major industrial cities and ports were also destroyed by US Air Force bombing, with the most extreme devastation in Hiroshima and Nagasaki after the nuclear bombings.

Seoul suffered a similar fate during the Korean War, as it became a battleground during the initial surprise attack by North Korean forces in June 1950, was later recaptured by US and South Korean forces after General MacArthur's Incheon landing, then was occupied by the Chinese army when it invaded South Korea. Seoul was again retaken in March 1951 by the US and South Korean forces when they counter-attacked. In 1953 when an armistice was declared, South Korea was one of the world's poorest nations, devastated in the aftermath of the Korean War, which had resulted in over one million civilians being killed. Seoul had been reduced to rubble with most of its population having fled during the early stages of the war. The state of the South Korean economy seemed so hopeless that General MacArthur said at the end of the Korean War that barring a miracle, it would take 100 years for South Korea's economy to be restored.

Yet within two decades, both Japan and South Korea had become fast-growing industrial economies. By 1964, Japan officially joined the ranks of the advanced industrial economies when it became a member of the OECD. South Korea became an OECD member in 1996.

Taiwan, Hong Kong and Singapore were also among the East Asian economies that experienced rapid economic growth since the 1960s, and have subsequently joined the ranks of the world's high income economies. Brunei, endowed with oil and gas resources, also has become one of Asia's high income economies.

The greatest transformative impact on the Asia-Pacific region occurred in 1978 after China's Senior Leader Deng Xiaoping shifted Chinese economic policy away from the traditional communist policy framework that had been the orthodoxy in the Soviet Union as well as in China under Chairman Mao. The gradual liberalization of the Chinese economy and the attraction of foreign investment into China's special economic zones created a long phase of very rapid growth in the Chinese economy, with average real GDP growth rates averaging 10 per cent per year, a pace that was sustained for three decades.

China's rapid economic ascent from a poor, low-income rural economy to a manufacturing export powerhouse since 1978 has lifted hundreds of millions of Chinese out of extreme poverty. It has also created a large new middle class consumer society in China that is becoming an important new market for other Asian economies.

However despite the East Asian economic miracle, Asia as a region still faces tremendous political and economic challenges in the next two decades.

Despite the tremendous achievements in poverty reduction in Northeast Asia, South Asia still has an estimated 500 million people who remain mired in poverty, with a significant proportion of the populations of India, Pakistan and Bangladesh still living in extreme poverty. In Southeast Asia the most populous nations, notably Indonesia and the Philippines, still have significant levels of rural poverty, although there has been substantial progress in poverty reduction over the last decade.

Megatrends

A number of megatrends will play an important role in determining the prospects for the Asia-Pacific region over the next two decades.

A key megatrend will be the impact of demographic change. Some of the advanced economies of East Asia, including the world's second and third largest economies, China and Japan, are experiencing demographic ageing, which will have significant implications for their future growth rates. However other populous Asian economies, including India and Indonesia, have much more youthful demographics, which is something of a double-edged sword.

Another megatrend will be the rapid growth in the number of Asian middle class households, which is expected to make domestic consumption a stronger growth engine for many Asian developing countries, as well as playing a more significant role as a global growth driver. China has already become a middle income economy, with per capita GDP approaching USD 7,000 per person. The spending power of the Chinese consumer is having an increasingly important global impact, as reflected in the global auto industry, with China having overtaken the US to become the world's largest auto market since 2010.

The economic ascendancy of China, which is projected to become the world's largest economy within about a decade, is transforming the global geopolitical and economic landscape. In the Asia-Pacific region, China is playing an increasingly important role in Asia-Pacific trade and investment flows, as well as becoming a much more significant player in global development finance and regional banking.

China's economic ascendancy is also reflected in China's rapid growth in military spending, as strong economic growth rates allow substantial annual increases in government expenditure, including for the defence budget. China's growing military power has created security concerns among many of its Asia-Pacific neighbours, including Japan, the Philippines, Vietnam and India. One of the key challenges that the Asia-Pacific region will face over the next decade will be to manage the risk of regional conflict occurring.

Another megatrend that will reshape the global political and economic landscape over the next two decades will be the rise of Asia's second BRICS economy, India. The Chinese economy has significantly outperformed the Indian economy in the pace of economic development over the last three decades. However with Chinese economic growth rates moderating due to key structural factors such as ageing demographics, the Indian economy may be able to grow faster than China on a sustained basis over the next two decades, if supported by progressive economic reforms and sound macroeconomic management. The economic ascendancy of Asia's second BRICS economy, if realized, will unleash a second wave of emerging Asian middle class consumer spending over the next two decades, following the first wave of Chinese consumer spending that is already underway.

The rapid growth of emerging Asian economies will also continue to drive the urbanization of developing Asia. The Chinese government has set a policy objective of increasing the share its total population living in urban areas from 53.7 per cent in 2013 to 60 per cent by 2020, with an additional 100 million rural migrant workers projected to be given residency rights in urban areas of China. While the size of China's population is being constrained by the long-established one-child policy introduced by Chairman Mao as well as the gradual impact of demographic ageing, India's youthful demographic and projected rapid economic growth signals rapid future growth of populations in urban areas. ASEAN nations will also face major challenges from urbanization, with ASEAN capital cities such as Jakarta, Manila and Bangkok set to experience significant further population growth over the next two decades.

Managing urbanization in developing Asia will therefore be one of the most important policy challenges facing Asian governments over the next two decades, requiring large infrastructure development programs as well as strategies to prevent some of the negative characteristics of urbanization, including crime, traffic congestion and adverse environmental impact effects due to carbon emissions, ground-level air pollution and pressure on water resources.

Risks and challenges

Despite the considerable progress in economic development achieved by many Asian economies since the 1950s, there are many downside risks and challenges facing the Asia-Pacific region in coming decades.

Political risk remains a key challenge in many parts of Asia. Unresolved territorial disputes still result in simmering political and military tensions in many parts of Asia, with India and Pakistan having ongoing military clashes along their border while their territorial dispute over Kashmir remains a key source of political and military friction. Territorial disputes in the South China Sea between China and several Southeast Asian nations, including the Philippines and Vietnam, have escalated in the last three years due to construction of structures on some of the shoals and reefs in the Spratly Islands. Meanwhile Japan and China continue to have a major territorial dispute over the sovereignty of the Senkaku/Diaoyu islets in the East China Sea. The Korean peninsula also remains one of the world's most dangerous military flashpoints, with the nuclear armed North Korean dictatorship remaining a key threat to regional stability. Therefore the political risk outlook for Asia over the next two decades still remains subject to a high degree of uncertainty.

Resource security will become an increasingly important challenge for the Asia-Pacific region, as Asian nations compete for scarce resources, notably oil and water. A key potential source of regional tensions and conflict is competition for scarce water resources. Both India and China are facing water crises over the next two decades, and there are concerns that the diversion of flows from the Himalayas could create potential for conflict between the two nations unless carefully managed through bilateral negotiations. Similarly the management of the water resources of the Mekong River is a political flashpoint, as the construction of dams along this major waterway is already creating regional tensions and creating major environmental problems for many communities living along this key waterway.

While globalization has been a very important driver for the successful economic development of many East Asian industrial economies since the 1950s, the Asia-Pacific region faces rapidly rising threats from the dark side of globalization. The proliferation of terrorist groups and organized crime organizations has been facilitated by the rapid growth of cross-border trade and investment flows, which have helped to disguise the activities of such criminal groups.

The increasing number of terrorist groups in Asia linked to Al Qaeda and ISIS has become a threat to peace and stability in the Asian region, with some nation states such as Afghanistan and Pakistan on the brink of becoming failed states due to insurgencies and attacks by extremist groups. Islamic terrorist groups linked to ISIS have also become an increasing security concern in Southeast Asian nations, including Indonesia, Malaysia and the Philippines. Even China, with its very powerful armed forces and police resources has faced significant threats and terrorist attacks from Islamic extremist groups that have built up amongst the Uighur population in Zhejiang province. The links that have developed between Uighur terrorists and Al Qaeda as well as ISIS are considered to be an important evolving risk that is a high policy priority for China.

There are also economic risks facing Asia over coming decades. Despite decades of rapid economic growth, the East Asian economies also face significant economic headwinds in coming decades. One such headwind is the impact of demographic ageing, which becomes an increasingly significant drag on potential economic growth rates in many of the advanced Asian economies. Furthermore, rising wage levels and slowing productivity growth rates are also creating pressures for the competitiveness of the manufacturing export sectors of industrialized Asian economies.

One of the most important structural changes influencing East Asian economies is the impact of demographic ageing, which has already been felt severely in Japan, where the population has been falling every year since 2004. China's population is also gradually ageing, and the implications of demographic ageing will have a significant effect on Chinese long-term GDP growth rates over the next twenty years. Ageing demographics will also have a significant impact on the long-term growth outlook for other East Asian economies, including South Korea and Singapore.

Another economic challenge facing East Asia is the impact of rising wage costs on competitiveness. Many East Asian economies such as Japan, South Korea, Hong Kong and Singapore, built their economies upon the rapid growth of low-cost manufacturing exports to the US and European markets. However rising wage costs have over time reduced their relative competitiveness in these low-cost manufacturing segments, forcing their economies to restructure towards higher value-added manufactures as well as other industry sectors, notably services.

The hollowing-out of the manufacturing sectors of Asia's most industrialized economies creates significant challenges for these economies, which need to find new growth industries for the future. The Chinese economy, which had benefited tremendously from the hollowing out of other Northeast Asian economies, notably Japan, over the last three decades, is now also facing the impact of rising wage costs. This is gradually eroding the competitiveness of Chinese low-cost manufacturing export industries in coastal Chinese provinces. Therefore China is entering a period of industrial transformation, and faces a protracted period of disruptive change across its key industries. In response, the Chinese government has recently introduced the "Made in China" strategy to transform the Chinese economy towards a higher value-added manufacturing sector by 2025. This is a significant challenge facing the Chinese economy over the medium to long-term and has become a high priority for the Chinese government.

Outlook

Despite these threats and challenges to the Asia-Pacific outlook, the region is expected to be the fastest growing part of the world economy for the next decade, underpinned by the expansion in consumer demand in Asian emerging markets. Based on current growth trends, the Asia-Pacific region is expected to account for around 40 per cent of world GDP by 2025, and the megatrends affecting the Asia-Pacific region will be increasingly important for the rest of the global economy.

The significance of the Asia-Pacific region will continue to rise, and the APAC region will account for an increasing share of global revenues for many global multinationals in the next decade and beyond. One of the most important megatrends in the Asia-Pacific region will be the rapid growth in the number of middle class households in Asian emerging markets, notably in China, India and ASEAN. This is likely to result in the further pivot of global multinationals towards the Asia-Pacific, as Asian markets become increasingly important drivers of new revenue growth for multinationals across a wide spectrum of industries ranging from manufacturing industries such as autos, electronics and consumer goods to services such as banking, insurance, health care and logistics.

Most importantly, if the Asia-Pacific region can maintain peace and stability to underpin strong regional economic growth, this will potentially lift hundreds of millions of people out of poverty over the next three decades.

Chapter 1

Asia's Consumer Spending Boom

Since the 1960s global consumer spending growth has been driven by the affluent societies in the US, Europe and Japan. However, the world economy is entering a new phase when the consumer spending of emerging Asia will become the most important driver for world consumer spending growth over the next two decades. This will be one of the key megatrends transforming the global economy, underpinned by strong GDP growth and rapid growth in the total number of middle class households in Asian developing countries, led by China.

Moderating long-term potential growth rates in the OECD countries has resulted in slower growth in consumer spending, notably in Japan where the falling population has been a major drag on household spending growth. Meanwhile the protracted effects of the global financial crisis in Europe have also resulted in weak consumer spending growth for close to a decade. Real retail spending growth in the European Union has been stagnant or declining in each year between 2008 and 2013, with very weak positive growth achieved in 2014.

In stark contrast to the performance of retail sales in Europe, Chinese retail sales growth has exceeded 10 per cent per year in

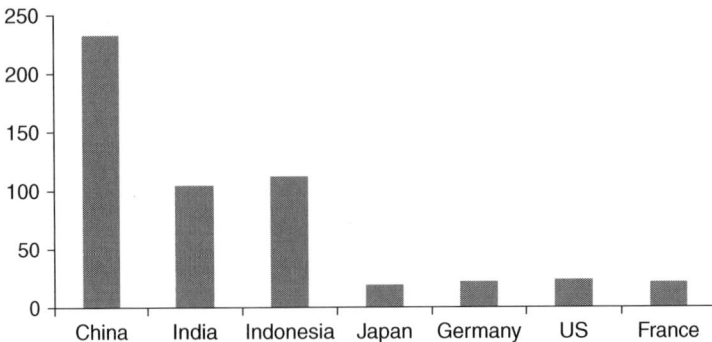

Figure 1.1   Household consumption growth, 2006–13

Note: Percentage change from 2006 to 2013.
Source: World Bank data.

real terms for every single year between 2005 and 2013. The rapid projected growth in the size of the consumer markets of China, India and ASEAN reflects rapid GDP growth, which is resulting in strong growth in per capita GDP levels as well as substantial growth in the total number of middle class households in Asian emerging markets.

The implications of sustained strong growth in consumer demand in Asian emerging markets is resulting in major shifts in the corporate strategies of multinationals, as they reposition their businesses towards the fast-growing markets of Asia. Multinationals have responded by increasing their foreign direct investment into Asian emerging markets, to expand their local presence and boost regional production to supply Asian markets.

The rapid growth of consumer demand in Asian emerging markets will also help to catalyse the growth of Asian companies in the manufacturing and service sectors, and will accelerate the rise of Asian emerging market multinationals. The tremendous expansion in the size of China's domestic consumer market has already helped the development of many Chinese multinationals in a wide range of industry sectors, including telecommunications equipment manufacturing giant Huawei and Chinese e-commerce leader Alibaba Group.

China's consumer market

Chinese per capita GDP when China's great economic reforms began in 1978 was an estimated USD 180 per year. China was an extremely poor nation, with a large proportion of the population living in extreme poverty. Within one generation, the nation has experienced a far-reaching transformation in living standards, buoyed by sustained rapid growth averaging 10 per cent per year for three decades. By 2014, Chinese per capita GDP had exceeded USD 7,400 with China no longer a low (or even lower middle) income country but defined as an upper middle income country according to World Bank classifications.

China's major coastal cities, notably Beijing, Shanghai, Shenzen, Tianjin and Guangzhou, have far higher per capita incomes than the Chinese national average. Beijing, which is China's most affluent major city in terms of household incomes, had reached per capita GDP levels of an estimated USD 16,000 by 2014, around double the national average. The per capita GDP of Shanghai was comparable, at around USD 15,700 in 2014. These levels of per capita GDP are similar to those of the lower range of advanced economies. When compared to European per capita GDP levels, they are similar to those of Hungary or Malta, and well above those of Romania or Bulgaria.

The sheer weight of total Chinese GDP is also propelling China higher in terms of its ranking in world consumer markets. China has become the world's second largest economy after the US, with its total GDP at around USD 10.5 trillion in 2015, compared to US GDP of 18 trillion. China's GDP is now more than double that of Japan, which is estimated to be USD 4 trillion in 2015.

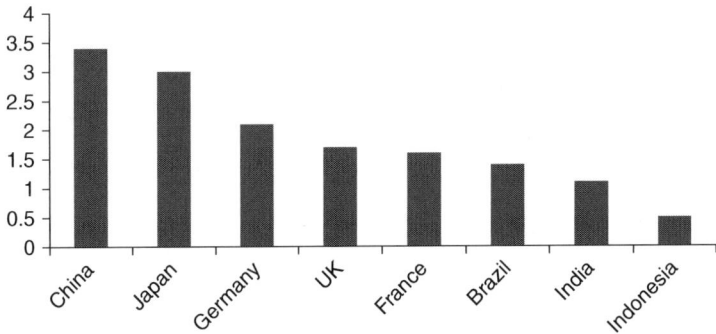

Figure 1.2　Size of consumer markets, household final consumption

Note: Trillion USD, nominal terms, 2013.
Source: World Bank data.

The rising affluence of Chinese households is becoming increasingly evident in key consumer industries in both manufacturing and services.

In the manufacturing sector, one of the most important indicators of the growing global importance of the Chinese consumer occurred in 2009, when the domestic sales of autos in China overtook the US for the first time. Chinese light vehicle sales reached 13.6 million in 2009, while US sales slumped sharply due to the impact of the global financial crisis, declining to 10.4 million light vehicles.

The Chinese auto industry has continued to grow rapidly since 2009, with total light vehicle sales in China reaching 23.5 million vehicles by 2014. By comparison, US light vehicle sales reached 16.5 million vehicles in 2014, a strong rebound of 58 per cent from the 2009 trough, but still considerably below the sales volume in China.

This rapid growth of Chinese auto sales has resulted in the Chinese auto manufacturing sector becoming the largest in the world, and, in turn, becoming a strategic focus for the world's largest automakers. While factors such as traffic congestion and regulatory controls to limit the number of vehicles in major Chinese cities will become increasingly important constraints on the growth of Chinese auto sales in some of these large cities, rapidly rising household incomes will continue to support strong demand for autos across many of the smaller cities and rural regions of China, where traffic congestion is not yet a key constraint.

In the service industry, there are also clear examples of the rapid rise of Chinese consumer spending power. An important segment of the services industry in China that is growing rapidly is e-commerce, which is already estimated to be a USD 400 billion industry and has overtaken the US, becoming the largest e-commerce market in the world in 2013. The rapid growth of e-commerce in China has been driven by wide use of the internet and mobile phones, supported by the strong logistics industry presence in many Chinese cities.

One of the most dramatic signs of the rising affluence of Chinese households is the number of international tourism visits by Chinese abroad. In 2005, China was the seventh largest source market for international tourism in terms of total spending. By 2012, China had become the world's largest source market for international tourism, with spending by Chinese tourists abroad reaching USD 102 billion, up around 40 per cent from 2011, according to the United Nations World Tourism Organization. (UN World Tourism Organization Press Release 13020, "China the New Number One Tourism Source Market in the World", UNWTO, Madrid, 4 April 2013.) The UNWTO statistics indicate that the total number of international trips by Chinese tourists rose from 10 million in 2000 to 83 million by 2012.

Chinese international tourism visits have continued to grow rapidly since 2012, with the total number of international trips by Chinese tourists rising to 103 million by 2014, according to UNWTO statistics. Total spending by Chinese tourists abroad rose to USD 165 billion by 2014. This rapid growth reflects rising per capita incomes, supported by other factors such as the large number of new airports that have been built in China over the last decade and the rapid growth of low-cost carriers in the Asia-Pacific commercial air transportation industry, which has facilitated the boom in outbound tourism.

It is in Asia where the impact of these large statistical increases is most evident on the ground. Nowhere is this more apparent than in Thailand, where Chinese tourist arrivals reached 4.7 million in 2014, up 48 per cent on the previous year. Compared with 2011, when there were 1.7 million Chinese tourism visits to Thailand, the scale of the increase is staggering, with an additional 3 million tourist visits just 3 years later.

One of the rather bizarre catalysts for the rapid growth of Chinese tourism visits to Thailand was the release of a Chinese movie called *Lost in Thailand* in 2012, which was made as a low-budget comedy about Chinese tourists visiting Thailand but became a big Chinese language blockbuster, triggering a rush of Chinese tourists to Thailand that has continued to gather momentum.

I had noticed the significant increase in Chinese tourists in Thai hotels even during 2012 and 2013, but during a visit to Bangkok in 2015, the hotel I was staying in, located in the most central tourist area of Bangkok, was filled with Chinese tourists. The shopping malls and streets were also packed with Chinese visitors, many laden down with purchases from the department stores.

With China in the process of negotiating the construction of major new Thai rail links that could eventually connect with China's high speed rail network, the rail linkages between southern China and Thailand could result in large new increases in Chinese tourism visits to Thailand using the future rail connectivity.

The Thai economy is heavily dependent on the tourism sector which accounts for around 8 per cent of GDP in terms of the direct impact effects of tourism output, and as much as 16 per cent of GDP after taking account of indirect multiplier effects. If large-scale increases in Chinese tourism inflows continue over the long term, this could have a very substantial positive impact on underlying economic growth in Thailand at a time when some of the other growth engines of the Thai economy have been sluggish.

While the impact effects of Chinese consumer spending in Thailand are particularly dramatic, there are similar effects evident in many other countries in the Asia-Pacific region in the last five years, as Chinese tourism visits have risen rapidly to many destinations.

Despite the geopolitical tensions between China and Japan over disputed sovereign territorial claims, which had even triggered widespread anti-Japanese riots in China in 2012, Chinese tourism visits to Japan boomed in 2014. Total Chinese tourism visitors to Japan in the 2014 calendar year reached 2.4 million, up 83 per cent from 2013, when political tensions had significantly dampened bilateral tourism flows.

When I visited Tokyo at the end of the Chinese New Year festival in 2015, I wanted to buy a small item from the duty-free shop at the airport in Tokyo. Normally Japan is a pretty efficient country and there aren't long queues. However, I found myself confronted with a very long queue of people waiting to pay at the checkouts and wondered what was going on. I soon realized that all the people in the queue were Chinese tourists, since they were all clutching their passports in their hands, and each seemed to be carrying many identical boxes that they wanted to buy. While I waited in the long line, I looked at these boxes, assuming they were chocolates. However, I later realized that the boxes contained cosmetics, and it seemed that Japanese cosmetics were particularly sought after by the Chinese tourists. No doubt the significant depreciation of the yen since 2012 had also made Japan an increasingly popular destination for Chinese tourists.

Another sight that has become increasingly common in airports is to see Chinese travelers buying infant formula milk powder in large quantities before catching their flight back home. This has become a new trend for Chinese shoppers ever since the Chinese milk powder scandal in 2008, when melamine was found in some milk powder products.

The flood of mainland Chinese travellers buying milk powder in Hong Kong became problematic some years ago, as local Hong Kong shoppers were finding it increasingly difficult to buy supplies for themselves. The Hong Kong government reacted by creating new rules restricting the amount of milk powder that could be carried. I remember finding out about this while in Hong Kong airport, when I heard repeated announcements on the public address system warning passengers that there were significant penalties for carrying milk powder above the individual quota out of Hong Kong. In a world where customs officials usually target criminals who may be carrying narcotics or terrorists with deadly weapons, it seemed to be a bizarre situation where the Hong Kong officials were instead focusing their efforts on their own most wanted list, namely families carrying too much baby formula. One would have thought that the Hong Kong shops could have just airfreighted in large volumes of baby formula from Europe or New Zealand rather than going down this rather draconian route.

Chinese tourists spend a significant part of their travel budget on shopping, which accounts for around one-third of their total travel expenditure. This further increases the benefit to the local economy of the countries they are visiting. Some of the drivers for this very high level of spending on shopping are due to scale of the counterfeit industry in mainland China, as well as relatively high taxes on luxury goods. This makes it particularly attractive for Chinese tourists to buy luxury goods and other products such as cosmetics while visiting other countries. US and European cities are particularly popular for shopping expeditions to acquire high-value branded goods.

India's consumer market

The Indian consumer plays a key role in the overall structure of the Indian economy, with private consumption expenditure having accounted for around 60 per cent of total GDP in the 2014–15 financial year. Taking into account government spending, which accounted for a further 11 per cent of GDP, the total share of consumption in GDP was 71 per cent of the overall economy.

Total private consumption in India in 2013 was around USD 1.1 trillion, compared to Chinese household consumption of USD 3.4 trillion and US household consumption of 11.5 trillion. India is already a very large consumer market by international standards when measured in terms of total consumer spending, comparable to household consumption of USD 1.3 trillion in Italy and USD 1.6 trillion in France in 2013.

A number of factors make India a key strategic market for global multinationals over the next decade and beyond.

Firstly, Indian potential GDP growth over the next decade is in the range of 7 to 8 per cent, and with accelerated large-scale infrastructure development, this rate could even reach 9 per cent. India has already grown at 8 to 9 per cent per year for a sustained period of time during the first term of the UPA government led by Prime Minister Manmohan Singh. Such high growth rates would, if realized, translate into strong growth in private consumption spending, driving the size of the Indian consumer market. In the 2013–14 and 2014–15 financial years, even though GDP growth momentum had moderated well below the 8 to 9 per cent range achieved a few years earlier, Indian private consumption grew at 6.2 per cent each year in real terms. This represents very strong growth when compared with consumer spending growth in OECD countries over the same time period, and continues to make India a very attractive market for global multinationals.

Secondly, Indian per capita GDP levels are still very low, with India still being towards the lower end of the lower middle income classification of the World Bank. Therefore sustained rapid economic growth would drive buoyant growth in consumer spending, as millions of households would enter the middle class each year. At such low levels of per capita GDP, rapid income growth would generate strong growth in demand for a wide range of consumer goods, including consumer electronics such as TVs, mobile phones, refrigerators, air-conditioners and kitchen appliances as well as fast-moving consumer goods such as processed foods, toiletries and soft drinks. The auto and motorcycle industry would also be a fast-growing sector, particularly given the relatively low level of car ownership per capita in India due to low income levels.

As India eventually progresses into the ranks of the upper middle income economies, the propensity to spend on services will rise, as households have more disposable income to allocate for services such as banking products, insurance, health care, education and communications services.

ASEAN consumer markets

Although the two Asian BRICS economies China and India will be the largest drivers of future consumer spending growth in Asia over the next three decades, the ASEAN region is also a significant source of new consumer demand. ASEAN's population of around 600 million persons combined with sustained rapid GDP growth make the region one of the most significant growth hubs for the global economy over coming decades. Moreover there is considerable industrial development momentum in some of the ASEAN economies driven by large new foreign direct investment inflows to establish low-cost manufacturing facilities in the region due to rising labour costs in coastal China.

The most important single consumer market in ASEAN is Indonesia, since Indonesian GDP accounts for around 40 per cent of total ASEAN GDP. The Indonesian population of 250 million combined with rapidly growing household incomes in major cities has sustained rapid growth in consumer expenditure in Indonesia over the last decade during the period of President Yudhoyono's presidency. Measured in USD current prices, the size of the Indonesian consumer market has doubled in the decade since 2004, when President Yudhoyono took office. While the future momentum of the Indonesian economy over the medium term will depend on whether President Jokowi's administration can continue to implement significant economic reforms, the Indonesian economy has the potential to grow at 5 to 6 per cent per year, which will support a firm pace of expansion in consumer demand.

The Indonesian consumer market is one of the most attractive long-term growth opportunities in the world after China and India, due to the large size of the Indonesian population and potential for sustained strong growth in GDP and household incomes.

Japanese automakers have established a dominant position in the Indonesian domestic auto market, which has grown rapidly over the last decade. Strong growth in Indonesian consumer demand for cars resulted in significant expansion of auto production facilities in Indonesia, with total auto production reaching 1.3 million units in 2014, while motorcycle sales were 7.9 million units.

One of the attractions of the Indonesian consumer market is that per capita GDP levels are on the threshold of moving into the upper middle income category, which will underpin demand growth for consumer durable goods and also gradually boost Indonesian demand for services, including banking, insurance, healthcare and tourism.

ASEAN also has other markets that offer very promising long-term potential, including Vietnam, which has a potential growth rate of around 6 to 7 per cent per year with a population of around 90 million, and the Philippines, which has been growing at 6 to 7 per cent per year since 2011 and has a population of around 100 million.

The combined size of the ASEAN consumer market is already around USD 1 trillion, comparable to the size of India's consumer market. Consequently the Southeast Asian consumer market will remain one of the world's most attractive consumer market opportunities over the next decade and beyond.

The implications for multinationals

Multinationals are increasingly positioning their global business strategies to focus on the fast-growing markets of the Asia-Pacific as the APAC share of world GDP and consumer expenditure continues to rise.

In the commercial aviation industry, Boeing has forecast that the Asia-Pacific will become the largest air travel market in the world, and by 2033, 48 per cent of global travel will be either to or from the APAC region. Boeing has forecast that over the period until 2033, the APAC region will need 13,460 new commercial airplanes, with a total value of an estimated USD 2 trillion. This equates to around 34 per cent of total global orders for new commercial airplanes. Of this total, China will be the largest single APAC growth market, requiring around 6,000 new airplanes with a value of USD 870 billion (Boeing, "Current Market Outlook 2014–2033", Boeing Commercial Airplanes, Seattle, 2014).

Airbus had 1,100 of its aircraft being operated by Chinese airlines by January 2015. As a result of the growing importance of the Chinese aviation market, Airbus has built a final assembly plant for Airbus A320 commercial airliners in Tianjin, as a joint venture with Tianjin Free Trade Zone and China Aviation Industry Corporation. The joint venture has already entered a second phase that will run until 2025, and will also expand aircraft deliveries to other parts of the Asia-Pacific (Airbus, "Airbus in China", www.airbus.com).

In the auto industry, the importance of the fast-growing Asian market is demonstrated by the rapid growth of BMW Group sales in Asia. The BMW Group sales of BMW, Mini and Rolls Royce cars in Asia were 286,300 in 2010, but have subsequently been rising rapidly each year, reaching 658,400 in 2014. Asia accounted for around 20 per cent of BMW Group global sales in 2010 in terms of total units sold by region, but by 2014, the share of Asian sales had risen to 31 per cent. In 2014, BMW Group sales in Asia measured by number of autos sold was up +13.8 per cent compared to the previous year. The Chinese market continued to be the largest market for the BMW Group in Asia and has grown rapidly, from 11.6 per cent of the BMW Group global sales in 2010 to 21.6 per cent of global sales by 2014. In 2014, BMW Group sales in China in terms of units sold were up +16.6 per cent compared to the previous year (BMW Group, Annual Report 2014).

In the luxury industry, the importance of the Asia-Pacific region has grown rapidly over the last decade, notably due to the fast growth of the Chinese consumer market. The Asia-Pacific region accounted for 36 per cent of LVMH Group revenue in 2014. Japan remains a key market, with 7 per cent of LVMH Group revenue in

2014 attributable to Japan alone, and 412 LVMH stores located in the country, as well as 870 LVMH stores in the rest of Asia (LVMH Group, "LVMH 2014 Annual Report").

The Asian region accounted for 30 per cent of the LVMH Group's wines and spirits revenue in 2014, 41 per cent of fashion and leather goods revenue, and 39 per cent of the Group's watches and jewelry revenue. With the Asian market already accounting for such a large share of the LVMH Group's revenue, it will be interesting to see how high the Asian market share will rise over the next decade, as large Asian emerging markets such as India and Indonesia grow in size. While Indian demand for luxury brands has been more constrained than in China due to the much lower per capita GDP levels, it is likely that as India moves into the upper middle income group of countries that the demand for luxury brands will rise sharply among India's fast-growing upper middle class households.

The changing competitive landscape in Asia

Although the size of consumer markets in developing Asia is growing rapidly, Western multinationals are also facing a fast-changing competitive landscape, as Asian multinationals are growing their regional footprints and competing for market share.

Japanese multinationals have been long-established as global competitors across many sectors of manufacturing and services. However multinationals from Asian emerging market countries are also becoming important competitors in many sectors.

In consumer electronics and communications equipment, the Korean giants Samsung and LG have invested heavily in establishing plants across the Asian region, with large-scale investments in countries such as India and Vietnam. Chinese multinationals are also competing for market share in this segment, with Huawei becoming a leading global player smartphone market. Huawei's sales in Asian markets outside of China accounted for 14.7 per cent of group revenue in 2014, and rose by +9.6 per cent in 2014 (Huawei Investment and Holding Co. Ltd, 2014 Annual Report). Huawei has become a global technology leader for communications equipment, with global revenue hitting USD 46.5 billion in 2014, up 20.6 per cent on the previous year. Notably the consumer business group of Huawei showed a 32.6 per cent increase in revenue in 2014, growing its global revenue to USD 12 billion.

The Chinese government's new "Made in China 2025" strategy for the future development of China's manufacturing sector has made the development of Chinese brands in global markets one of its key strategies for the next decade.

Asian automakers are also expanding their regional footprint, with Hyundai having become one of the leading auto brands in the Indian domestic auto market as well as having made India an important hub for production of Hyundai cars for export markets. Tata Group's JLR division has entered the Chinese auto market with a new plant having been built in Jiangsu province for production of the Land Rover Evoque sports utility as well as a Jaguar model.

In the banking sector, large Asian banks are increasingly seeking to use their balance sheets to expand their regional footprint. Japan's banks have a long history in trade finance and corporate banking in Asia. China's largest banks, including ICBC and Bank of China, have been expanding their branch network across Asia as part of a wider global push. Singapore's OCBC, DBS and UOB have been building their presence in other ASEAN countries. UOB has retail operations in Thailand, Malaysia and Indonesia. DBS also has a large regional footprint, including operations in mainland China, Hong Kong and Taiwan.

OCBC acquired the Wing Hang Bank in Hong Kong in 2014, and is one of the Singaporean banks that has received a license to open a bank branch in Myanmar, with the new branch in Yangon commencing operations in April 2015. OCBC also has a major banking presence in Malaysia and Indonesia (OCBC Bank, Annual Report 2014).

Malaysia's banking giants Maybank and CIMB have also been building their regional presence with operations across Southeast Asia, including retail banking as well as Islamic banking operations in Indonesia. Maybank has an 80 per cent stake in PT Bank Internasional Indonesia, the ninth largest commercial bank in Indonesia.

Thai companies are also broadening their strategies to build their presence in other Southeast Asian markets, with Siam City Cement and Siam Cement both having operations in other Southeast Asian countries. Thai Beverage PLC, Thailand's largest producer of beverages, has expanded its presence in other ASEAN markets through the controlling interest in Fraser and Neave Limited, which has given it a strong position to expand into other Southeast Asian beverage markets (Thai Beverage Public Limited Company, Annual Report 2014).

The changing structure of Asian consumer demand

While the overall outlook for consumer spending growth in the Asian region remains very positive, buoyed by rapidly rising incomes in the Asia's two BRICS giants China and India, as well as fast growth in household incomes in Southeast Asia, there are important shifts in the long-term outlook looking beyond the medium-term.

One important factor that will increasingly create differentiation in the pace of growth of consumer spending is the impact of ageing demographics. The importance of this factor is demonstrated by the declining population of Japan, which is acting as a key constraint to long-term growth in household expenditure. Over the next two decades, ageing demographics will also become an increasingly significant factor in other Asian economies, including China, South Korea and Thailand. This will impact not only on the overall growth rate of consumer spending, but also the distribution of spending, as health care and social services become more important due to the rising share of the elderly in the overall population.

However the relatively youthful demographics of much of Southeast Asia as well as South Asia create a different consumer growth dynamic, as the large cohorts of young workers entering the workforce over the next two decades create a rapidly growing market for consumer goods and sectors such as tourism and communications.

Rapidly rising household incomes across Asia will also support strong growth in demand for financial services, including banking, insurance and asset management, as rising per capita household incomes allow higher discretionary savings among the growing ranks of the Asian middle class.

Another key growth sector will be the demand for education services. Asia is already a key source of global demand for international education services, with many higher income Asian families having sent their children to study in schools and universities in the US, UK and Australia during the last three decades. However the significant increase in wealth in emerging Asia is fuelling sustained rapid growth in demand for international education services, and this is creating opportunities for new market players to compete in this segment.

Singapore has already established its credentials as an international education hub, through the development of education exports from its own major universities, the National University of Singapore, Singapore Management University and Nanyang Technological University. Singapore has also attracted leading international universities to establish campuses in Singapore, such as Duke-NUS Medical School and the INSEAD Asia Campus.

Malaysia has also begun to develop its international education exports, with Sunway University having established itself as a leading Malaysian university with around 30 per cent of its student population coming from abroad.

Another area of rapid future growth in consumer demand is private health care services, as rising numbers of affluent households in Asian emerging markets seek high quality medical services due to weak public health infrastructure. Due to high government debt levels and large fiscal deficits in many Asian developing countries, governments have been unable to allocate sufficient financial resources to develop healthcare infrastructure, and public health systems are extremely weak in many Asian countries including much of Southeast Asia and South Asia.

This has created rapid growth in demand for private healthcare services in emerging Asia, with strong private healthcare systems having developed in Malaysia, Thailand and India. As increasing numbers of households enter the middle class in South Asia and Southeast Asia, the demand for private healthcare services will rise rapidly.

In addition to domestic demand for such private healthcare services, medical tourism is also expanding rapidly, as patients travel to other countries in order to obtain healthcare services. Medical tourism segments in the private healthcare sectors of Thailand, Malaysia, Singapore and India have been growing in recent years due to rapid growth in demand for these services.

The impact of Asian consumer demand growth

Over the next two decades, consumer demand growth in China, India and ASEAN will be one of the most important growth drivers for the global economy. This rapid growth in Asian emerging markets consumer demand will also create an increasingly significant domestic demand growth engine for the emerging Asian economies, reducing their traditional dependence on export markets in the OECD. This will create greater diversification in the structure of the global economy.

This strong growth in Asian consumer markets will have positive transmission effects to other regions of the global economy,
helping to create new growth markets for Europe and Japan during a period when their domestic consumer markets are projected
to experience relatively slow growth.

It will also help to create new sources of demand for other
developing regions of the global economy, including Sub-Saharan
Africa, the Middle East and Latin America, helping to boost
South-South trade and investment flows.

Chapter 2

The Impact of Ageing Demographics on Asia

Japan's demographic tsunami

I entered the discreetly located member's club at the five-star hotel in central Tokyo, and was greeted at the door by the club manager. I mentioned the name of the Japanese entrepreneur I was supposed to meet, and the club manager immediately ushered me in to the elegantly furnished club, taking me to the table where the businessman was already seated, waiting for me with Japanese punctuality. He clearly was appreciative that I was also very punctual. Over cups of Japanese green tea, we discussed the Japanese economy and business conditions. He explained to me that he had sold out of his previous business activities a few years ago, and he had switched his business strategy so as to ride the demographic wave that was transforming Japan. His new business comprised a chain of pharmacies with adjacent medical clinics in major Japanese cities, and he had already built up a substantial number of such co-located facilities.

This is what economists would refer to as a form of tied-in sales. The doctors in the medical clinics would write prescriptions for the patients visiting their clinics, and the prescriptions would be filled by the adjacent pharmacies. The businessman told me that business was brisk, and the outlook was only getting better each year for his business as Japanese society continued to age rapidly. He told me that he was still acquiring prime real estate in major cities so that he could open even more pharmacies and medical centres.

I asked him about his views regarding how the Japanese economy would cope with the problem of ageing demographics and rising social welfare and health care costs, and he said that in his opinion, Japan was facing an economic and social tsunami due to these factors. He emphasized the word "tsunami" by mentioning this several times in his conversation, to highlight how severe the impact of demographic change would be on Japan. He told me that the short-term time horizon of politicians seeking re-election had resulted in many years of lethargic reforms, and the nation was already in a demographic crisis.

Japan's demographic crisis

Japan's population is not just ageing but is actually in decline. The United Nations 2014 population projection data showed that the population of Japan started to decline in 2010 (United Nations, World Urbanization Prospects, 2014). The initial pace of contraction is very gradual, but is projected to increase over time. In 2014, the total drop in the Japanese population was 268,000 persons, similar to the 244,000 decline in 2013. However, by 2025 the annual drop in population is projected to double, falling by 475,000 in 2025 compared to the previous year.

The Japanese government's 2010 Population Census of Japan estimated that the population was 128 million in 2010. According to Japan's National Institute of Population and Social Security Research (NIPSS), based on their Population Projections for Japan in January 2012, the total size of the Japanese population will decline to 116 million by 2030 in their central case scenario.

This implies a 12 million decline in Japanese population over the period from 2012 to 2030.

In the very long term, the NIPSS projects further significant declines in the total size of the Japanese population. According to its central case projection, the population is forecast to fall

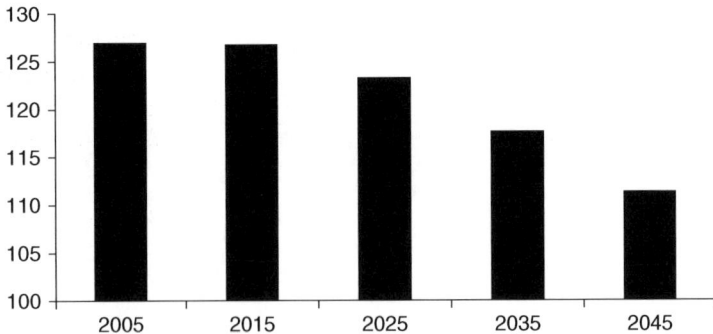

Figure 2.1 Japan's shrinking population, 2005–45 (millions of persons)

Source: UN population projections, 2014.

to just 87 million by 2060, which will be 41 million persons less than in 2010.

The demographic impact of such large changes in the total size as well as the age distribution of Japan's population has far-reaching consequences for the overall economy.

The first and most obvious impact is that the decline in total population size year after year means that the total Japanese consumer market size will shrink. For both Japanese companies and multinationals selling their products and services in the Japanese domestic market, this means that consumer demand for many types of products and services are in long-term decline.

Certain segments of the economy will of course benefit from ageing demographics, such as the health care sector, as exemplified by the case of the Japanese entrepreneur recounted above, with his pharmaceutical retail chain which has seen strong growth in business due to the rising number of senior citizens.

The impact of Japan's ageing society has already been dramatic in some areas. The total number of births in Japan halved between 1973 and 2010, with one million fewer births per year by 2010 compared with 1973. The total number of births in 2010 was 1.07 million. The cumulative impact of this structural trend has been to lower the total number of Japanese aged below 15 from 27 million in the early 1980s to just 15 million by 2015, with the number projected to continue to decline over coming decades, reaching ten million by 2046.

The immediate consequences have been far-reaching for Japanese schools, with the collapse in total numbers of births since 1973 having resulted in school infrastructure being far in excess of requirements. Since 1984 around 3,500 Japanese schools have been closed, and the rate of annual closures is increasing.

A report published by Professor Hiroya Masuda, Visiting Professor at the University of Tokyo Graduate School and the Declining Population Issue Study Group (Masuda, H., Discuss Japan, "The Death of Regional Cities", No. 18, Japan Foreign Policy Forum, Ministry of Foreign Affairs of Japan, 20 January 2014) has assessed the implications of Japan's ageing demographics for the population of Japanese municipalities.

Based on NIPSS demographic projections and the Study Group's assumptions about continued internal population migration at current rates into the large urban centres, their report concluded that 896 municipalities, or around half of all Japanese municipalities, could face a decline of 50 per cent or more in the total female population of reproductive age during the 2010–40 period. This will result in the economic and social decline of many of these municipalities, with the report warning that up to 523 of these municipalities could have such low populations by 2040 that they are no longer viable as municipal areas. The report characterizes these demographic developments as a type of 'population black hole', as fertility rates in big cities in Japan and many other countries are now far below the population replacement rate.

The impact of demographic ageing on the labour force is also becoming increasingly significant, as the number of young workers entering the workforce each year continues to decline, while the ageing cohorts of the baby boomer generation are retiring from the workforce. The significant mismatch between the numbers of workers entering and leaving the workforce each year has already resulted in the size of the Japanese workforce beginning to decline.

The Japanese working age population peaked in 2005 at 87.3 million and had declined to 81.7 million by 2010. According to projections by the NIPSS, further drastic declines will occur over the next decade, with the size of the population of working age falling to 70 million by 2027 and 44 million by 2060. This implies that by 2060, the Japanese population of working age will be just half the size of the working age population in 2005.

For Japan's corporate sector, the implications for their business strategy are very significant, and both the declining size of the domestic Japanese consumer market and the shrinking size of the Japanese workforce will reinforce corporate strategies to continue to hollow-out domestic manufacturing operations and expand facilities in fast-growing emerging markets with plentiful, low cost, labour supply.

Other countries that have confronted problems with ageing demographics and declining labour supply have addressed the issue by increasing immigration rates, but Japan retains a strong national identity as a homogeneous society (*tanitzu minzoku*). The Japanese government has been reluctant to allow a large-scale influx of migrants, which remains a highly charged issue politically. While the Abe administration is trying to make some adjustments to its immigration policies to allow more foreign workers into Japan, these measures are still very limited and will have only a modest impact on the overall decline in Japan's population.

The Japanese Ministry of Health, Labour and Welfare has estimated that 2.5 million caregivers will be needed in Japan to look after the elderly population by 2025, with a projected shortfall of 300,000 caregivers. In 2013, the number of caregivers in Japan was estimated at 1.8 million persons.

So far, the pace of change is glacial. A total of 78 persons from the Philippines and Indonesia passed the caregivers examination in Japan in 2014, while only 26 people from the Philippines, Indonesia and Vietnam passed the nursing exam.

However, the Abe government is making reforms, with Justice Minister Yoko Kamikawa having convened an expert committee on immigration to consider reforms. The Japanese government has drafted new legislation that will give foreign nurses and caregivers special visa status, although this will mainly be for students enrolled in nursing and caregiving courses in Japan.

The overall demographic challenges facing Japan are severe, with the impact of ageing demographics expected to be a long-term structural drag on GDP growth, as the population of working age continues to decline. While increasing immigration of foreign workers may help to mitigate the problem, the cultural barriers to substantial immigration programs make this an unlikely policy response. Based on the current demographic path that Japan is projected to follow based on both Japanese government and United Nations population projections, the Japanese economy is facing a growing crisis due to the impact of ageing demographics. A rapidly increasing proportion of the total population will be senior citizens, imposing rising health care and social welfare costs on the Japanese government budget at a time when the gross government debt of Japan is already the highest in the world. The nature of structural policy reforms by the Japanese government to address this demographic crisis will be crucial. It is already starting to pursue labour force reforms to encourage a higher female participation rate in the work force as well as immigration reforms to allow foreign workers with essential skills in areas such as nursing and aged care to work in Japan, but the pace of reform will need to accelerate. Meanwhile the Japanese government will also need to make further reforms to contain rising health care and social services costs due to the rising share of the population of senior citizens and the declining size of the Japanese work force.

China

One of the major challenges facing the Chinese economy over the next two decades will be the gradual ageing of the Chinese population. China officially introduced a one-child policy for families in 1980, and this regulation, combined with other factors such as rising education and urbanization, has resulted in a significant decline in birth rates over the last three decades. The fertility rate in China declined from around two in the early 1990s to an estimated 1.5 by 2010, which is well below the natural replacement rate, resulting in a slowdown in the rate of population growth in China. Furthermore, the population of China is due to start declining by 2032, according to the UN 2014 population projection.

While the impact of ageing demographics is still relatively moderate, it will increase over the next decade, as the number of senior citizens increases more rapidly. Meanwhile, due to the declining birth rate, the number of young people aged below 15 is falling, and this has started to lower the annual number of young people entering the labour force. China's working age population started to decline in 2012, falling by 3.45 million. In 2013, the total size of the working age population dropped by 2.44 million persons, and in 2014, fell by a further 3.71 million persons.

The declining size of the work force will over the long term put increasing pressure on Chinese wages. As the available supply of surplus labour that was a key competitive advantage of China in low-cost manufacturing has gradually declined, it has already become more difficult for coastal Chinese provinces to attract migrant labour from inland provinces. These difficulties have been compounded by the Chinese government's policy thrust over the last decade to accelerate the development of western Chinese provinces, with large-scale infrastructure spending and urban development. This has created more job opportunities for workers in their home provinces in western China, reducing the attractiveness of moving to coastal Chinese cities to fill manufacturing sector jobs.

However there is also an important silver lining due to the gradual decline in the annual number of young workers joining the labour force. One of the key policy concerns of the Chinese government for decades has been to create sufficient new employment growth to provide jobs for the millions of new workers joining the work force each year. With the Chinese economic growth rate gradually moderating, the number of new jobs that need to be created each year is also declining significantly, helping to avert the risks of rising unemployment and potential social unrest.

While China's population will be ageing significantly over the next three decades, the total size of the population is projected to gradually increase until 2030, and then start to decline at a moderate pace until 2035. Consequently the population in 2025 is expected to be approximately the same as in 2035, at 1,450 million people. Beyond 2035, the pace of decline will increase. Over the fifteen year period between 2035 and 2050, the total population of China is projected to decline by 64 million persons.

However the Chinese population is projected to age rapidly according to the United Nations population projections measuring the old age dependency ratio, which calculates the share of population aged 65 and over to the working age population aged 15 to 64. This ratio is projected to rise from 13 per cent in 2015 to 24 per cent by 2030 and 39 per cent by 2050. As in other countries with ageing demographics, such as many Western European countries and Japan, this implies a rising burden of health care and social services costs in future years as the share of the elderly population increases.

However unlike advanced economies such as EU countries or Japan, Chinese per capita GDP levels are still considerably lower than OECD standards, indicating that a large share of the working age population will not have accumulated substantial private savings for their retirement, and pension entitlements will also be much lower. With average life expectancy also increasing, a key policy challenge for the Chinese government will be to provide adequate care for the elderly population; the question of who will fund this looms large. It is likely that the extended family system will continue to play a key role in caring for the elderly, although the burden on the working age population will be significantly greater than for past generations since the ratio of elderly citizens to the working age population is projected to rise significantly.

Therefore, the issue of demographic change has become an increasing focus of policy attention within the Chinese government, as concerns rise about the long-term economic implications of population ageing. The Chinese government has already made some significant amendments to the one child policy in response. In 2013, new legislation was passed by the Standing Committee of the Chinese National People's Congress to allow couples to have two children if one of the partners is an only child. Initial predictions by experts in China anticipated that this change in policy could lift birth rates in China by between one million and two million annual births. As the new legislation was passed at the end of 2013, the full impact of the new policy was not able to be fully assessed based on annual births in 2014, although the total number of births increased by 470,000 in 2014. With total annual births having been around 16 million in the years preceding the change in the legislation, the impact of the new rule does seem to have had a significant impact, although it will be necessary to see the overall impact over a number of years to fully assess whether the new rule is increasing the total number of births each year in a sustainable way or whether the effect was only a temporary spike.

Other factors could also impact on the birth rate in a manner that offsets any positive impact from the new legislation, including the rapid urbanization of western Chinese provinces, rising education standards and increasing female labour force participation rates.

Therefore while the long-term demographic projections for China do indicate that there will be increasing challenges from ageing demographics, the overall impact of demographic ageing over the next thirty years is not as severe as in Japan. Moreover the Chinese government may be successful in its efforts to relax the one child policy framework and boost the birth rate through these reforms. While these may not completely offset the current rising trend for the dependency ratio, it may help to mitigate the effects. Nevertheless the fiscal implications of rising aged dependency ratios will result in higher health care and social services costs for the Chinese government over coming decades.

South Korea's ageing population

South Korea's current population is estimated to be 50 million people with the current rate of annual increase of the population being very slow. By 2035, the South Korean population is projected to peak at 52.4 million people, which implies that the population will increase by 2.4 million people over the next two decades.

However due to ageing demographics and increasing life expectancy, the old age dependency ratio is expected to rise dramatically, from 18 per cent in 2015 to 37 per cent by 2030 and 66 per cent by 2050.

The fertility rate for women has been trending downwards for the last four decades, and has reached around 1.3 children per woman, far below the natural replacement rate of the population, which is 2.1 children per woman. It is also difficult to envisage that South Korea will allow significant immigration from abroad as a means of mitigating its ageing demographics.

Although South Korea is projected to have net immigration inflows over the next two decades, the annual rate of immigration is projected to remain very low. South Korea, like Japan, has a very homogenous culture reflecting past immigration policies, though South Korean President Park Geun Hae has led policy reform initiatives to allow greater immigration inflows of skilled workers. The total share of immigrants including foreign-born South Korean citizens in the total population remains very low, at less than 3 per cent of the population, which is slightly higher than Japan, but still low compared to many other advanced nations.

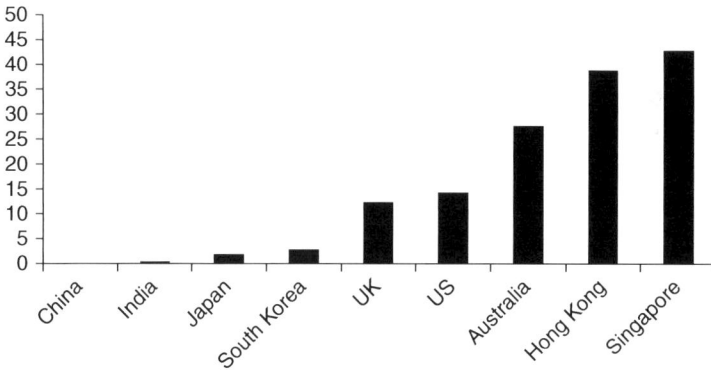

Figure 2.2 Immigrants as share of population, citizens born abroad and resident foreigners

Source: UN data.

Research by a wide range of institutions, including the IMF and OECD, has pointed to the significant future impact on the Korean economy from ageing demographics.

"Korea is on the verge of an unprecedented demographic shift, which will severely strain its public finances. Over coming decades, rapid ageing is set to transform Korea from one of the youngest populations in the OECD to among the oldest in record time. This shift will put tremendous pressure on the pension system as well as health and long-term care spending."

Feyzioglu, T., Skaarup, M. and Syed, M., "Addressing Korea's Long-term Fiscal Challenges", IMF Working Paper WP/08/27 (IMF, Washington D.C., 2008).

The IMF has continued to highlight its concerns about the impact of demographic ageing on South Korea in subsequent years, with its 2013 Article IV Report on South Korea stating that:

"Going forward, population ageing will be a major further drag on potential growth. On current trends, the working age population is projected to peak in 2016, and Korea is expected to become one of the oldest countries in the OECD by 2050, with the dependency ratio increasing rapidly. As a result, without offsetting policies, Korea's potential growth would decrease to around 2 – 2.5 per cent by 2025."

Due to the impact of ageing as well as other factors, the OECD has estimated that South Korea's potential GDP growth rate in the period from 2008–13 was 3.7 per cent growth per year, and will moderate to 2.9 per cent per year from 2014–2030. However as the impact of demographic ageing becomes more severe, the potential output growth rate is projected to moderate to just 1.6 per cent growth over the 2030–50 period (OECD, "Growth Prospects", 2014).

Therefore South Korea is amongst the Asian countries facing the most severe impact from demographic ageing. As the supply of young workers entering the workforce gradually declines, this will put pressure on Korean multinationals to accelerate their hollowing out to fast-growing emerging markets.

Demographic trends in South Asia

In sharp contrast to Northeast Asia, the demographic projections for South Asia show that the structure of the population distribution will be much more youthful than Northeast Asia. The population of South Asia is projected to increase from 1,793 million in 2015 to 2,085 million in 2030.

With the South Asian fertility rate at 2.5 in 2015, this still remains above the natural replacement rate. Therefore the number of births remains relatively high, and there are relatively large cohorts of young people entering the working age population every year in the next two decades.

Consequently the old age dependency ratio remains very low over the next two decades, rising from just 8 per cent in 2015 to 9 per cent by 2020 and 11.6 per cent by 2030. Even by 2050, the old age dependency ratio rises to only 19 per cent. This is far lower than China's old age dependency ratio in 2050, which is projected to be 39 per cent, or Korea's old age dependency ratio of 66 per cent in 2050.

This is a positive situation for South Asia from the perspective of fiscal implications of an ageing population and is also attractive for global multinationals looking for production hubs with large pools of labour supply. The rapidly rising size of the total population of South Asia also creates a rapidly growing consumer market.

However there are also significant downside risks from a fast-growing youthful population. If governments are unable to meet the aspirations of large numbers of young people entering the work force, the result could be an accumulation of frustration and resentment among those who cannot get suitable jobs, which could erupt into social unrest.

There are already significant parts of India where Naxalite insurgents have considerable control over local areas, benefiting from the extreme level of poverty in some of these regions. The Indian government has begun to respond to the economic underpinnings of this insurgency by attempting to boost economic development in these areas, so as to address the root cause of local support for this Maoist insurgency movement.

The proliferation of the Naxalite insurgency in the last two decades highlights India's vulnerability to social unrest if large segments of the Indian population remain in poverty and do not see steady progress in living standards.

Nepal, a low income country with very limited domestic growth drivers, has also suffered a Maoist insurgency that started in 1996 and lasted for a decade, culminating in a peace agreement in 2006 and elections in 2008 that resulted in a government led by the Communist Party of Nepal-Maoist taking office. Considerable political instability has since ensued with a number of elections having been held; Nepal remained under various forms of communist-led governments until the 2013 elections, when the Nepal Congress party was able to form a coalition government. However the communist parties still have a large number of seats in parliament and have also mobilized large-scale public protests against the government. Political instability has left Nepal as a very poor, low-income nation, with the nation suffering even further economic devastation following a massive earthquake in 2015.

Overall, the youthful demographics of the Indian subcontinent are a double-edged sword. While young demographics are an important potential source of competitive advantage as there are ample supplies of young workers entering the working age population each year, their aspirations also need to be met by sufficient new job creation so that they have a reasonable standard of living in line with national standards. Rapid increases in population also create significant new challenges for governments in order to provide basic infrastructure and health care facilities.

In India, the total population is projected to increase from 1,282 million in 2015 to 1,476 million in 2030 according to UN central case population projections. By 2050, India's population is projected to rise to 1,620 million persons, a further increase of 144 million persons in the population. This represents an increase of 194 million people over the next 15 years, which will result in significant growth in the size of Indian cities and a rising urbanization ratio, boosted by continued rural-urban migration flows to cities for those in search of employment and access to essential infrastructure and services.

India's fertility rate, which was 2.5 children per woman in 2015, is not projected to drop below the 2.1 natural replacement rate until after 2030, and therefore the old age dependency ratio will remain low for decades ahead. The old age dependency ratio was 8.3 per cent in 2015, and is projected to only be 12 per cent by 2030 and around 19 per cent by 2050.

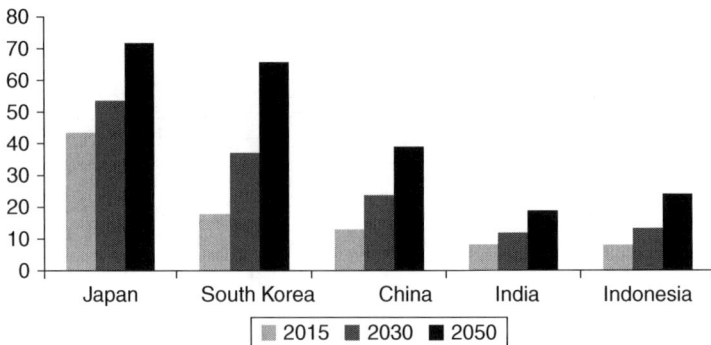

Figure 2.3 Old age dependency ratios in Asia

Source: UN population projections.

Demographic trends in Indonesia

Indonesia is Asia's third most populous country after China and India, with a population of around 254 million people in 2015. By 2030, the size of Indonesia's population will reach 293 million, according to United Nations population projections, an increase of 39 million people. By 2050, the population size is projected to reach around 320 million.

Like India, Indonesia's old age dependency ratio was very low in 2015, at only 8 per cent. By 2030, the old age dependency ratio will only rise to 13.5 per cent, which is still low compared to trends in Northeast Asian countries.

With the fertility rate remaining above 2 until 2030, Indonesia retains a youthful demographic profile. However as with India, the large number of young school-leavers and university graduates entering the labour force each year will be a key challenge for the Indonesian government, in order to provide sufficient jobs, infrastructure and essential services.

After 2030, Indonesia does start to experience more significant population ageing, with the old age ratio reaching 24 per cent by 2050. However this is still moderate compared to Northeast Asian countries.

The relatively youthful demographic profile of Indonesia over the next three decades should give Indonesia a competitive advantage in trying to attract manufacturing investment into the country, although significant economic reforms in to improve the business climate are also needed over the medium-term.

Asia's demographic outlook

Demographic patterns across Asia are projected to show wide variations across the region over the next three decades, with Northeast Asia expected to experience significant ageing of their populations and rapidly rising old age dependency ratios. For Japan and South Korea, the economic implications of demographic ageing are severe over the next three decades, resulting in rising fiscal costs related to health care and social services. The sharp decline in the number of young workers joining the labour force is also likely to underpin the hollowing out of manufacturing industries.

The shrinking size of the total population in Japan is also creating new dynamics in the economy. Demand for products and services for the share of the population that is below the age of 15 will decline rapidly, while goods and services for the senior citizens is likely to grow rapidly over the medium-term.

In China, the impact of ageing demographics is already resulting in a gradual decline in the working age population, with the
old age dependency ratio also set to rise rapidly over the next three
decades. However the Chinese government has already started
making changes to its 'one child' policy, which may gradually help
to mitigate the implications of demographic ageing.

Meanwhile in South Asia and Indonesia, the pace of demographic ageing is relatively slow, and starting from a low base, so
the impact will be very gradual. However these nations will face
challenges of a different nature to Northeast Asia, as large numbers
of young workers entering the workforce each year will put considerable pressure on governments to deliver sufficient jobs growth
to meet the aspirations of their rapidly growing populations.

Chapter 3

Building a New Financial Architecture in Asia

Reshaping the global financial architecture

In April 2015, Indonesian President Joko Widodo made a speech at the Asian-African Conference in Jakarta in which he called for a reshaping of the global economic order. His speech was made to an audience mainly comprising government leaders from developing countries in Asia and Africa, and he expressed his frustration with the Bretton Woods system that was established in 1944.

> *"Those who say the global economic problems shall only be solved by the IMF, World Bank and ADB, these are obsolete ideas. There needs to be change. It's imperative that we build a new international economic order that is open to new emerging economic powers."*
>
> Indonesian President Joko Widodo, Speech to
> 60th Asian-African Conference in Jakarta, 22 April 2015.

In Asia, the creation of a new financial architecture was proposed almost two decades ago. In 1997, amidst the carnage of the East Asian financial crisis, Japan proposed the creation of an Asian Monetary Fund (AMF) that would play a role in crisis prevention and resolution for Asian countries. Eisuke Sakakibara, the Japanese Vice-Minister for International Finance, was one of the key advocates for the creation of this new institution. This proposal created a political clash with the US, and the idea was strongly opposed by the US government, particularly by the US Treasury, on the grounds that this initiative would duplicate the role of the Bretton Woods institutions. At the time, support for the AMF initiative faded in Asian capitals, due to the strength of US opposition to the idea and the political and economic importance of the US relationship to many Asian countries.

However the seeds of the concept of an Asian financial architecture had been sown, and by 2000, finance ministers of the ASEAN countries together with Japan, China and South Korea (ASEAN+3) launched the Chiang Mai Initiative by creating a series of bilateral swap agreements to provide foreign exchange liquidity in future balance of payments crises amongst the ASEAN+3.

With the global financial crisis of 2008–09 having pushed the US and EU to their financial limits in terms of the ability of their governments to resolve the banking sector crises that had occurred, the case for Asian countries to be able to play a greater role in crisis prevention within Asia became more evident.

Following the global financial crisis, the ASEAN+3 countries recognized that the Chiang Mai Initiative would need to be substantially expanded in order to be effective. In 2009, ASEAN+3 finance ministers agreed to the Chiang Mai Initiative Multilateralisation (CMIM), creating a joint reserves pool of USD 120 billion. The size of this reserves pool was expanded further in 2012. At the ASEAN+3 Finance Ministers and Central Banks Governors Meeting held in Manila in May 2012, governments agreed to double the size of the CMIM to USD 240 billion as well as to develop a crisis prevention role.

While the capabilities of the CMIM to act in the event of a financial crisis in an Asian country remain untested, Asian countries have clearly made progress on the path towards greater regional monetary co-operation.

Other forces are also creating momentum for a stronger regional financial architecture. As Asian banks from Japan, China, Singapore and Malaysia continue to expand their international banking operations across Asia, there is an increasing need for greater cross-border supervisory and regulatory co-operation amongst Asian financial regulatory and supervisory bodies.

However the greatest impetus for increased financial co-operation amongst Asian countries has come from China, which has been the driving force in launching a number of new multilateral development finance institutions for Asia in 2014, in parallel with the creation of the new BRICS development bank.

Reshaping development finance in Asia

In July 2014, the BRICS nations agreed to create a new development bank that would have initial capital of USD 50 billion.

Their decision reflects the growing discontent amongst developing nations that the governance structure of the Bretton Woods institutions has not evolved to reflect the increasing weight of emerging markets in global GDP. The new bank, if successfully implemented, could give the BRICS nations greater influence in global development financing.

China has also launched other new initiatives to increase infrastructure financing for Asian developing countries. In October 2014, 21 Asian countries agreed to establish the Asian Infrastructure Investment Bank, to which China agreed to provide up to 50 per cent of the initial capital. In November 2014 at the APEC Summit, President Xi also announced the creation of a new Silk Road Fund to improve connectivity in Asia, for which China will provide USD 40 billion of capital funding.

The new BRICS Development Bank, as well as the AIIB and Silk Road Fund, will face considerable hurdles, including establishing efficient governance and a world-class prudential regulatory structure that will avoid the pitfalls of overt politicization of the new institutions. However with the correct design, the new BRICS Development Bank could become an important new source of financing to address the economic development and infrastructure financing needs of developing countries worldwide. The establishment of the BRICS Development Bank at the same time as the AIIB and Silk Road Fund has the potential to significantly reshape the global financial architecture for development finance.

BRICS discontent with the Bretton Woods architecture

The decision by the BRICS nations in July 2014 to establish a new development bank in which the BRICS nations would have at least 55 per cent of the capital is a response to mounting discontent with the voting structure of the Bretton Woods institutions, which remains heavily dominated by the US and Europe.

When the IMF and the IBRD were created at the Bretton Woods Conference in 1944, the governance and voting structure of these institutions was dominated by the US and Europe, with a total of 44 founding member nations. With the decline of colonialism during the 1950s and 1960s as the former European colonies gradually gained independence, the number of member countries of the IMF and World Bank has risen from 44 to 188. Moreover, the share of world GDP accounted for by developing countries has risen significantly. The world economy has changed very dramatically in the seventy years since the Bretton Woods Conference, but the IMF and World Bank continue to have governance structures that have not evolved sufficiently since 1944.

Despite sustained efforts by developing countries to argue for reforms within the Bretton Woods institutions to reflect the greater economic weight of developing nations, the pace of reforms to the distribution of voting rights has been slow. Meanwhile the status quo in terms of the current distribution of voting rights remains distorted, most notably for China amongst the BRICS nations. For example, the US controls 16.75 per cent of voting rights in the IMF, while China, the world's second largest economy, has 3.81 per cent. Indeed, France, which had a GDP value in nominal USD terms that was around one-third the size of Chinese GDP in 2013, has 4.29 per cent of IMF voting rights, slightly larger than China's voting rights. For the BRICS as a whole, their share of IMF voting rights currently totals 11.04 per cent of total IMF voting rights, whereas their share of GDP is 21.2 per cent.

Table 3.1 BRICS voting rights in IMF compared to GDP
(GDP share measured in nominal USD terms; IMF Voting Rights as of August 2014)

	Share of IMF Voting Rights	**Share of World GDP**
China	3.81	12.4
India	2.34	2.6
Russia	2.39	2.8
Brazil	1.72	3.0
South Africa	0.78	0.5
TOTAL	11.04	21.2

Sources: IMF.

With China and India having grown more rapidly than the US and Europe for decades and projected to continue to do so over the next two decades, the distortion between the BRICS share of IMF voting rights and share of world GDP is likely to continue to widen unless substantial reforms are made within the Bretton Woods institutions in terms of governance and voting rights structures.

Based on long-term projections of world GDP, China is expected to become the world's largest economy by around 2030 if it can sustain annual GDP growth rates of around 6 per cent to 7 per cent per year over the next decade. Based on these growth rates, by 2030, China is projected to account for 19.9 per cent of world GDP, while India is projected to account for 5.5 per cent of world GDP. Combined, the Asian BRICS alone would therefore account for over 25 per cent of world GDP, whereas at present their combined IMF voting rights total only 6.15 per cent. Unless there is far more rapid progress in IMF voting right reforms than is evident currently, the Asian BRICS would confront a major asymmetry between their weight in the global economy and their role in the governance of the IMF.

What has also provoked the developing nations in regard to the governance of the Bretton Woods institutions has been the agreement between the US and Europe that the Managing Director of the IMF should be European and the President of the World Bank should be from the US. This custom has been carried out since the foundation of the IMF and World Bank, with no developing country national ever having led either of these multilateral institutions during the past 70 years. President Obama attempted to make amends for the unfairness of this situation by nominating a US citizen of Korean ethnicity to become the World Bank President in 2012.

However this does not fundamentally redress the increasing imbalance between the weight of GDP of the BRICS in the global economy and their voting rights in the Bretton Woods institutions.

Reshaping the financial architecture

With efforts to reshape the governance structure of the IMF and World Bank in favour of developing countries having been painfully slow, one of the initiatives that had been under discussion since 2012 amongst the BRIC countries was the establishment of their own development bank.

The plan to establish a BRICS development bank was formally approved by the BRICS at their summit in South Africa in 2013, and detailed planning was subsequently undertaken in the lead-up to the 6th BRICS Summit in Fortaleza in July 2014. At Fortaleza, the formal decision was taken by the BRICS to establish the BRICS development bank, to be called "New Development Bank" (NDB), with initial authorized capital of USD 100 billion and initial subscribed capital of USD 50 billion and also a Contingent Reserve Arrangement (CRA) with capital of USD 100 billion.

An Inter-Governmental Agreement was signed on 15 July 2014 by Brazil, China, India, Russia and South Africa to establish the NDB and CRA. The initial subscribed capital of the NDB will be provided equally by the five founding member countries.

The primary role of the NDB will be to provide finance for infrastructure and sustainable development projects, while the CRA is intended to be an external account support facility to help developing countries manage balance of payments crises.

The NDB will operate through the provision of loans, equity participation, guarantees and other financial instruments. Furthermore, the BRICS governments intend that the NDB will have the discretion to work in co-operation with international organizations as well as public and private organizations, particularly with international financial institutions and national development banks.

The Fortaleza Declaration stated that the NDB will help to strengthen co-operation among the BRICS, and will also serve to supplement the work of multilateral and regional financial institutions for global development. However the Fortaleza Declaration also pointedly went on to say that the BRICS countries were "disappointed and seriously concerned" that the 2010 IMF reforms had not been implemented, and that the IMF governance structure needs to be modernized to reflect the increased weight of emerging market economies and developing countries.

The genesis of the NDB has at its core the response of the BRICS nations to reshaping the international financial architecture to reflect their growing economic weight. The NDB creates a dynamic mechanism to achieve this outside of the Bretton Woods institutions, albeit the BRICS countries have stated their intention to work in co-operation with the existing multilateral and regional financial institutions.

From the BRICS perspective, the NDB also offers considerable flexibility for the BRICS and other developing countries to expand their subscribed capital for the NDB as the weight of their own economies increases in the global economy. In contrast, this has proven to be very difficult to do within the Bretton Woods governance structure.

Size of capital of the New Development Bank

While the initial capital for the NDB is to be provided in equal share by the five BRICS countries, the initial total capital of USD 100 billion for the CRA will be strongly underwritten by China, which will provide USD 41 billion of the initial capital. With China holding foreign exchange reserves of USD 3.65 trillion at the end of July 2015, the depth of China's international reserves will provide the key underpinning for the NDB and CRA, as well as being a potential source of considerable new capital as the NDB and CRA commence operations. The important role that China will play for the NDB is reflected in the decision to locate the NDB in Shanghai.

The total initial capital of the NDB will not necessarily be constrained to the USD 50 billion from the BRICS, since other developing countries will also be invited to join and subscribe capital to the NDB.

By way of comparison, as at June 2014, the total subscribed capital of the World Bank was USD 233 billion, with paid-in capital of USD 14.4 billion and Total Shareholder's Equity of USD 39 billion.

Therefore if the NDB is able to attract significant additional subscribed capital from other sovereign states in addition to the BRICS, it could considerably increase the size of total development finance that the NDB is able to provide.

One of the strengths of the World Bank is its very strong credit rating, reflecting its sound financial position, as well as the strength and diversity of its government shareholders. Standard and Poor's rated the World Bank as a AAA foreign currency credit rating in its April 2014 rating, and Moody's gave the World Bank a Aaa long-term issuer credit rating in its January 2014 rating. These strong credit ratings from international rating agencies combined with the extremely sound financial management and liquidity position of the World Bank help to give it excellent access to international capital markets for its program.

In comparison, the NDB could have a less favourable financial profile in the view of international capital markets, due to the smaller number of government shareholders and their lower sovereign credit ratings than the major shareholders of the World Bank. In addition, the financial governance and loan portfolio of the NDB will not have an established track record in the early years, which will also give it a less favourable credit rating in international financial markets, making the cost of borrowing higher.

However the NDB is likely to benefit from having good access to funding from the state-owned banks of the BRICS countries, notably from Chinese state-owned banks, which would provide a very large potential source of financing for the NDB.

The eminent Professor Stephanie Griffith-Jones (2014) has recently estimated that with initial capital of USD 100 billion, the NDB could be lending up to USD 34 billion annually in 20 years time, which is roughly equivalent to the current annual lending of the World Bank.

While the exact annual lending levels of the NDB will be determined by a complex mix of factors, the key point is that the governance structure of the NDB does allow for the rapid future growth of the Chinese and Indian economies to be easily translated into increased capital subscriptions to the NDB. If the total size of the Chinese and Indian economies does indeed amount to 25 per cent of world GDP by 2030, this could result in very sizeable increases in the NDB's total capital and in its annual lending for infrastructure and sustainable development projects in developing countries.

China's parallel initiatives

With China's foreign exchange reserves estimated at USD 3.65 trillion in July 2015, China is in a unique position amongst the large emerging markets to be able to fund significant development finance initiatives such as the NDB.

China has begun to play a more significant leadership role in global development finance, recognizing that such initiatives will help to strengthen its political and economic ties with other developing nations. In addition to the creation of the NDB in July 2014, China also has led an initiative to create an Asian Infrastructure Investment Bank (AIIB), with a Memorandum of Understanding signed by 21 Asian countries on 24 October 2014 to establish the AIIB.

The AIIB will have initial authorized capital of USD 100 billion. China initially stated that it was willing to provide up to 50 per cent of the initial capital for the AIIB, although with many other nations having joined the AIIB during 2015, and after the final negotiations about the size of each member's subscriptions, the final size of China's capital subscription was lowered. The headquarters of the AIIB will be located in Beijing.

The creation of the AIIB has created concerns in some quarters about a potential rivalry with the World Bank or the Asian Development Bank, with some major Asia-Pacific countries having initially remained on the sidelines of this new AIIB initiative.

The US stance on the creation of the AIIB appeared at the outset to be similar to its response to Japan's proposal in 1997 to create an Asian Monetary Fund. Initially, the US efforts to persuade major developed countries not to join the AIIB seemed to be working.

However for many Asian developing countries, the AIIB represented an additional source of much-needed infrastructure financing for Asia, and hence the Chinese initiative to create this new bank for infrastructure finance was widely welcomed by many Asian developing countries. Twenty-six Asia-Pacific nations had joined the AIIB by March 2015, including India, Singapore and New Zealand.

The momentum behind the AIIB was further boosted in March 2015 when the UK announced its decision to apply for membership of the AIIB. From the UK perspective, this decision was taken due to the importance of the Asia-Pacific region to UK firms, with the AIIB membership seen by the UK government as an important means to strengthen UK investment and trade ties with the Asia-Pacific. Becoming a founder member of the AIIB also would give the UK a role in establishing the governance and ethical standards for the AIIB from the outset.

The UK decision triggered an angry response from the US, which still regarded the new AIIB initiative as a potential rival to the Bretton Woods system of development financing through the World Bank together with regional development banks such as the Asian Development Bank in Asia.

The UK decision to apply for membership of the AIIB also triggered a wave of applications for AIIB membership by other European countries, including Germany, France, Italy, Switzerland, Portugal and Luxembourg. In the Asia-Pacific region, South Korea and Australia, both of whom had initially been undecided about joining the AIIB, both submitted their applications to join once the wave of European applicants became evident.

In April 2015, the AIIB announced that a total of 57 nations were admitted as founder member nations of the AIIB, including Australia, Brazil, Saudi Arabia and many of the EU countries. The US and Japan did not apply to join.

With such a large international group of nations now part of the AIIB a key area of focus has been on the governance structure of the new organization, particularly in regard to the system of voting rights and management structure.

As with the NDB, the AIIB will also create a mechanism for China and other developing countries to reshape the global financial architecture for development finance.

China has further reinforced its efforts to play a much larger role in international development finance by committing USD 40 billion to establish a new Silk Road infrastructure fund that will boost infrastructure connectivity in emerging Asia. The announcement was made by China at the APEC Leaders Summit in Beijing in November 2014.

From the Chinese perspective, the NDB, AIIB and Silk Road Fund achieve a number of strategic objectives.

Firstly, these new development finance institutions will give developing countries a major source of international development financing that will not be under the auspices of the Bretton Woods institutions with its outdated system of voting rights that do not properly reflect the rising share of developing countries in world GDP.

Secondly, China will be a key source of capital funding for these new development finance institutions, which from a foreign policy perspective helps to boost China's geopolitical influence amongst developing countries, albeit China is positioning itself more as the primus inter pares among the members of these new institutions, rather than as the dominant shareholder that will drive decision-making.

Thirdly, the creation of these new development institutions will become an important counterbalance to the political weight of the West through the Bretton Woods institutions, giving China a greater role and voice in global development finance. This will become increasingly important politically and economically for China once it becomes the world's largest economy, as the current voting rights China has in the World Bank and IMF trivialize its stature in the global economy.

The challenges ahead

The governance of the new multilateral development finance institutions will be very much under scrutiny. To a large extent, this reflects international perceptions about issues such as corruption in developing countries, with the rankings of the BRICS countries still relatively low by international standards, as reflected in Transparency International's Corruption Perceptions Index. In the Transparency International 2014 rankings of 175 countries, South Africa had the best ranking amongst the BRICS, at 67th, with Brazil in 69th place, India 85th, China 100th and Russia at 136th. This is within an international ranking spectrum in which Denmark was rated 1st, and North Korea and Somalia were ranked equal in last place, at 174th.

Therefore a key challenge for the founding countries involved in establishing the NDB and AIIB will be to establish governance structures and decision-making systems that have a high degree of transparency, integrity and independence from political influence in making lending decisions.

There are well-established international best practices for governance of financial institutions, with the BRICS central banks as well as other central banks from developing countries having considerable experience in such principles through their regulatory and supervisory roles in their domestic banking systems. Therefore there is considerable capacity and knowledge within the BRICS to establish such best practice standards for the NDB and other new multilateral development finance institutions being created by the developing countries.

Another major challenge that the BRICS and other developing countries will face when attempting to reshape the international financial architecture comes from the significant constraints on most developing countries in terms of their foreign exchange reserves.

While the establishment of the NDB, AIIB and Silk Road Fund have the ability to rapidly transform global development finance, it is unlikely that the developing countries as a group can play a significant role in international crisis prevention and resolution for developing countries in the near to medium term, with even some of the largest developing countries facing considerable challenges due to volatile international capital flows.

The limitations on the foreign exchange reserves of both Russia and India have been tested by recent economic crises, with India's economic crisis in 2013 triggering a protracted depreciation of the rupee that required the Indian central bank, the Reserve Bank of India, to intervene in currency markets over a period of months, depleting foreign exchange reserves for these interventions to smooth the depreciation of the rupee. Russia's economic crisis that started in 2014 triggered capital flight in 2014 that was estimated by the Central Bank of Russia at USD 128 billion (The Moscow Times, 10 November 2014). The Central

Bank of Russia is estimated to have used USD 80 billion of its foreign exchange reserves for foreign currency intervention to stabilize the sharp depreciation of the ruble during 2014 (Reuters News, "Global Forex Reserves", 17 December 2014). Total Russian foreign exchange reserves are estimated to have declined from USD 510 billion at the end of 2013 to USD 416 billion by mid-December 2014.

The ability of China to play a far greater role in global crisis prevention and stabilization could change significantly if China is able to eventually introduce full currency convertibility and establish the Chinese currency as a key global reserve currency, but this is still a long-term goal.

The future shape of Asia's financial architecture

Asia's growing share of world GDP and the rapid growth of financial assets in Asian financial centres have been accompanied by the rapid growth of Asian financial systems as well as total Asian official foreign exchange reserves.

This rapid growth of Asian financial assets has also driven the growth of Asian bank balance sheets, with banks from a number of Asian countries having established regional footprints as they expand their international banking activities.

The fast-growing size of the Asian middle class that is projected over the next twenty years implies that the financial assets of middle class households in the region will grow rapidly, driving further strong growth of Asian bank balance sheets.

Deepening financial intermediation and the rapid growth of cross-border financial services provision by Asian banks will create an increasing need for greater co-operation amongst Asian financial regulatory and supervisory bodies to ensure the stability of Asian financial systems.

Beyond supervisory and regulatory co-operation amongst Asian financial regulators, there has also been growing momentum amongst Asian countries for creating an Asian regional capability for financial crisis prevention and resolution. This has been gradually progressing under the Chiang Mai Initiative since 2000.

Regional financial co-operation has also gathered new momentum in 2014, as China has led the creation of several new multilateral development financing institutions for developing countries, including two new institutions that will be focused on infrastructure lending to Asian developing countries.

The long-simmering discontent among developing countries about the Bretton Woods financial architecture, notably about the current allocation of voting rights, has resulted in a revolution in global development finance that is being led by China.

China's rapid economic ascent over the last two decades has led to its having become the world's second largest economy, with accumulated foreign exchange reserves of USD 3.65 trillion at the end of July 2015. China therefore has acquired the financial capacity to act as the financial bulwark for a number of new initiatives for development financing that will be led by developing countries.

Having been thwarted from playing an increasingly important decision-making role in the IMF and World Bank due to the anachronistic allocation of voting rights, China is playing a leadership role in creating new intergovernmental development finance institutions that will be largely governed by developing countries. China will use its vast international reserves to give financial strength to these institutions, although other developing countries will also provide capital.

The NDB, AIIB and Silk Road Fund combined have the potential to significantly increase the total multilateral financing available for development financing over the medium-term, potentially giving developing countries a much greater role and voice in reshaping global development finance over the next decade and beyond.

However at present, the capacity of the BRICS and other developing countries to play a large role in crisis prevention and resolution for developing countries is much more limited, due to constraints on foreign exchange reserves of most large developing countries, including the BRICS, with the exception of China, which had USD 3.65 trillion in foreign exchange reserves at the end of July 2015.

Over the next two decades, significant further progress is likely to take place in the creation of a much stronger Asian financial architecture for financial regulation and supervision, as well as crisis prevention and management and development financing.

A crucial driver for the future evolution of Asia's financial architecture will be the emergence of China as the world's largest economy as well as eventually shifting to full currency convertibility. Currency convertibility will also most likely lead to the Chinese currency playing a significant role as an international reserve currency, will give China a much greater capability to act as a source of liquidity for regional financial crisis prevention and management.

While Japan's initial proposal at the time of the East Asian financial crisis for the creation of an Asian Monetary Fund was unsuccessful, the foundations have subsequently been laid by the ASEAN+3 governments for the creation of an Asian regional financial institution that has a role in regional liquidity management and crisis prevention. These foundations have been laid through the Chiang Mai Initiative and the subsequent Chiang Mai Initiative Multilateralisation.

In order for the CMIM to play a role in crisis prevention and resolution, Asian governments will need to build a stronger regional financial surveillance capability, and that may become increasingly institutionalized under an Asian financial regulatory and supervisory body created by the ASEAN+3.

With China already having created an Asian multilateral architecture for development finance, the creation of the equivalent to an Asian Monetary Fund would then create a new Asian financial architecture that will play a similar role to the current Bretton Woods financial institutions but with a regional focus on Asia.

With Asia projected to account for an increasing share of world GDP over the next two decades, and the current Bretton Woods financial architecture and voting rights heavily dominated by the US and EU nations, it is increasingly necessary for Asian countries to establish their own regional financial architecture with sufficient resourcing for crisis prevention and resolution in the Asian region.

With China likely to become the world's largest economy in about ten years, a key policy issue will be when the Chinese leadership decide to allow full convertibility for the Chinese renminbi (CNY). China has been taking gradual steps towards currency liberalization, including creating offshore renminbi settlement centres in a number of major international financial centres, including Hong Kong, Singapore, UK and Canada. An estimated 18 per cent of China's trade was settled in Chinese currency in 2014.

While the Chinese government may only gradually shift to full currency convertibility, it is a long-term objective that they will pursue through a process of further exchange rate liberalization. The eventual move by China to full currency convertibility will also accelerate the development of an AMF, since China will be able to more easily expand the AMF's capital by using its own currency rather than having to utilize its foreign exchange reserves.

However there is a risk that the new financial architecture being created could become too heavily dominated by China in terms of voting rights in the various new multilateral institutions being created. While the NDB seems to have addressed this issue from the outset by allocating equal voting rights to all the BRICS countries, the voting rights distribution of the AIIB may be vulnerable to the same weaknesses as the Bretton Woods institutions. This could eventually create the same kind of problems that the Bretton Woods institutions have experienced if there is insufficient flexibility built in to the voting rights formula to accommodate the rising economic weight of other economies. India and Indonesia are projected to also be rising global economic powers, and if the voting rights distribution is not designed to accommodate their future expansion, then this could result in the AIIB also experiencing difficulties as some members seek a redistribution of voting rights.

Outlook for the Asian financial architecture

For the first time since the end of the Second World War, the global financial architecture created by the Bretton Woods Conference in 1944 is being redrawn. China is leading this process, although many other developing countries are also taking part in the new multilateral institutions that are being created. The rising importance of the Asia-Pacific economies in the global economy has created increasing political momentum for reforms that will reshape the international financial architecture.

The initiatives led by China to create the NDB, AIIB and Silk Road Fund will significantly reshape the financial architecture in Asia, with China set to play a much greater role in development financing across emerging Asia. While these initiatives are mainly focused on creating new multilateral institutions for development finance, other Asian multilateral institutions that will play a greater role in crisis prevention and management are also likely to emerge in future.

A key challenge for the success of this new financial architecture is how well the new institutions can perform given the geopolitical tensions that still exist between a number of the major Asian nations. Therefore the establishment of a framework for political co-operation and conflict resolution in Asia that can prevent escalation of disputes between Asian nations will be crucial for the future success of Asia's ambitions for economic and financial integration.

Chapter 4

Asian Megacities

Managing Urban Growth

In much of developing Asia, the rapid pace of urbanization and population growth is creating vast urban conurbations with populations that exceed ten million people. In Asia, there are currently 16 such megacities, including Tokyo, Delhi, Shanghai, Beijing, Mumbai and Jakarta. These megacities are creating a wide array of challenges for governments, due to problems of traffic congestion, costs of provision of essential infrastructure and services, as well as managing environmental problems such as air and water pollution, groundwater depletion and threats from flooding.

With many developing Asian countries still projected to have significant population growth over the next two decades, addressing the rapid growth of Asia's largest cities will be a high priority for governments.

In addition to the economic and social costs of the future growth of Asian megacities, there is also growing competition among global cities to attract new investment in industries. Cities that become increasingly uncompetitive in this new Asian urban landscape therefore could face significant economic costs if they are unable to generate rapid output and jobs growth. Even worse, uncompetitive cities could face an exodus of corporations, which may be attracted to relocate to more competitive cities.

India's megacities

Between 2015 and 2050, India's population is projected to increase by 350 million persons, according to United Nations population projections, with India set to overtake China as the world's most populous country by 2028 (United Nations, World Urbanisation Prospects, 2014).

Of Asia's 16 megacities in 2015, four of these are in India. By 2030, the number of Indian megacities will rise to seven. By that time, 69 Indian cities will have a population in excess of one million persons.

The tremendous pressures that India has faced since independence due to rapid population growth can be best understood by looking back at India's population in 1950, which was just 376 million people, and comparing it to the population in 2015, which had reached 1,282 million. With such a massive increase in the total size of the Indian population since 1950, amounting to around 900 million persons, the pace of urbanization has been extremely rapid.

The Indian government's persistent fiscal difficulties due to high government debt and fiscal deficits have limited government expenditure and capital investment plans for managing India's rapid urban development. Consequently India's large cities have suffered many negative impact effects from urbanization, including increasing traffic congestion, environmental problems, and lack of adequate infrastructure for power, roads, public transportation systems and other forms of public infrastructure.

Meanwhile the rapid rate of population growth has created increasing urban sprawl in Indian cities. In Delhi, which is already one of India's megacities, the population in 1950 was only 1.3 million people. By 2015, the population of Delhi had reached 25 million, making it one of Asia's largest megacities.

This was certainly not the size of population that New Delhi was originally designed for. New Delhi was built as the modern capital for the British colonial government of India based on the design of British architect Edwin Lutyens in 1913. The city was built on a grand scale on an open, undeveloped plain, which gave Lutyens almost unlimited scope for creating his own grand vision for a capital city. With wide open spaces and classic design, the new city was a masterpiece of elegant design for a modern capital city.

For the modest population of New Delhi in the next three decades, the city was spacious, with the roads having plenty of capacity to cope with population growth. The hinterland of the city was still rural. My father recounted anecdotes of having seen tigers jumping across the road in rural areas near Delhi soon after the Second World War.

One of my favourite memories of Lutyens' elegant architectural design of the centre of New Delhi is of riding on the back of my cousin's motorcycle up the long Parisian-style boulevard that Lutyens designed leading up to the Viceroy's House, now the official residence of the President of India, known as the *Rashtrapati Bhavan*. We managed to go right up to the gate of the Presidential residence, and by coincidence, we were behind an official car that was entering the residence. The security guard lifted the barrier, and let the official government vehicle through, and surprisingly also waved us through.

These were happier times in the world, before the era of widespread terrorism and extreme security controls. These days all government buildings in central Delhi are heavily protected with military and reinforced guard posts, but in those days, there was little in the way of security.

We parked the motorcycle in the driveway at the entrance to the residence, and my cousin thought that since we had already reached the doorstep of the President's official residence, we should try our luck at visiting inside the residence to look around. We went to the front door of the Presidential residence, and since the door was closed, knocked on the door. This was the Indian equivalent of entering the Buckingham Palace main gates, ringing the doorbell and asking to meet the monarch. A butler dressed in a very smart uniform opened the door, and asked us who we were. After a rather brief conversation we were duly sent packing, albeit very politely. Unfortunately we were not invited for tea with the President of India that day!

Since those halcyon days the population of Delhi has continued to grow at a rapid rate. With the population of the city having already reached 25 million people, traffic in New Delhi is badly congested, and although Lutyens' architectural design still makes New Delhi one of the most beautiful cities, much of the city's grandeur has been eroded by the effects of traffic congestion and poor maintenance of infrastructure. By 2050, the United Nations projections indicate that Delhi's population will have reached 36 million, adding another 11 million people into the congestion.

By 2030, there will be seven Indian megacities with a population exceeding ten million persons, with Delhi projected to remain India's most populous city. The scale of increase in Delhi's population over the next ten years is equivalent to another new megacity being added on to the existing population, with another ten million residents expected to live in Delhi by 2030.

This is resulting in the rapid expansion of urbanization in Delhi's hinterland, with satellite cities being built in the surrounding areas, such as Gurgaon, which has emerged as a fast-growing satellite city with a major new office and residential district.

Mumbai is also projected to have a very large increase in total population size by 2030, with an estimated additional 6.8 million persons projected to live in the city by that time.

Kolkata, Bangalore and Chennai are also projected to see further large increases in population, making these existing megacities considerably larger. In addition, Hyderabad and Ahmedabad will join the ranks of India's megacities by 2030.

The next Indian city that is on the threshold of becoming a megacity is Poona, whose population is rapidly approaching the megacity level, albeit not expected to cross that threshold by 2030.

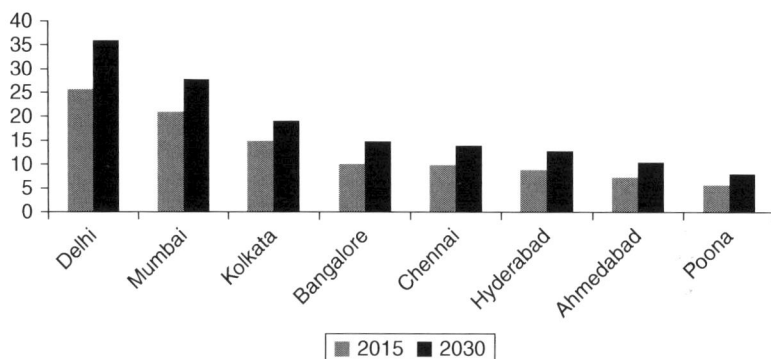

Figure 4.1   Indian megacities to 2030 (population in millions)
Source: UN, World Urbanisation Prospects, 2014.

According to United Nations population projections, the urban population of India is expected to increase from 31 per cent of the population in 2014 to 40 per cent of the population by 2030. This implies that an additional 200 million persons will live in India's cities by 2030, in just 15 years time.

In order to cope with this huge increase in the total size of India's urban population, the Indian government will need to make urban development one of its most important economic priorities. This has been recognized by the BJP government, and Prime Minister Modi has spearheaded the Indian smart city initiative as one of the key policy responses to tackle this challenge.

India's 100 smart cities strategy

Since Prime Minister Modi took office following the BJP election victory in 2014, one of the most visionary policy announcements that he has made is for a plan to build 100 smart cities in India.

This reflects a very important step in improving Indian economic competitiveness, and Prime Minister Modi has fully understood the importance of modern cities for national competitiveness. Many of the high growth industries of the future are knowledge industries, and the plan to build 100 smart cities recognizes that if India is to attract knowledge industries and global multinationals, the nation will have to develop advanced urban centres that offer efficient power, transport and communications infrastructure as well as being liveable cities for companies to establish facilities such as R&D centres, IT centres and service centres for back office functions.

A number of smart cities are already in the advanced planning stages in India, several of which are located in Gujarat, the state where Prime Minister Modi had previously been chief minister for over a decade. One of India's first smart cities that will become operational is likely to be Gujarat International Finance Tec-City (GIFT), which is intended to be a financial centre that provides an alternative hub with modern infrastructure to Mumbai. Infrastructure development is already underway in GIFT, and the new city is expected to become one of the first new Indian greenfield smart cities.

Gujarat is also developing two other smart city projects. One is the Dholera smart city, which is intended to become an IT hub, and the second is Surat Dream City, which is expected to become the home of a second Indian diamond exchange.

The Indian government has developed a physical infrastructure strategy for the new smart cities which will address a range of key infrastructure needs in the smart cities. These will include:

- waste management to dispose of waste and treatment of sewage;
- water management to use modern technology to manage water resources, including water meters, monitoring of water quality and surveillance of the water system for leakages;
- urban transport systems to provide integrated transport within the city and good connections to rail, road and airport infrastructure, with intelligent traffic management systems;
- energy systems to ensure optimal use of renewable energy and power plants to deliver continuous power supply; and
- e-governance to maximize e-government delivery, including video surveillance.

The integrated management of the energy and water grids using advanced monitoring systems can play a major role in improving the overall efficiency of cities and reducing use of energy and water resources. Efficient integrated management of a city's electricity systems together with advanced renewable energy technology can significantly lower the electricity consumption of a city, reducing total energy costs and lowering carbon emissions. There is also significant loss of water resources in conventional water grids in older cities due to leaking pipes that often are not detected for long periods of time. A smart city water grid has sophisticated sensor systems and meters which monitor the water grid continuously and detect leakages, preventing significant wastage of water resources.

For example, the Civil Engineering department of the Indian Institute of Technology Delhi estimated in a study in 2012 that water losses through the Delhi water grid are around 40 per cent, due to a number of factors, including leaking pipes and theft of water through illegal connections (Times of India, 14 June 2012).

Consequently the long-term efficiency gains from smart city infrastructure can be very significant. However, the infrastructure financing requirements for such large-scale urban development across India will require substantial government infrastructure funding as well as considerable private sector funding.

While Indian private sector real estate developers will be key partners for these projects, the scale of urban development envisaged will also require foreign infrastructure investment. India already has a number of urban development projects that have international private sector partners.

Smart City, a subsidiary of Dubai's Tecom Investments, is developing a smart city in Kochi, which is already in the early stages of development. The new project is called SmartCity Kochi, and is a joint venture between the Government of Kerala and Smart City. The Government of Kerala has a 16 per cent stake in the project. Smart City is a leading developer of knowledge cities, and Tecom Investments has a long track record of developing smart cities and townships in the Middle East, including Dubai Internet City and Dubai Media City. SmartCity Kochi is designed to be a knowledge city that will attract companies in information and communications technology, finance and media.

Singapore is developing the masterplan for the creation of a new smart city on a greenfield site which will be the capital of the Indian state of Andhra Pradesh. Andhra Pradesh lost its capital city when the state was split into two to create a new state called Telangana in 2014. Hyderabad, the former capital of Andhra

Pradesh, will remain the transitional capital city for the Indian state until its new capital city is built. The Singapore government signed a memorandum of understanding with the Infrastructure Corporation of Andhra Pradesh in late 2014 for the development of a masterplan for the new city. Two Singapore urban development firms with a long track record of urban development, Surbana International Consultants Holdings Pte Ltd and Jurong International Holdings Pte Ltd, were selected to develop the masterplan for the new city. The two firms merged in June 2015, creating a new firm called Surbana Jurong Private Limited.

Surbana Jurong completed the final masterplan for the new city, which is to be named Amaravati, in July 2015. The vision is for a new smart city which will have the capacity for a population of 10 million by 2050, which would place it among the ranks of India's megacities if that population threshold is reached. The Andhra Pradesh government has ambitious plans for the development of the new central business district and key state government buildings by 2018.

There has been a rush of other governments to offer their support for the development of smart cities in India, in order to strengthen their political and economic ties with Asia's second-largest BRICS economy. During Prime Minister Modi's visit to France in April 2015, French President Hollande offered to provide Euro 2 billion to finance French assistance for the development of three smart cities in India, including Puducherry, which was once a French port city and has strong historical ties with France, as well as Nagpur.

The advanced technological requirements that will be created by such large-scale smart city development projects will create major new business opportunities for a wide range of multinationals, including global firms with expertise in smart city technology such as Cisco Systems and IBM. Some of the other multinationals that are global leaders in smart city technological development include Hitachi, Toshiba, GE, Schneider Electric and Siemens. There are also likely to be considerable opportunities for construction engineering companies to help to develop such a large number of major new urban development projects, as well as for environmental companies that can build wastewater treatment plants and sewage treatment plants.

With a single greenfield smart city such as GIFT or the new capital of Andhra Pradesh estimated to cost over USD 10 billion each, building 100 smart cities by 2022 as planned by the Indian government could cost in excess of USD 1 trillion, although it is extremely ambitious to expect that all these new cities will be completed within the next decade. The Indian government has also announced significant initiatives for modernizing infrastructure in India's existing cities, which will also be crucial for addressing the infrastructure needs of India's rapidly growing urban population. While these new urban development plans for smart cities are very ambitious, by setting clear targets and deadlines, Prime Minister Modi is aiming to achieve far-reaching results and focus the efforts of the Indian government on a fixed timeline.

President John F. Kennedy did not galvanize the US space program into action by saying that the US would put a man on the moon eventually, when circumstances permitted and the right technology had been developed. He set a clear target in May 1961 of putting a man on the moon "before this decade is out". On 20 July 1969, Apollo 11 landed on the moon.

"First, I believe that this nation should commit itself to achieving the goal, before this decade is out, of landing a man on the moon and returning him safely to the Earth."

US President John F. Kennedy, Speech to Joint Session of US Congress, 25 May 1961, Washington D.C.

It is clear that urban development in India is set to accelerate over the medium term, and this could provide a significant boost to economic growth and industrial development over the next decade and beyond.

There are already a number of smart cities that have been built elsewhere in Asia that India can look to as prototypes for designing its own smart cities. In South Korea, a new smart city has been built on a greenfield site on reclaimed land at Incheon, near Seoul's Incheon International Airport. The new smart city is called Songdo International Business District, and was built at an estimated cost of USD 40 billion.

Having stayed in Songdo smart city during 2014, I was very impressed to find a modern city with beautiful office towers, five star hotels, large landscaped parks and pleasant shopping malls. While some sections of the city were still under construction, the new smart city was fully operational with a large population, bustling shopping malls and plenty of restaurants. They even staged a huge fireworks display while I was visiting, which attracted very large crowds. The apartments in Songdo smart city are indeed very smart, with high technology sensors that measure energy consumption and control security.

China has also been working on a number of smart city projects, a number of which have been developed with Singaporean collaboration. The Sino-Singapore Guangzhou Knowledge City project is currently being developed northeast of Guangzhou city centre, in relatively close proximity to both Guangzhou and the international airport. Singbridge, owned by Singapore's Temasek Holdings, is the co-master developer of the project together with the Guangzhou Development District Administrative Committee.

Singapore and China also have also established a joint project for the development of a smart city called the Sino-Singapore Tianjin Eco-city. The city is intended to create an environmental services industry cluster, and will be an integrated city with offices, residential developments and shopping malls.

China's megacities

China has been through four decades of very rapid transformation in its urban landscape, with the total share of the population living in urban areas having risen from 18 per cent in 1978 to 51 per cent by 2011.

In 2015, China already had six megacities, and despite China's relatively advanced level of economic development and infrastructure quality compared to other lower income Asian developing countries, China's large cities also face severe pressures due to traffic congestion, air and water pollution and industrial waste. By 2030, these six megacities will all have a significant expansion of population size, with Shanghai projected to exceed 30 million persons, and Beijing reaching around 28 million persons. Chengdu, which was not a megacity in 2015, is projected to have a population of ten million by 2030, joining the ranks of China's megacities.

Other Chinese cities are also projected to reach close to the megacity threshold by 2030, with Wuhan, Hangzhou and Dongguan all expected to have a population of around nine million persons.

The emergence of Dongguan to reach the threshold of megacity status is remarkable, since in 1980 when China's economic liberalization was just beginning, its total population was only 137,000 persons. By 1990, its population had reached 550,000, and by 2000, it had grown to 3.6 million. Located on the Pearl

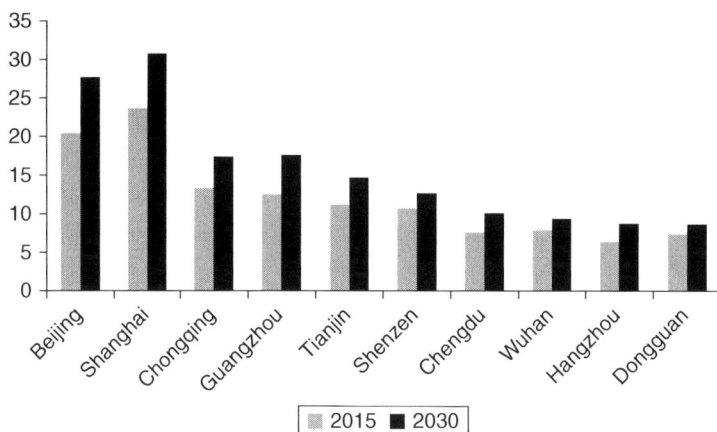

Figure 4.2   Chinese megacities to 2030 (population in millions)
Source: UN, World Urbanisation Prospects, 2014.

River delta, its rapid expansion was attributable to foreign direct investment by companies from Hong Kong and Taiwan seeking to relocate their low-cost operations to benefit from the low labour costs in the Pearl River delta. By 2050, Dongguan is projected to have a population size of 8.7 million, close to reaching the threshold of a megacity.

The Chinese government has also projected significant further rural to urban migration over the next decade, with Premier Li having stated in 2012 that further urbanization in China has considerable potential to lift domestic demand. The Chinese government has targeted an increase in the share of the total population living in cities over the medium term outlook, rising from 54 per cent in 2012 to 60 per cent by 2020.

However due to the Chinese government's regulatory control over the issuance of resident permits to people moving from one region to another, the government has significant ability to channel the flow of rural migrants towards second and third tier cities, to avoid further rapid expansion of Chinese megacities.

This, combined with the gradually ageing demographics of China over the next three decades, does make the outlook for the future growth of megacities in China less fearsome than in India, where the government has little ability to influence which cities internal migrants choose to move to.

Chinese local governments in the largest cities are also using regulatory measures to try to manage the problems of urban traffic congestion. A number of measures have been introduced in large cities such as Beijing and Shanghai to limit the number of people buying new cars, through mechanisms such as lotteries and auctions for obtaining permits to buy new cars. Combined with continuing large investments in public transport infrastructure, the Chinese government is attempting to mitigate the impacts of rising levels of car ownership on traffic congestion.

The fiscal capacity of the Chinese government for infrastructure development has been very strong during the last three decades, and the Chinese government still has considerable scope to deploy central government funding for infrastructure development in Chinese megacities. The government is already investing heavily in addressing key challenges such as air pollution and water shortages, such as major new energy and water infrastructure projects to address the environmental challenges facing Beijing.

Megacities in other South and Southeast Asian nations

While India and China have the largest populations in the world and face the greatest challenges from rapid urbanization and the expansion of many of their largest cities, a number of other developing Asian economies are also tackling major social, economic and environmental problems with the growth of their own megacities. These megacities included Dhaka, Karachi, Manila and Jakarta as well as Bangkok in 2015. By 2030, Lahore is also projected to become a megacity.

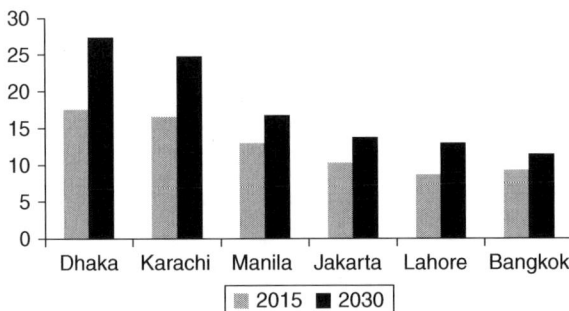

Figure 4.3   South and SE Asian megacities to 2030 (population in millions)

Source: UN, World Urbanisation Prospects, 2014.

Dhaka has a current population of around 18 million persons, with Bangladesh being classified as a low income country by the World Bank. By 2030, the United Nations projects that Dhaka's population will have risen to 27 million people. With the Bangladeshi government having limited fiscal resources to devote to urban development, the outlook for the governance of this megacity is not positive.

One of the many crises that Dhaka is facing is the large share of the population that are extremely poor, with an estimated 3.5 million people living in around 4,000 slums in Dhaka, based on a government estimate stated in the Bangladesh Parliament (Financial Express (Dhaka), 25 February 2013). Lack of government resources for investment in housing programs will result in further increases in the size of Dhaka's slum population over the next 15 years as the population increases by a further nine million people.

Dhaka also faces extreme traffic congestion, due to the weak public transport system, which forces a large proportion of Dhaka's population to use cars, motorcycles or bicycles for transport. Despite considerable planning for a mass rapid transit system (MRT) for Dhaka, there were protracted delays in the process. The Japan International Co-operation Agency has provided funding for the MRT in a deal signed with the Bangladesh government in 2013, and the tendering began in 2015.

To compound the problems that the Bangladeshi government faces, Dhaka is also extremely vulnerable to flooding since it is located on a low-lying area adjacent to three major rivers, and some areas of central Dhaka are below sea level. There have been many serious floods in Dhaka during the last four decades, with protracted flooding in 1987, 1988, 1998 and 2004 that resulted in much of the city being flooded. With fears that climate change will result in even more severe weather events, Dhaka needs large-scale further infrastructure investment in flood prevention systems, but the acute lack of fiscal resources has constrained the ability of the government implement such infrastructure spending.

With the Bangladesh economy showing sustained strong growth, the role of Dhaka as the commercial and financial capital has continued to grow, and the further rapid expansion of Dhaka's population will continue to intensify the problems from urbanization that the megacity already faces.

Bangkok, built on swampland, faces increasing vulnerability to flooding due to its gradual subsidence each year, caused by a number of factors including groundwater depletion and the impact of urbanization in reducing the effectiveness of drainage systems as canals have been in-filled. Meanwhile the size of the total population is projected to increase rapidly over the next decade, increasing the impact of future flood events in Bangkok.

Jakarta, like Dhaka and Bangkok, is also vulnerable to flooding, with regular floods having disrupted the city in recent years during periods of heavy rainfall. However the Indonesian government has substantially improved its fiscal position during the last decade, and with a low government debt to GDP ratio and moderate fiscal deficits, the government can afford to undertake more substantial infrastructure development to address the infrastructure and urban development problems of Jakarta.

The traffic congestion problems of Jakarta are severe, but construction of a MRT system commenced in 2013, with financing from the Japan International Co-operation Agency. The first line of the MRT system is due for completion in 2018.

The government has also undertaken flood mitigation measures through the Jakarta Urgent Flood Mitigation Project, dredging 11 rivers in the area with financing from the World Bank.

With President Jokowi having a strong focus on infrastructure development, the prospects for addressing Jakarta's problems as a megacity are improving, thanks to a combination of strong political will at the highest level, combined with Indonesia's relatively strong fiscal position and its sustained strong economic growth over the past decade. The combination of domestic fiscal resources and access to large-scale development financing from donor nations such as Japan does allow scope for Indonesia to make more rapid progress in addressing the challenges that Jakarta faces as one of Asia's megacities.

The future of Asian megacities

Rapid future growth in the size of many of Asia's megacities signals increasing social, economic and environmental problems in South Asian and Southeast Asian megacities. The relatively limited financial resources of the governments in both these regions to address the mounting challenges faced by megacities signals rising economic and social challenges as these megacities continue to grow in size.

However the outlook for megacities in China may be less bleak, since the Chinese government has a relatively strong fiscal capability to fund long-term infrastructure projects to address many of the key environmental and social problems facing their megacities. Moreover the government has significant regulatory tools to manage the future growth of Chinese megacities, and may be able to divert some of the potential population growth that would have flowed into megacities into China's medium sized cities.

There is also the possibility that Asian regional co-operation initiatives for infrastructure development could provide significantly greater resources to assist the economic development of low income Asian countries, which may also boost efforts to improve infrastructure financing for Asian megacities in Asia's low income nations.

Chapter 5

Emerging Manufacturing Hubs in Asia

The hollowing out of Northeast Asian manufacturing

At a roundtable lunch I was chairing for Malaysian CEOs in 2010, one of Malaysia's leading entrepreneurs, the Chairman of Top Glove, Tan Sri Lim Wee Chai, was the guest speaker. He gave a fascinating and insightful assessment of the changing competitive landscape for the rubber glove industry in Asia.

He explained that his original production facilities for rubber gloves had been in Malaysia, which has long been a leading global production hub for natural rubber and had been a competitive location for producing these products. However as Malaysia continued to develop rapidly and experienced rising wage costs, Top Glove eventually opened manufacturing facilities in China, since labour costs were still relatively low in coastal China and the Chinese domestic market for rubber gloves was growing rapidly.

However Tan Sri Lim went on to explain that as China had continued to develop and because Chinese labour costs had started rising rapidly in recent years, Top Glove had decided to significantly increase production in Malaysia, which had become relatively more competitive again in terms of labour costs, as well as from the point of view of factors such as logistics costs for raw materials and the very high quality standards in Malaysia.

Since that time, global multinationals have increasingly voiced their concerns about rising labour costs across a wide range of Chinese manufacturing industries, and many multinationals have decided to establish new production facilities for their low-cost manufactures in other locations, including in Vietnam, Bangladesh and Cambodia.

The economic development of East Asia has been driven by export-led growth, as East Asian nations became low-cost manufacturing hubs for consumer markets in the US and Europe. Japan was the first of the East Asian economies to become an advanced economy, initially based on a model of low-cost production of manufactures. As domestic wages continued to rise, Japan's competitiveness as a low cost manufacturing hub was gradually eroded by other competitor nations.

A similar pattern of industrialization has been replicated in other East Asian economies, including South Korea, Hong Kong, Taiwan and Singapore, where the gradual erosion of manufacturing competitiveness due to rising wages has resulted in a shift of production to other low-cost locations.

This pattern of industrial development and shifting competitive advantage was originally described as the "flying geese" model of industrial development by Kaname Akamatsu in the 1930s and became better known internationally following several articles he published in international economic journals during the 1960s. In the "flying geese" model of industrial development, nations first develop competitive advantage in low-cost manufacturing with a relatively unskilled, low paid workforce, but as labour costs rise and the industrial workforce becomes more skilled, the structure of industrial production moves into higher value-added products, losing competitiveness in low value-adding industries. As the manufacturing sector loses competitiveness in low value-added segments of industry, these move to other countries, resulting in a hollowing-out of the manufacturing sector.

China's competitiveness in manufacturing

Since 1978, China became the foremost beneficiary of the hollowing out of more advanced East Asian economies, as multinationals from Japan, South Korea, Taiwan and Hong Kong established factories in mainland China in order to tap the large pool of low-cost labour.

However after over three decades of rapid economic growth during which low-cost manufacturing exports played a key role in China's rapid economic development, rising wage costs are eroding China's competitiveness as a low-cost manufacturing export nation. When China first began liberalizing its economy in 1978 and attracting foreign direct investment into low-cost manufacturing, average per capita GDP in China was around USD 180 per year. Since then, Chinese economic growth accelerated to around 10 per cent per year for the next three decades, albeit moderating somewhat during the last four years. This has resulted in Chinese per capita GDP rising to around USD 7,000 per year by 2014.

For a nation with a population of 1.3 billion people, this represents a tremendous achievement and has lifted most of China's population out of absolute poverty. However it also has resulted in higher Chinese labour costs which have gradually reduced China's competitiveness in low cost manufactures.

A number of factors are driving the rapid increase of labour costs in China.

Firstly, the large manufacturing centres of coastal China have been dependent on inflows of migrant workers from inland Chinese provinces to provide a large pool of low-cost labour for their manufacturing plants. However the Chinese government has invested heavily in infrastructure and urban development in inland Chinese provinces over the last decade, due to concerns that rising inequality between coastal and inland provinces could eventually generate social unrest. This has brought more rapid economic development of inland provinces, creating more dynamic employment growth in inland Chinese provinces, resulting in some tightening of the pool of migrant labour flowing to coastal provinces as well as pushing up wage costs for migrant workers.

Secondly the marginal productivity of capital in China is gradually declining due to the rapid pace of modernization of China's capital stock, which has resulted in diminishing marginal productivity gains for additional new investment in physical capital and infrastructure. The slowdown in productivity growth implied by the declining marginal productivity of capital means that rapid wage growth can no longer be largely offset by rapid growth in productivity, and that unit labour costs are rising more rapidly, gradually eroding manufacturing competitiveness.

Thirdly, China is gradually facing the impact of ageing demographics, reflecting factors such as the long-term implications of China's one child policy, which was first introduced in 1980. This is already beginning to reduce the number of new workers joining the workforce each year, and this trend will intensify for future cohorts of new workers joining the labour force over the next two decades.

Rising wage costs are already creating significant economic challenges for China's low-cost manufacturing sector, with multinationals already having begun relocating production for some very low-cost industries such as garments to countries such as Bangladesh and Cambodia, where labour costs are still considerably lower than coastal China.

With hollowing out of Chinese manufacturing industry in other important sectors such as electronics having already commenced, the Chinese economy is likely to experience significant economic restructuring over the next two decades. China will need new growth industries that will absorb the displaced labour from low-cost manufacturing industries that are no longer able to compete globally.

The pace of economic restructuring and hollowing out in China may be significantly more protracted than in less populous economies such as Japan, South Korea, Taiwan and Hong Kong. This is because China has a very large workforce distributed across a large geographic area. Consequently there are still significant variations in manufacturing wage costs across China. Therefore although there may be significant hollowing out of low-cost manufacturing in coastal Chinese provinces, companies can lower their labour costs by shifting their production facilities to Chinese inland provinces as well as to other countries with lower labour costs.

In previous decades, the weak domestic transport infrastructure combined with the mainly export-dominated structure of manufacturing production would have made it very difficult for inland provinces to compete with coastal Chinese provinces in terms of overall production costs. Even infrastructure in coastal China was quite poor just twenty years ago, and rural China was even more backward.

I recall visiting a steel mill in Shanghai in the 1990s, and facing long delays during the drive back from the steel mill as the narrow road was heavily congested with small trucks carrying all types of steel products. Larger trucks could not be used because the road was not wide enough. The global market for traded thermal coal was also boosted during the last decade because of China's poor transport infrastructure from inland coal mining provinces to the coastal regions where coal was needed for power generation. Therefore it was cheaper for thermal coal to be imported from Australia and Indonesia into the coastal ports rather than trying to transport the coal from inland provinces to the coast.

However a number of factors have significantly changed that equation.

Firstly, the rapid growth of China's domestic consumer market has made domestic demand an increasingly important end market for Chinese manufacturing production, reducing the need for factories to be located on the coast so that products could easily be shipped to foreign markets.

Secondly, the massive infrastructure investment program by the Chinese government over the last decade into inland Chinese provinces has created much stronger internal connectivity, with high speed rail networks, strong road infrastructure and a large number of new airports serving major cities in inland China. These developments have made inland Chinese provinces more attractive as hubs for manufacturing, as reflected in the auto industry, which is well distributed in many provinces across the nation.

While this will not stop the process of hollowing out of Chinese manufacturing, it could significantly slow the pace of hollowing out in China compared to other East Asian nations such as Japan that have previously experienced eroding manufacturing competitiveness.

This shift of low cost manufacturing out of China, even if it occurs at a relatively gradual pace, will create major new growth opportunities for the next wave of industrializing Asian economies that are able to attract low-cost manufacturing.

Rising manufacturing wage costs in coastal Chinese provinces have already eroded China's competitiveness in some segments of manufacturing. Global multinationals began shifting their production hubs for low-cost textiles away from coastal China some years ago, with Vietnam, Cambodia and Bangladesh among the nations that attracted new investment inflows for textiles production.

The ASEAN region is likely to emerge as one of the major new hubs for low-cost manufacturing in Asia, since a number of nations with relatively large populations, notably Indonesia, Philippines and Myanmar, have significantly lower wage costs than China. Clearly wage costs alone are not the only factor determining relative competitiveness, and the overall country risk characteristics of the different ASEAN countries will be important in the decision by multinationals about which Asian nation to locate new production facilities in. Political stability, infrastructure quality, rule of law, workforce skills, local market size and issues such as corruption levels all play a part in the location decision.

The Greater Mekong Subregion

One of the major new growth hubs for low-cost manufacturing in Asia will be the Greater Mekong Subregion (GMS).

The GDP of the GMS was around USD 1.1 trillion in 2014, which was larger than the size of the Indonesian economy, at around USD 860 billion. The GMS comprises the fast-growing ASEAN frontier economies of Vietnam, Myanmar, Cambodia and Laos, as well as Thailand and two fast-growing regions of China. Vietnam, Myanmar, Cambodia and Laos are forecast to maintain very strong GDP growth rates over the medium to long-term. Moreover, their per capita GDP is set to increase rapidly, helping to underpin strong growth in consumer spending.

The GMS has considerable competitive advantages that support its future growth as a manufacturing hub, notably relatively low manufacturing wages compared to Northeast Asian countries, as well as geographical proximity to China, which may allow relatively easy integration of ASEAN manufacturing production into the Chinese industrial supply chain. The total trade flows between China and the other countries of the GMS reached USD 153 billion in 2013, reflecting the importance of the GMS as an economic area.

Due to the ASEAN Free Trade Agreement and the China-ASEAN Free Trade Agreement, cross-border trade in goods will also be largely tariff-free, which will allow the development of manufacturing production hubs in the GMS that can supply intermediate goods and finished goods to other nations in ASEAN as well as into China.

Chinese Premier Li Keqiang made major new funding commitments to boost the economic development of the GMS at the 5th Leader's Summit of the GMS held in Bangkok on 20 December 2014, with a strong focus on infrastructure development to boost transportation links between China and ASEAN countries.

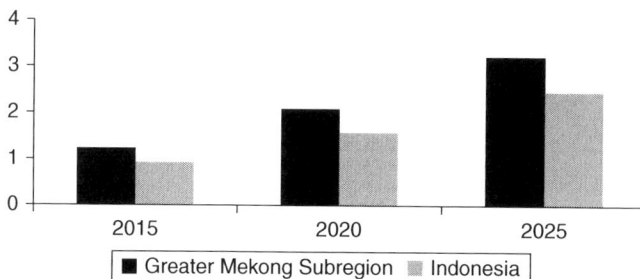

Figure 5.1 Greater Mekong Subregion compared to Indonesia (nominal GDP, USD billion)

Source: IMF; author's estimate.

With China's industrial heartland in the coastal regions of the Pearl River Delta and Yangtze River Delta facing increasing pressures on competitiveness due to rising labour costs, the GMS offers considerable potential as an alternative location for the establishment of low cost manufacturing. Average manufacturing wages in Vietnam, Myanmar, Cambodia and Laos are considerably below the average manufacturing wages in most Chinese provinces. Yunnan and the Guangxi Zhuang Autonomous Region also have relatively lower wage costs compared to the national average, and considerably lower than industrial hubs such as Shanghai, Guangzhou, Tianjin and Beijing.

Strengthening infrastructure connectivity

A major competitive weakness of the GMS is relatively poor infrastructure connectivity, which has been a constraint on economic development. If infrastructure connectivity is strengthened in Southeast Asia to allow high speed rail networks and modern roads to link provinces such as Yunnan in southern China to the Indian Ocean via Thailand and Myanmar, this could significantly improve freight logistics for southern China for both imports and exports. It will also create significant opportunities for the development of major ports and free trade zones in Thailand and Myanmar, boosting their economic development as entrepots. China's One Belt One Road strategic initiative launched in 2013 will help to boost infrastructure in inland Chinese provinces and China's development financing initiatives will improve funding for infrastructure development in ASEAN, strengthening connectivity in the GMS.

With China having launched a number of strategic policy initiatives during 2014 to boost financing for development, the GMS is likely to have access to significant new sources of infrastructure development finance. The new Asian Infrastructure Investment Bank that was founded by China and 20 other Asian countries in November 2014 will be one important new source of financing for GMS projects, with an initial authorized capital of USD 100 billion intended for developing Asian nations. China also established the Silk Road Fund in November 2014, with a commitment of USD 40 billion for financing projects that will improve connectivity in Asia.

In addition to its initiatives to establish multilateral institutions for development finance, China is also providing significant bilateral development finance for other Asian developing countries. Chinese Premier Li Keqiang pledged USD 11.5 billion in financial assistance for the GMS during the 5th GMS Leaders Summit, comprising USD 1 billion in infrastructure aid funding, and USD 10 billion in special loans for GMS projects.

One of the major announcements made during Premier Li's visit to Bangkok for this summit was for a bilateral infrastructure project between Thailand and China with a construction value of USD 10.6 billion for two railway lines to be built linking Thai cities. This could also eventually be linked to China's high speed rail network, creating high-speed rail connectivity between Thailand and China.

Japan and Thailand are also planning to co-operate on the construction of four new railway projects in Thailand. These are for a high speed railway from Bangkok to Chiang Mai, which will be around 720 kilometres in distance and will be funded with low cost development financing by Japan, a railway from Bangkok to Sa Kaew, a rail link from Kanchanaburi to Bangkok and Laem Chabang, and a railway link between Mae Sot and Mukdahan. The GMS nations also have access to other important sources of infrastructure financing, including multilateral lending from the World Bank and Asian Development Bank, as well as bilateral lending from Japan. In the case of Myanmar, there have been significant new official aid and lending commitments by OECD countries following the political and economic liberalization of Myanmar since 2011.

While economic co-operation in infrastructure development in the GMS is showing signs of accelerating, the GMS also has significant political challenges to resolve in relation to management of the water resources of the Mekong River. Regional efforts to boost the economic development of the GMS could help this issue.

There have been long-running disputes between a number of sovereign states in the GMS about dams that have been built or are planned for the Mekong River, because of the implications of such infrastructure projects for the millions of people who rely on the Mekong River for their food security. Greater regional co-operation amongst GMS leaders may also help to create a regional platform for managing and resolving such disputes over the water resources of the Mekong River.

The Vietnamese manufacturing sector

The Vietnamese economy, which is at the heart of the GMS, has stabilized considerably since 2010. Previous high inflation rates, which were a key macroeconomic problem, have moderated to just 4.0 per cent year on year in 2014, from a peak of 23 per cent year on year in August 2011. This has allowed significant easing of monetary policy, supporting economic recovery.

A substantial improvement in Vietnam's export performance over the last three years has also resulted in foreign exchange reserves increasing significantly since 2011. Vietnam's foreign exchange reserves had fallen to a critically low level in 2011, estimated at around USD 13.5 billion, but subsequently rebounded to an estimated USD 35 billion by mid-2015. With Vietnam's electronics industry cluster growing rapidly and a new petrochemicals industry cluster currently under construction, Vietnam looks set to be an important segment of the GMS manufacturing export sector.

Vietnam is also attracting significant new investment inflows into its textiles industry, which is already one of Vietnam's key manufacturing exports. In 2014, Vietnamese exports of textiles and clothing reached USD 24.5 billion, increasing by 18 per cent year-on-year. If the Trans-Pacific Partnership free trade agreement is successfully concluded, this will provide a significant boost to Vietnam's textiles and clothing industry by providing Vietnam with tariff-free access for its garments exports to the key US market, which is already a large market for Vietnamese garments exports.

The EU-Vietnam free trade agreement which was agreed in principle in August 2015 will also boost Vietnamese exports over the medium term, as the bilateral FTA will remove tariffs on 99% of goods traded over the next seven years. The overall impact on Vietnam's export industry is expected to be significant, as the EU is already Vietnam's second largest export market, accounting for Euro 22 billion or 18% of total Vietnamese exports in 2014.

The new FTA will be positive for the export growth of the Vietnamese electronics and clothing industries, as it will give duty free access for Vietnamese products into the EU market. If the TPP deal is also concluded, this will represent a further boost for Vietnamese manufacturing exports into the markets of the TPP member countries, notably the US.

Due to rules of origin requirements, the EU-Vietnam FTA will encourage multinationals to build up their textiles and electronics supply chain in Vietnam so that a high share of value-adding for the final product is completed in Vietnam. If the TPP is also successfully concluded, this will also have strict rules of origin requirements, which will catalyse more foreign direct investment into Vietnam's textiles and clothing industry.

A new wave of shifting manufacturing production is currently underway in the Asian electronics industry, as multinationals shift their production of electronics products such as semiconductor chips, mobile phones and printers away from coastal China towards other lower cost production hubs. Vietnam has been a key beneficiary of this trend, with Samsung opening a mobile phone plant in Vietnam in 2009, which was a major step for Vietnam in establishing its electronics industry. Another key investment that boosted Vietnam's electronics industry was the decision by Intel to build a semiconductor chip testing and assembly plant in Vietnam that opened in 2010. Many other multinationals have subsequently followed, including Kyocera, Canon, LG Electronics and Nokia. LG Electronics recently announced that it would switch production of TV sets from its Thai plant to its Vietnam facility as Vietnam provided the more efficient and lower cost production centre.

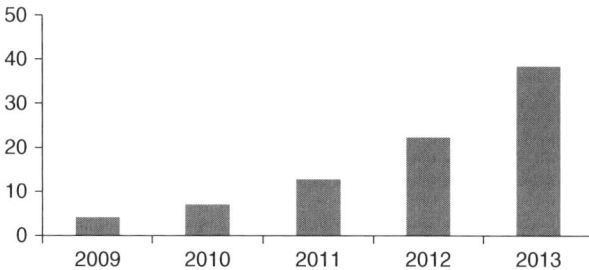

Figure 5.2 Vietnam electronics exports, 2009–13 (USD billion)
Source: UN International Trade Center data.

Samsung has become a major investor in Vietnam, with production facilities in Ho Chi Minh City, Bac Ninh and Thai Nguyen. Samsung announced plans in late 2014 to build a second smartphone factory in Vietnam involving an investment of USD 3 billion, and is expected to reduce production of mobile phones in China due to rising wage costs. Samsung already accounts for around 20 per cent of total Vietnamese exports, and has around 73,000 employees in Vietnam; Samsung recently announced that it is planning to hire 60,000 new employees in Vietnam.

Overall a number of factors are supporting Vietnam's further development as a major Asian manufacturing hub, helped by the new FTAs that Vietnam has been negotiating and also because of its competitiveness due to low manufacturing wage costs compared to China.

Myanmar: gateway to southern China

Myanmar currently does not have any competitive strength in manufacturing, having been heavily reliant for decades on imported manufactures, mainly from China. However with the rapid economic liberalization underway, Myanmar does have the potential to become a manufacturing export hub, based on its very low wage costs, if some of the key infrastructure constraints are addressed. If Myanmar's power, rail and port infrastructure is modernized, this could create significant potential for Myanmar ports to become entrepots for trade with China, allowing inland provinces in southwest China better access to global markets for their manufacturing exports as well as for imports of raw materials.

China has already invested in building oil and gas pipelines from Kyaukpyu port in Myanmar to Yunnan province in southern China, adjacent to the Myanmar border. Both the pipelines were funded by Chinese investment, and the length of the pipelines in 2,400 kilometres, serving the Chinese cities of Kunming and Chongqing.

China also has proposed plans to build a railway from Kyaukpyu to southern China. Once this railway link is built, it will create significant potential for Myanmar to rapidly expand its role as a logistics and manufacturing hub for the Chinese market.

There is also planning underway for the development of Dawei port in Myanmar, with Thailand and Myanmar having established the Dawei Special Economic Zone Development Company for the purpose of developing the port. The Japanese government has also proposed to help with the development of Dawei port, and will help with the planning of the project. The Myanmar government has approved the construction of a 140 kilometre road from Kanchanburi in Thailand to Dawei, so that the new port can become a major logistics hub for Thai industry.

The Dawei port development is expected to be an infrastructure megaproject, with a deep sea port to be built, along with major road linkages, as well as new power projects to provide electricity for the industries expected to locate in the Dawei Special Economic Zone.

The new Silk Road Economic Belt

The improved connectivity planned for Myanmar is part of a much broader vision for the improved connectivity of China, ASEAN and Central Asia with Europe. The Chinese government has announced major new strategic plans to develop a new Silk Road Economic Belt that links China with Central Asia and ASEAN, extending through to the Middle East and Europe.

> *"The envisaged economic belt along the Silk Road is inhabited by nearly three billion people and it represents the biggest market in the world, with enormous, unparalleled potential for trade and investment co-operation between the countries involved."*
>
> Chinese President Xi Jinping, "Work Together to Build the Silk Road Economic Belt", Speech at the Nazarbayev University, Astana, Kazakhstan, 7 September 2013.

China has already established a direct rail link between Chongqing and Duisberg in Germany, with the first cargo trains having already commenced using this route in August 2014. The railway route goes through Kazakhstan, Russia, Poland and Belarus, and reduces the shipment time from five weeks by sea to just two weeks by the new rail link. While the cost is still significantly higher than sea freight, the much lower time required for rail shipment is an important advantage for many companies.

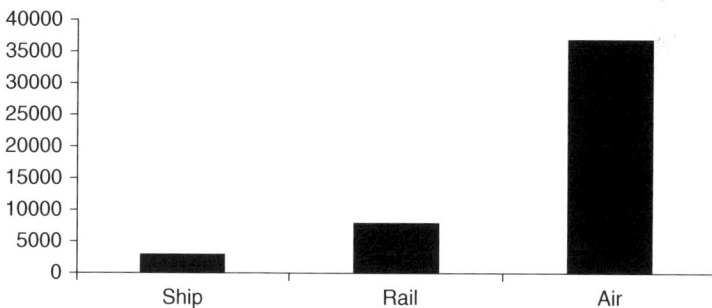

Figure 5.3 China–Europe freight cost (40 foot container equivalent weight, USD, 2014)

Source: Various freight forwarding estimates.

Improved connectivity in the Southeast Asian economies of the GMS will assist the economic development of the inland Chinese provinces in southwest China such as Yunnan province, which is already growing more rapidly than the Chinese national average. The economic development of the GMS will therefore help to realize a key strategic priority of the Chinese government, for reducing the economic development gap between inland Chinese provinces and the more advanced Chinese coastal provinces.

The accelerated economic development of the GMS has become a key policy focus for national leaders from China as well as ASEAN. With China taking a key leadership role within the GMS by providing major new funding for improving infrastructure connectivity at a regional as well as bilateral level, the economic development of the GMS is set to accelerate over the next five years. In addition, China has launched other development finance initiatives in 2014 that will also help to fund GMS infrastructure projects, notably the Asian Infrastructure Investment Bank and the Silk Road Fund.

The GMS regional economy is already growing at around 6 per cent per year, with an economy whose total size is larger than the Indonesian economy. The new initiatives to accelerate economic development of the GMS could further boost the GMS economic growth rate over the medium term outlook.

With concerns among some ASEAN countries having risen in recent years about China's territorial claims in the South China Sea, this latest strategic initiative led by China for the accelerated economic development of the GMS will provide an important platform for regional co-operation and strengthening economic ties between China and Southeast Asia.

Greater regional co-operation among the GMS countries may eventually help to create a more stable regional platform for joint economic co-operation and dispute resolution relating to the use of the water resources of the Mekong River. Disputes over the use of the water resources of the Mekong River remains an important political risk for the GMS countries, so a key priority for the success of the GMS will be to manage and resolve these disputes about the use of the Mekong River water resources.

The Indonesian manufacturing sector

During the first half of the 1990s, the Indonesian manufacturing sector experienced a period of rapid growth during which manufactured exports grew at a pace of around 20 per cent per year. At this point, Indonesia appeared to be industrializing rapidly, with manufacturing set to become an important growth sector and a major source of new employment growth.

However this period of rapid manufacturing growth ended with the onset of the East Asian crisis in 1997, which resulted in a protracted period of political turmoil, economic recession and a banking sector crisis. Indonesia eventually emerged from this dark period in its economic development with gradual economic stabilization and recovery under President Yudhoyono after he was elected to office in 2004. However growth in the manufacturing sector had slowed down to around 7 per cent per year between 1997 and 2004.

The Indonesian economy experienced a decade of sustained strong growth under President Yudhoyono, proving to be resilient even during the depths of the global financial crisis, when financial markets had anticipated that Indonesia might be vulnerable to capital flight and another economic crisis. Having demonstrated its macroeconomic resilience in 2009–10, Indonesia's strong macroeconomic performance earned sovereign rating upgrades and it became one of the most favoured emerging markets for global investors.

Much of its strong growth performance was underpinned by rapid growth in commodity-related exports, notably of thermal coal, as rapidly growing Chinese imports of thermal coal created expectations of a protracted period of strong export growth of Indonesian thermal coal.

However, since 2011, thermal coal prices have fallen sharply, due to rapidly expanding global supply of coal compounded by a recent sharp decline in Chinese thermal coal imports from Indonesia.

The impact of falling coal prices since 2011, as well as subsequent price declines for other major commodity exports from Indonesia such as for copper and LNG, have resulted in a significant slowdown in Indonesian export growth and have triggered a sharp deterioration in Indonesia's current account balance from sustained surpluses prior to 2012 to chronic deficits since then.

Partly reflecting this deterioration in Indonesia's external trade position, the pace of GDP growth in Indonesia has slowed down to around 5 per cent per year by 2014, compared with around 6.5 per cent during 2010–12.

Indonesia's dependence on commodity exports has again been exposed as a key macroeconomic vulnerability, and one of the key challenges that Indonesia will face over the next two decades is to develop its industrial economy and become a hub for Asian manu-facturing exports.

Over the next two decades, Indonesia's working age population is projected to increase by around 20 million persons. This implies that around 1.5 million new workers will enter the workforce each year, and the manufacturing sector will need to play a key role in generating sufficient new employment to absorb these cohorts of new workers entering the labour market. If Indonesia fails to cre-ate sufficient jobs growth, there could be growing risks from rising discontent and social unrest, as occurred during the Arab Spring in a number of Middle Eastern countries such as Tunisia and Egypt. The World Bank has estimated that around 28 million Indonesians live below the poverty line, defined as around USD 1.25 per day (World Bank, Indonesia Overview, 17 April 2015). If a measure of USD 2 per day is used to define the poverty line, the World Bank estimates that around 50 per cent of Indonesian households are living on incomes that are around the poverty line.

In order to address the challenges of large numbers of young workers entering the workforce as well as underemployment, one of the key policy issues that the Indonesian government needs to address is to make Indonesia more competitive as a manufactur-ing hub for exports. There are many reasons why Indonesia has not yet become a successful manufacturing export hub in the way that other East Asian economies such as South Korea, Thailand or most recently Vietnam have achieved. The business climate in Indonesia remains unattractive for foreign multinationals, as reflected in Indonesia's rank at number 114 on the World Bank's Ease of Doing Business Index for 2015, out of 189 economies measured.

This reflects a wide range of factors, including government red tape, complex legal and regulatory approval processes, a difficult legal system for contract enforcement, and lengthy approvals for construction permits. Foreign manufacturers also have to con-tend with weak power and transport infrastructure and difficult labour laws. As if these hurdles were not enough, the Indonesian government's latest contribution to the competitive landscape was a proposed new law that would have prevented foreigners from working in Indonesia unless they spoke Indonesian to an approved standard. However this proposed law did not proceed.

While Indonesia will most likely continue to attract large foreign direct investment flows into manufacturing facilities for the sub-stantial domestic market of 240 million persons, the key challenge is to become a competitive hub for manufacturing exports. If Indonesia fails to build itself up as a competitive industrial hub, the long-term political and economic consequences could be severe for its economic stability.

India's future role as a manufacturing hub

Prime Minister Modi was elected to office in May 2014, bringing a new sense of urgency to building India's manufacturing sector. According to the most recent National Accounts estimates produced by the Indian Government, the manufacturing sector output accounted for around 18 per cent of total GDP, which is significantly lower than other Asian industrial nations such as China and South Korea. In China, manufacturing accounts for an estimated 32 per cent of GDP, while in South Korea, manufacturing accounts for around 31 per cent of GDP.

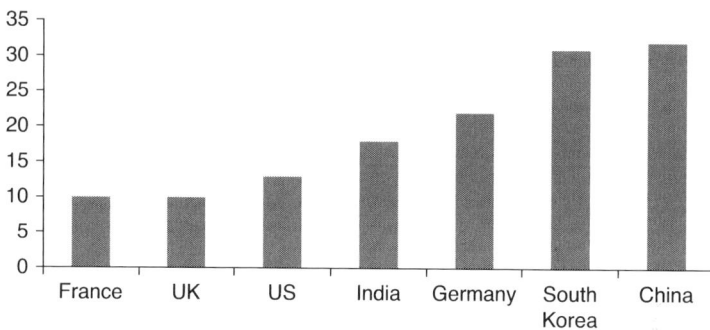

Figure 5.4   Manufacturing output as share of GDP, 2013
Source: World Bank, Indian government data.

India's large population and youthful demographics will result in very large cohorts of workers entering the workforce over the next decade, with around 12 million workers projected to join the workforce each year. This will require sustained rapid economic growth in order to absorb the large inflows of new workers. The Modi government has therefore set a target to lift manufacturing output from 18 per cent of GDP to 25 per cent of GDP by 2022. If this ambitious goal can be achieved, it will generate an estimated 100 million new jobs in the manufacturing sector by 2022.

One of the important advantages that the Indian manufacturing sector has is the large domestic consumer market, with private consumption accounting for 60 per cent of GDP. Therefore if the Indian economy moves on to a high growth path with sustained average GDP growth of 8 per cent or more annually, this would fuel rapid growth in consumer spending and help to boost manufacturing growth.

If India can also improve its competitiveness as a manufacturing export hub, this could also significantly contribute to manufacturing sector growth outperforming GDP growth. The Modi government has embarked on very significant plans for boosting infrastructure development, which would be a key enabler of manufacturing sector competitiveness.

India has already made substantial progress in becoming more globally competitive in some key industries, including the auto sector. Prior to the commencement of economic liberalization in 1991, India only had two main models of passenger cars. One was the Ambassador car, which was the 1950s Morris Oxford model, and the other was the Premier Padmini, which was based on the Fiat 1200 *GranLuce Berlina*, a Fiat model introduced into the Italian market in 1957.

The liberalization of the Indian auto sector and the introduction of foreign competition has resulted in a dramatic transformation of the Indian auto market over the last 25 years, with many major global automakers establishing production facilities in India. India's own domestic automakers have also become much more internationally competitive, with Tata Motors now a significant player in international markets following its acquisition of Jaguar Land Rover from Ford in 2008.

The size of India's domestic auto manufacturing industry has grown substantially since liberalization, with total domestic production of passenger cars at 3.1 million vehicles in 2013–14, with an additional 800,000 commercial vehicles also manufactured in India during that financial year. Automakers are also exporting cars made in India, with Hyundai currently producing around 700,000 autos per year in India, of which around 200,000 are exported. Ford opened a new auto plant in Sanand in Gujarat in March 2015 which will have the capacity to produce 240,000 cars per year, with around 50 per cent of production intended to be exported to other emerging markets worldwide.

In 2014, around 600,000 autos produced in India were exported, and India is expected to become a significantly larger production hub for auto exports over the next five years.

The transformation of India's auto industry from a heavily protected uncompetitive industry into a leading sector of Indian manufacturing exports over the last two decades indicates that India does have the potential to become one of Asia's leading manufacturing hubs over the next twenty years.

Bangladesh

With its large pool of low-cost labour, Bangladesh has already emerged as an important new manufacturing hub for the international garment industry as an alternative location to coastal China. The ready-made garments industry in Bangladesh has boomed over the last decade, with an estimated 5,000 garment factories and 4.2 million employees in the industry. Total exports of garments in 2014 were estimated at USD 23 billion, accounting for around 80 per cent of Bangladesh's total exports.

Bangladesh has a population of 160 million persons, and has been experiencing sustained strong economic growth over the last decade due to the large foreign direct investment inflows into the garment industry as well as the very rapid growth in total exports.

Although Bangladesh still remains a low income country, its macroeconomic performance has significantly improved due to hollowing out of the low-cost garments industry in coastal China and the shift by multinationals to Bangladesh.

Continued economic growth at a pace of around 6 per cent per year should push Bangladesh per capita GDP into the lower middle income category within the near future. If Bangladesh can sustain average GDP growth per year of around 6 per cent or higher, this should allow domestic consumer demand to become an important driver of industrial development and manufacturing output.

Structural trends

Although Asia will continue to be the world's leading region for low-cost manufacturing, the location of low-cost manufacturing will continue to shift over the long-term, reflecting the changes in relative competitiveness of different industrial hubs. One of the key structural trends will be the gradual erosion of competitiveness of low-cost manufacturing in coastal China, which will result in a major shift in manufacturing investment flows towards other low-cost manufacturing locations in inland China and also into other industrial hubs such as Thailand, Vietnam, Cambodia, Indonesia, India and Bangladesh.

The ASEAN region is expected to be a major beneficiary of the shift of low-cost manufacturing out of coastal China. The Greater Mekong Subregion, which also includes some adjacent Chinese provinces, is expected to be one of the most significant beneficiaries of these trends.

For global multinationals in the manufacturing sector, the next two decades will be a period of significant change as they reshape the geographic distribution of their manufacturing production to adjust to rapidly rising wage costs in China and shift low-cost manufacturing operations to new manufacturing growth hubs in Southeast Asia and South Asia.

While China's manufacturing sector is facing eroding competitiveness in low-cost manufacturing, especially in coastal Chinese provinces, a number of low income developing countries may benefit from a period of rapid industrialization due to the hollowing out of low cost manufacturing in China. Vietnam, Cambodia and Bangladesh have already been significant beneficiaries of this megatrend, but other Asian emerging markets such as India, Indonesia, Thailand, Philippines and Myanmar could also attract substantial new foreign direct investment inflows into their manufacturing sectors.

Chapter 6

China

Asia's Fragile Superpower

China's economic ascendancy

Since economic reforms led by China's senior leader Deng Xiaoping commenced in 1978, China's economic ascent over the next 35 years to 2014 has been spectacular. The number of people living in extreme poverty in China has been estimated to be 81 per cent of the total population in 1981, when China was still predominantly an agricultural economy and a large share of the total population lived in rural areas. An estimated 94 per cent of the rural population lived in extreme poverty in 1981, with around 45 per cent of the urban population also living in absolute poverty (Addison and Nino-Zarazua, 2012).

During the period from 1980 until 2010, China grew at an annual average rate of 10 per cent per year, as economic liberalization resulted in strong inflows of foreign direct investment by global manufacturing multinationals to benefit from China's low labour costs. The economic development of the Yangtze River Delta around Shanghai and the Pearl River Delta centred around Guangdong province became the new growth drivers for the Chinese economy.

This resulted in the rapid urbanization of coastal China, as industrialization created rapid jobs growth and attracted large inflows of Chinese workers into these coastal regions.

As a result of the rapid growth of China's manufacturing sector and the industrialization of coastal China, poverty rates in China fell rapidly during the 1980s and 1990s. According to World Bank data on per capita GDP levels in current USD terms, China's per capita GDP rose from an estimated USD 193 in 1980 to USD 314 by 1990, still a relatively modest improvement. However over the next decade, per capita GDP levels tripled to USD 949 by 2000. The decade between 2000 and 2010 was the most transformational for the Chinese economy, as per capita GDP rose to USD 4,433 by 2010, making China an upper middle-income country. Since that time, China's per capita GDP levels have continued to grow rapidly, as strong growth in household incomes as well as some appreciation against the USD since 2010 have propelled Chinese per capita GDP to around USD 7,500 by 2014.

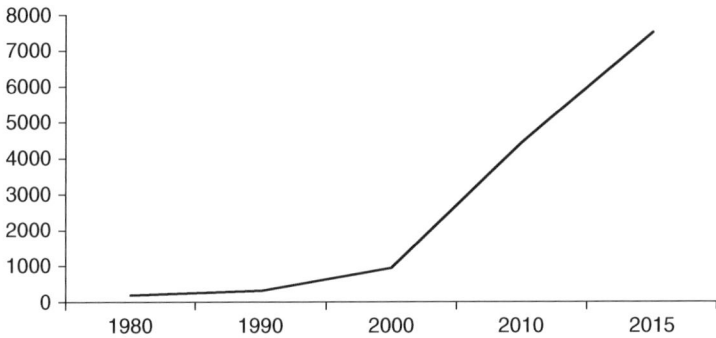

Figure 6.1   China's economic miracle (per capita GDP in nominal USD)
Source: World Bank data.

The rapid pace of economic development has resulted in far-reaching progress in poverty alleviation in China, with the total number of people living in absolute poverty having been reduced by an estimated 750 million persons in the three decades since 1980 (World Bank, "Poverty Overview", 2015).

The rapid economic growth rate of China since 1980 has also resulted in the total size of Chinese GDP escalating rapidly, from USD 200 billion in 1980 to USD 390 billion by 1990, with China becoming a USD one trillion economy in 1998. By 2010 China leapt forward to become a USD six trillion economy, and by 2014, it had crossed the threshold of the USD ten trillion mark.

The rapid growth of China's total GDP resulted in China overtaking Japan in 2009 to become Asia's largest economy, and by 2014, the size of Chinese GDP was more than double Japan's annual GDP output, with the widening gap between China and Japan having been accentuated by the sharp depreciation of the Japanese yen against the USD and also China's CNY since late 2012.

Having overtaken Japan to become the world's second largest economy, there is much debate amongst economists about when China's GDP will become larger than the US economy, putting it in the number one position. Based upon current GDP growth trends with China growing in the range of 5.5 per cent to 6.5 per

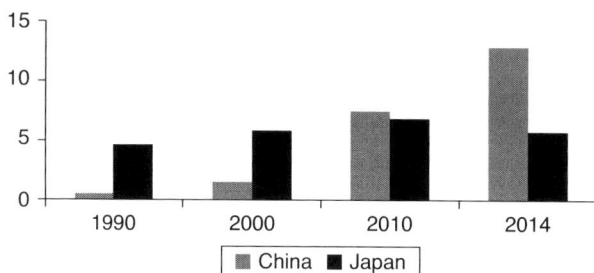

Figure 6.2 Asian economic powers: rising dragon, setting sun (GDP in nominal USD, trillion)

Source: IMF data.

cent per year over the medium term outlook to 2020 and then gradually moderating to a potential growth rate of around 5 per cent growth by 2030, Chinese GDP is likely to overtake US GDP by around 2030, measuring GDP in nominal terms. On a per capita basis, Chinese GDP per capita would remain far below US per capita GDP levels by 2030. Chinese per capita GDP is projected to rise from just 14 per cent of US per capita GDP in 2015 to around 25 per cent of US per capita GDP by 2030.

However if China has a hard landing or protracted growth slowdown sometime in the next decade, this could delay the date by which Chinese GDP would overtake US GDP. China's economic growth momentum has moderated significantly during the 2011–15 period compared to the rapid 10 per cent average annual real GDP growth achieved in the first three decades after its economic reforms began. There are also increasing signs of economic imbalances in the Chinese economy which have raised concerns about whether China may experience a hard landing or protracted period of weaker growth due to the impact of these imbalances. Nevertheless, China's estimated long-term growth path is likely to make it the world's largest economy within the next two decades, with significant geopolitical and economic implications for the rest of the world as the size of the Chinese trade and investment flows become increasingly important.

China's economic slowdown

Since 2010, China's GDP growth rate has begun to moderate. In part, this reflects cyclical factors due to the surge in GDP growth in 2009–10 following large fiscal and monetary stimulus measures introduced in 2008 to tackle the global financial crisis. However there are also structural factors that will gradually lower China's potential GDP growth rate over the long-term.

One of the important structural changes that is occurring in China is the impact of demographic ageing on Chinese GDP growth, as the size of the working age population drops at an increasingly rapid pace over the next two decades. A second important factor that will lower China's potential growth rate is the declining marginal productivity of capital. Following decades of large-scale infrastructure development and industrial modernization in China, the gains from further incremental investment are expected to gradually moderate.

These two factors will act as significant drags on China's long-term potential growth rate, which will slow to a range of around 5.5 to 6.5 per cent annual GDP growth over the medium term until 2020, and then moderate further to around 5 per cent annual GDP growth by 2030. Such low growth rates for China would have signaled a hard landing for the Chinese economy ten years ago, but given the structural changes occurring in the Chinese economy and the significant rise in per capita GDP that has occurred over the last decade, these more moderate GDP growth rates are becoming the new normal for China. Estimates of what would constitute a hard landing for China will also gradually have to be lowered.

One of the key concerns about the Chinese economy a decade ago was about Chinese GDP growth slipping below the 8 per cent per year GDP growth rate, creating a hard landing for the Chinese economy. A major fear relating to such a hard landing was that there would be increasing unemployment as GDP growth below 8 per cent would not have generated enough jobs for the annual number of young people joining the work force. However that equation has changed rapidly due to ageing demographics, since the number of new entrants to the labour force is gradually declining each year. This means that GDP growth rates of around 6 to 7 per cent are sufficient over the medium term outlook to generate enough jobs to maintain a stable labour market without rising unemployment. The required rate of GDP growth for labour market stability will drop further by 2025, as the impact of ageing demographics continues to drive down the working age population. By 2030, the definition of what would be a hard landing may drop significantly further. If the potential GDP growth rate is around 5 per cent per year by 2030, the definition of a hard landing may need to be adjusted down to around 3 per cent growth, as continued demographic ageing significantly lowers the number of young workers entering the workforce each year. One uncertainty beyond 2030 is whether current changes to regulations regarding the one child policy will significantly boost birth rates and have an upward impact on the number of young people joining the labour force beyond 2030.

President Xi Jinping has stated that the Chinese government has calculated that a 7 per cent GDP growth rate will suffice to meet China's development goals until 2020.

"The slowdown of the Chinese economy is an intended result of our own regulatory initiatives. This is because, according to a thorough calculation done at the time we set our mid- and long-term development goals to double the 2010 GDP and per capita income by 2020, it is judged that a 7% annual growth rate would suffice. Moreover, we have recognized that to ensure long-term economic development China has to press ahead with structural reform, even if this requires some sacrifice of pace."

Chinese President Xi Jinping, "Work Together for a Better Asia Pacific",
Speech to the APEC CEO Summit, Bali, Indonesia,
7 October 2013. In Xi Jinping, The Governance of China,
(Foreign Languages Press, Beijing, 2014).

In its own calculations of the long-term potential growth rates for different economies, the OECD has estimated in 2014 that China's long-term potential growth rate will moderate significantly over the next fifteen years, from an average potential GDP growth rate of 9.2 per cent per year between 2008 and 2013, to an average pace of just 5 per cent from 2014 until 2030. (OECD, "Growth Prospects and Fiscal Requirements Over the Long Term", *OECD Economic Outlook*, Chapter Four, Vol. 2014/1. [OECD] (Paris, 2014)).

However in its very long range forecast for the period from 2031 until 2060, the OECD projects that China's GDP growth rate will slow significantly more, to an average of 2.4 per cent GDP growth over this timeframe. This will result in a very sharp slowdown in per capita GDP growth rates in China, from an average annual per capita GDP growth rate of 8.5 per cent during the 2008–13 period to just 2.8 per cent annual average growth from 2031 until 2060, according to the OECD long-range projections.

The Chinese government recognizes that the structural changes in the Chinese economy due to ageing demographics and slowing productivity growth will drag down China's long term growth rate, and is responding to the projected growth slowdown by trying to develop new economic strategies to make the economy more efficient and competitive.

Economic reforms in manufacturing

One key area where the Chinese government is increasingly focusing its economic policy is on undertaking significant economic reforms to reshape its economy to manage the transition from a low-wage economy that specialized in low-cost manufacturing exports towards an upper middle-income economy that will need to compete for global export markets with lower wage economies in other emerging markets.

Rising manufacturing wages in coastal Chinese provinces have already resulted in the commencement of hollowing-out of some of China's export industries, such as low-cost textiles and garments, as well as low-cost electronics industry production. Average wages of factory workers in China rose 11.6 per cent in 2014, continuing to drive up wage pressures. Whereas rapid productivity growth in past decades had mitigated the impact of rising wages on unit labour costs, the gradual slowdown in productivity growth has begun to drive up unit labour costs. The appreciation of the Chinese currency against the USD over the last decade, from an annual average of CNY 8.28 per USD in 2004 to CNY 6.16 per USD by 2014, has also reduced export competitiveness.

This poses a significant challenge to the long-term outlook for China's low-cost manufacturing industries that have been a key driver of Chinese economic growth since the commencement of economic liberalization in 1978. Much of the growth of coastal China has been fuelled by low-cost manufacturing exports which have also underpinned the economic development of the Pearl River Delta and the Yangtze River Delta, and the hollowing-out of the manufacturing export industries in these regions would pose a significant structural shock for the Chinese economy.

In order to address these challenges to China's manufacturing sector outlook, in May 2015 the Chinese government announced a new ten-year strategic plan called "Made in China 2025", that has the objective of transforming the manufacturing sector towards production of higher value-added products.

A key element of the new policy is to develop China's competitiveness in higher value-adding, leading edge segments of the manufacturing sector. Ten key sectors have been identified as strategic industries that will be development priorities for this plan. These comprise:

- new information technology,
- precision numerically controlled machine tools and robotics,
- aerospace equipment,
- ocean engineering equipment and high-end vessels,
- advanced rail transportation equipment,
- energy-saving vehicles and new energy vehicles,
- power equipment,
- agricultural machinery,
- new materials such as polymers, and
- bio-medicine and high performance medical devices.

A key policy focus of the "Made in China 2025" strategy is to build China's own company brands globally, rather than maintaining the current strategy that has been in place since 1978 of producing low-cost manufactures for foreign firms which are then marketed globally by foreign firms. China has already started to make progress with some of its IT and communications hardware company brands, such as Lenovo and Huawei, but a substantial increase in China's own manufacturing brand positioning abroad is seen as essential to the long-term success of Chinese manufacturing.

China is also making reforms to improve the efficiency and competitiveness of its domestic industrial enterprises, and some significant reforms have been introduced in the oil and gas industry to force the state-owned enterprises to allow greater competition from private sector firms in some segments, such as development of unconventional energy resources and in LNG trading.

An equally important part of the economic transition away from dependence on low value-added manufactures will be the gradual shift in the structure of the domestic economy towards the service sector economy, which already accounts for an estimated 47 per cent of GDP. Rising per capita GDP levels are expected to translate into a higher share of household income being spent on services, which is a structural trend that has occurred in other industrializing economies such as Japan, South Korea and Hong Kong as a result of rising per capita GDP levels.

Higher household incomes per capita are therefore expected to drive a greater share of household expenditure towards services such as banking, insurance, communications, logistics, education and health care, gradually resulting in a structural transform-ation of the Chinese economy towards the service sector. Within the retail sector, e-commerce has grown very rapidly, reaching an estimated total value of USD 450 billion in 2014, and is expected to be another high growth segment of the service sector economy.

Fragile China: key vulnerabilities

The rapid expansion of the Chinese economy since 1980 had been driven by strong growth in exports and investment, which had gradually resulted in exports and investment becoming increas-ingly important growth drivers for the overall economy while private consumption as a share of total GDP had declined from around 50 per cent of GDP in 1980 to just 35 per cent by 2008. Meanwhile investment as a share of GDP had risen to around 50 per cent, which is extremely high by international standards. The importance of exports as a contributor to annual GDP growth had become one important source of vulnerability for China, and this vulnerability was exposed during the Global Financial Crisis, when Chinese exports fell sharply due to the collapse of domestic demand in the US and Europe.

Concerns about the fragilities of the Chinese economy have escalated since the Global Financial Crisis of 2008–09, due to the very large fiscal and monetary stimulus measures that were uti-lized by the Chinese government to avert an economic recession. In November 2008, during the depths of the international finan-cial crisis, the Chinese State Council announced a stimulus plan that would involve spending RMB 4 trillion (USD 586 billion) over two years to stimulate economic recovery.

At the time, all the high frequency economic indicators were signaling that China was heading for a severe economic slowdown, and indeed for the 2009 calendar year, the export data showed a −16 per cent decline in value terms compared to 2008. This resulted in net exports contributing −3.9 percentage points to GDP growth. Had the government's investment stimulus program not kicked in to boost the economy, Chinese GDP growth was almost certainly heading for a hard landing in which GDP growth could have fallen to 5 per cent or lower. However as a result of the stimulus package investment contributed 8 percentage points to GDP growth in 2009, and the Chinese economy recorded GDP growth of 9.2 per cent for the calendar year 2009.

While the bulk of the stimulus package was spent on infrastructure development, the structure of the stimulus package was only partly financed by central government expenditure, which accounted for around 30 per cent of the total stimulus package. A significant portion of the stimulus spending was financed by local governments. The largest part of local government financing was raised through the creation of local government special purpose financing vehicles that used land owned by local governments as collateral to borrow from state-owned banks. This off-balance sheet special purpose vehicle was used because local governments were not permitted to directly borrow funds. Overall, local governments are estimated to have spent RMB 2.8 trillion on stimulus-related activities, much of this funded by bank loans. By the end of 2010, the total amount of local government debt had reached RMB 10.7 trillion, which was equivalent to 27 per cent of Chinese GDP with half of these debts accruing to local government financing vehicles (IMF, "People's Republic of China", 2011). A report by China's National Audit Office released in 2013 found that total local government debt rose significantly by 2013, reaching RMB 17.9 trillion yuan.

Overall, around two-thirds of the Chinese stimulus package in 2009–10 was estimated to have been funded by borrowing, and the result was a massive expansion in bank credit during 2009. Bank loans rose from around RMB 4.6 trillion in 2008 to RMB 9.6 trillion in 2009, with broad money supply measured by M2 rising by +27.7 per cent in 2009 (European Commission, "China", 2010). With substantial stimulus continuing in 2010, the broad money supply measure M2 showed another strong increase of +18.9 per cent.

Overall the total expansion of credit in the Chinese economy during 2009 and 2010 combined exceeded 50 per cent, with credit expansion of +31.7 per cent in 2009 followed by a further +19.9 per cent rise in 2010. This rapid expansion in credit, mainly funded by state-owned banks, was the starting point for further fragilities and risks that have subsequently developed in the Chinese economy.

One of the early consequences of the flood of new bank credit was a surge in real estate loans, which rose 50 per cent in 2009. The residential construction sector saw rapid growth in new home sales and home prices showed rapid growth in 2009–10, forcing the government to adopt cooling measures in 2011 to ward off a property bubble from developing. With underlying speculative demand for property remaining high in China in 2011 and 2012, the relaxation of cooling measures in 2012 resulted in another pick-up in property prices in late 2012 and 2013. By September 2013, new home prices were rising in 69 of the 70 cities measured in China's new home price index, with Beijing new home prices up 16 per cent year-on-year, while Shanghai new home prices were 17 per cent higher. In Shenzen and Guangzhou the price rises grew even more rapidly, up 20 per cent year-on-year. This forced another round of tightening measures in late 2013 and early 2014 directed at the residential property sector, particularly at investors who owned multiple properties.

The tightening measures applied in late 2013 and during 2014 had a significant impact on new home prices, which started to record negative year-on-year changes during 2014, and remained negative into early 2015, with Chinese average new home prices down 6 per cent year-on-year in April 2015, the eight month of consecutive declines. With investor confidence in property purchases dampened by the combination of tighter regulatory controls on mortgage lending and declining new home prices, new residential construction starts began to slow, with real estate developers in smaller Chinese cities facing supply gluts of newly built apartments, forcing deep discounting.

By November 2014, investor attention had turned towards investing in equities, and the Shanghai 225 Index recorded strong gains during late 2014 and the first half of 2015. By the middle of 2015, the Shanghai stock market was up +157 per cent year-on-year.

Meanwhile the stimulus measures in 2009–10 were still working through the Chinese economy, with local governments facing the consequences of the large-scale borrowings they had made through local government financing vehicles in order to fund infrastructure projects. With a large proportion of these projects estimated to be unable to generate sufficient returns to repay the bank debt, the Chinese central government had to develop strategies to rescue the local governments. Meanwhile the slump in the residential property sector had resulted in lower new land sales by local governments to property developers, which choked off a key source of fiscal revenue for local governments.

With local governments facing substantial quantities of debt maturing in 2015, the Chinese Ministry of Finance announced in March 2015 that it was providing a RMB one trillion (USD 160 billion) program to swap local government debt raised through local government financing vehicles for municipal bonds, to help local governments to deal with rolling over their debt as well as lowering interest payment costs significantly. A second tranche of another RMB one trillion was announced by the Ministry of Finance in June 2015.

The Ministry of Finance and People's Bank of China have also been working to stabilize the problems of the shadow banking system, which had been largely unregulated until 2013. With central government lending guidelines having restricted banks from lending to many sectors after 2011, borrowers had turned to shadow banks for credit, resulting in a rapid increase in the role of shadow banks in the overall provision of credit in the financial system. The scale of lending through the shadow banking system began to raise concerns about potential systemic risks by 2013, resulting in new regulations being issued by the People's Bank of China to strengthen regulatory supervision of the shadow banks. Since then the expansion of credit from the shadow banking system has slowed sharply.

Consequently China is facing a complex risk landscape over the medium-term, creating significant vulnerabilities.

Firstly, China remains heavily dependent on fixed asset investment growth as a key economic growth driver. The real estate sector is an important part of total investment, and the slowdown of the residential real estate sector during 2013–15 acted as a drag on total investment growth, resulting in weaker demand for key industries that are significant suppliers of industrial materials for construction, including steel, chemicals, cement and plate glass. China is therefore vulnerable to any protracted weakness in the residential construction sector. The total credit exposures of to the Chinese real estate sector were estimated at USD 1.9 trillion or around 19 per cent of GDP, excluding mortgages, by the end of 2014 (IMF Financial Stability Report, April 2015). Moreover the IMF has estimated that Chinese real estate developers have issued USD 130 billion in external bonds since 2010, creating risks of transmission effects to international financial markets in the event of severe financial stress in the Chinese real estate industry.

Secondly, the rapid surge in mainland equities markets in late 2014 and the first half of 2015 resulted in an increase of the Shanghai stock market index of 157 per cent year-on-year by mid-June 2015, and created vulnerability to a bursting of the stock market bubble, since a high share of the total index is owned by retail households and there had been significant use of leverage.

The sharp correction of the mainland Chinese stock markets in late June, July and August 2015 highlighted the risks to the economy from a bursting of the stock market bubble. The Chinese government responded with emergency measures such as monetary policy easing and the creation of a stock market stabilization fund in order to try to stabilize the Chinese stock market.

Thirdly, the local government bad debts sitting on bank balance sheets could eventually have to be treated as non-performing loans, although the central government has managed to push this problem into the future with its debt swap program for local government special vehicle debts.

Fourthly, the extent of non-performing loans within the shadow banking system also remains opaque, with concerns about the potential exposure of shadow banks to smaller real estate developers who are facing difficulties due to the slowdown in the property market.

Fifthly, significant reform and consolidation is taking place in some industry sectors that are facing over-capacity problems, such as the steel industry. Capacity utilization in the Chinese steel industry is estimated to be only 66 per cent, and Chinese domestic steel consumption fell by 3.4 per cent in 2014 according to the China Iron and Steel Association (Wall Street Journal, 29 January 2015). This is also impacting new investment growth, which has already been hit by the slowdown in residential investment.

A sixth key structural challenge has been the eroding competitiveness of China's low cost manufacturing sector. With rising manufacturing wage costs and yuan appreciation against the USD, China's export sector has faced increasing headwinds since 2012. In August 2015, the Chinese central bank, the People's Bank of China, surprised international financial markets with a series of small devaluations of the yuan against the USD over three days. This created turmoil in global currency markets, with many other emerging markets' currencies depreciating alongside the yuan. This creates new policy risks for China, particularly of capital flight if investors anticipate further yuan devaluation moves under China's new exchange rate mechanism.

Consequently the Chinese government is handling considerable imbalances in the economy concurrently, which is a very difficult balancing act. History has shown that when economies accumulate substantial economic imbalances, an unexpected shock can cause an implosion and protracted economic and financial crisis.

However China still has significant buffers against such shocks, due to the lack of capital account convertibility, which impedes capital flight, and also its large holdings of foreign exchange reserves, which were still at USD 3.65 trillion in July 2015, albeit having declined by USD 340 billion from their peak level in June 2014. Furthermore, the central government still has relatively low levels of government debt as a share of GDP, at just 22 per cent in 2013. However the fiscal leeway is not as large as this statistic may suggest, since contingent liabilities for local government debt as well as for state-owned enterprises would push this figure to above 50 per cent of GDP. Nevertheless there is some leeway, albeit limited, for additional fiscal measures in the event of a sharp economic slowdown.

Transmission risks of a hard landing

The probability of a hard landing over the medium term outlook is mitigated by the Chinese government's ability to use fiscal and monetary policy measures to try to prevent a sharp slowdown. The Chinese government has shown that it has a wide range of measures in its toolkit to manage the Chinese economy, both to contain overheating, and to manage a slowdown. Nevertheless the accumulating imbalances and fragilities in the Chinese economy do make the possibility of a hard landing an important downside risk. Moreover, as former US Federal Reserve Chairman Alan Greenspan famously stated, the business cycle has not been repealed. While his comments were about the US economy, other countries including China are not immune from the business cycle.

"There is no evidence, however, that the business cycle has been repealed. Another recession will doubtless occur someday owing to circumstances that could not be, or at least were not, perceived by policymakers and financial market participants alike. History demonstrates that participants in financial markets are susceptible to waves of optimism, which can in turn foster a general process of asset-price inflation that can feed through into markets for goods and services. Excessive optimism sows the seeds of its own reversal in the form of imbalances that tend to grow over time. When unwarranted expectations ultimately are not realized, the unwinding of these financial excesses can act to amplify a downturn in economic activity, much as they can amplify the upswing."

Alan Greenspan, Testimony on US Federal Reserve's Semi annual Monetary Policy Report before the Committee on Banking, Housing, and Urban Affairs, US Senate, February 26, 1997.

If the Chinese economy were to experience a hard landing over the medium term in which GDP growth slowed down to below 5 per cent per year, this would have far wider transmission effects than a Chinese recession would have had even a decade ago. In 2005, China accounted for 4.8 per cent of world GDP, whereas in 2015, it accounted for around 14.5 per cent of world GDP, making up an additional 10 per cent share of world output over the past decade.

Consequently the transmission effects of a hard landing in China would be much more severe than in past decades, since China accounts for a larger share of world trade and investment flows. China has also become a much more significant domestic consumer market in sectors such as autos, where China is now the largest auto market in the world.

For the Asia-Pacific economies, the risk of a China hard landing has become an increasingly important downside risk and vulnerability, as the rapid growth of China has resulted in large increases in bilateral trade shares with China. For many Asia-Pacific economies, China is now their largest export market, including for South Korea and Australia. Australia's vulnerability to a Chinese hard landing has risen very substantially over the last two decades, as China's share of total Australian exports has risen to around one-third of total exports. Total Australian exports of goods and services to China reached AUD 97 billion in 2014, with iron ore exports accounting for around half of merchandise exports. China has also become the largest export market for South Korea, accounting for around 25 per cent of total exports in 2014. Similarly China has become an increasingly important export market for most ASEAN nations, with ASEAN exports to China having grown at a double digit annual pace over the last decade. While this has been a powerful export growth driver for ASEAN, it has also increased the vulnerability of Southeast Asian economies to an economic downturn in China.

Therefore the rise of China has become a double-edged sword for other Asian nations, as it has helped Asian countries to diversify away from traditional export markets such as the EU and US, but has increased their vulnerability to a future recession in China.

China's rise as a world superpower

Although the Chinese economy does face imbalances and fragilities in the medium term outlook, nevertheless China's long-term potential GDP growth rate over the next two decades is still considerably faster than the US, EU or Japan. Therefore China's economy is projected to increase in importance as a share of world GDP over the next two decades. The geopolitical and economic importance of China will continue to increase and the impact of China upon the rest of the world will rise further. There are a number of key dimensions to China's increasing impact on the global economy.

Firstly, China has already demonstrated its willingness to play a new leadership role in global development finance through leading the initiatives to establish the AIIB, the BRICS New Development Bank and the Silk Road Fund. The impact on global development finance is likely to be far-reaching, catalysing new financing flows for infrastructure development in many Asian and other developing countries.

Secondly, Chinese multinationals are expanding their global footprint, as the Chinese government continues to encourage Chinese firms to build their global brands. This is a central strategy of the new "Made in China 2025" policy, and the development of Chinese brands globally is likely to accelerate over the next decade. Chinese banks and insurance companies are also expanding their global footprint, and major Chinese banks such as Bank of China and ICBC will continue to build their global branch network and build up their international trade finance and corporate banking businesses worldwide.

Thirdly, the importance of the Chinese economy for the rest of the Asia-Pacific economies will continue to grow, as the further substantial expansion in the size of the Chinese economy over the next decade will boost bilateral trade and investment ties with other Asia-Pacific nations considerably further. For most, if not all, Asia-Pacific nations, the sheer size of the Chinese economy will make it the largest export market within the next decade, where it does not already occupy the number one position. China will also become an increasingly important source of capital flows into many Asia-Pacific nations, through bank lending, foreign direct investment as well as portfolio capital inflows.

Fourthly, the rising importance of Chinese domestic consumption combined with rising per capita GDP levels in China will support further strong growth in demand for world agricultural commodities, particularly as environmental problems such as water shortages limit the ability of China to supply its domestic food requirements. This should continue to support rising demand for imports of grains, dairy products, meat products and fisheries products. In 2009, China imported USD 2 million of live or processed lobster from the US, but by 2014, this had risen to USD 90 million (Associated Press, 17 February 2015). The value of Chinese wine imports has risen from USD 800 million in 2010 to USD 1.5 billion by 2014. The rapid growth in the size of the Chinese consumer market will sustain strong long-term growth in demand for agricultural commodity and processed food imports, which will not only benefit OECD agricultural exporters such as the US, Australia and New Zealand, but will also offer important market opportunities to other developing country food exporting nations in Sub-Saharan Africa such as South Africa and Kenya, as well as Latin American agricultural exporters such as Brazil, Chile and Argentina.

Fifthly, China will continue to place high strategic importance on energy security, as its reliance on imported oil and gas continues to increase over the next two decades. This is a key strategic concern for China, and a major focus of economic and foreign policy is on building its relationships with key energy exporters. China has already developed a number of oil and gas pipelines from neighbouring countries, including gas pipelines from Central Asia, oil and gas pipelines from Myanmar into southern China, and large-scale new gas pipeline deals with Russia. Construction of Gazprom's Power of Siberia gas pipeline from Russia to China has already begun, for a USD 400 billion, 30-year deal to supply gas to China through a 3,968 kilometre pipeline. Negotiations have also been underway for a second Russia-China gas pipeline called the Altai pipeline which would also be a major new source of gas supply for China. The first Central Asia-China gas pipeline from Turkmenistan through Kazakhstan and Uzbekistan was commissioned in 2009, with additional pipelines added subsequently. The Central Asia-China gas pipeline will have a capacity of 55 billion cubic metres by 2015, equivalent to around 20 per cent of annual Chinese gas consumption.

Sixthly, China as a leading economic power is also pursuing trade liberalization initiatives in the Asia-Pacific region. Since China joined the World Trade Organisation in 2001, it has been actively building up its network of bilateral and regional free trade agreements, notably the China-ASEAN Free Trade Agreement which was implemented in 2010. New bilateral free trade agreement deals were signed in 2014 with South Korea and Australia, which will take effect when ratified by the respective parliaments. China has also led an initiative at the APEC Summit in 2014 to develop a feasibility study for a Free Trade Area for the Asia-Pacific, and this long-term initiative could eventually bring substantial economic benefits to Asia-Pacific countries.

Seventh, China is leading a strategic initiative for the economic development of infrastructure connectivity to link China with Central Asia and ASEAN through to Europe and the Middle East. This is the New Silk Road initiative, which has also been named the One Belt, One Road initiative to develop an economic corridor linking these regions.

While all of these strategic trends offer considerable positive economic effects for the rest of the Asia-Pacific region and the global economy, the world's attention is currently focused on how China's rise as a military superpower will impact the rest of the Asia-Pacific.

> *"China's ascendancy is accompanied by massive socio-economic change and, in some instances, dislocation internally. China's ability to continue to manage its emergence as a great power side by side with its internal transformation is one of the pivotal questions of our time."*
>
> *Henry A. Kissinger, Speech on 'Power Shifts and Security',*
> *Global Strategic Review 2010 Keynote Address, 10th September 2010,*
> *International Institute for Strategic Studies. Published in*
> *'Power Shifts', Survival, Vol. 52, No.6, Dec 2010-Jan 2011,*
> *International Institute for Strategic Studies, Routledge Journals.*

As China has emerged to become the world's second largest economy and also a major military power in the Asia-Pacific, tensions have risen between China and several ASEAN countries over territorial disputes in the South China Sea and between China and Japan in the East China Sea. These escalating geopolitical tensions have raised concerns in the Asia-Pacific region about China's rise as a military superpower and whether this is becoming a threat to decades of peaceful economic co-operation and rapidly rising regional trade and investment flows that have served the economies of the Asia-Pacific so well since China began its economic reforms under senior leader Deng Xiaoping.

Chapter 7

Can Japan Avert a Debt Crisis?

After the bubble

Japan as a nation had been devastated by the intensive bombing raids of the US Air Force during World War Two. Most of Japan's major cities had been destroyed by conventional aerial bombing prior to the final devastation caused by the dropping of the atomic bombs on Hiroshima and Nagasaki. The initial process of reconstruction was gradual, but accelerated during the 1950s, as Japan became a key base and supplier for the US military during the Korean War, which helped to boost Japan's economic recovery.

From the 1950s until the 1980s, Japan's economy experienced very rapid economic growth, emerging from the destruction of World War Two to become Asia's first developed economy. During the two decades after the end of the Allied occupation of Japan, the Japanese economy grew at an annual average rate of 8 per cent per year. By 1964, Japan became the first Asian nation to join the OECD club of developed nations.

The Japanese economy experienced sustained rapid economic growth over much of the next thirty years, as rapid industrial development and export growth drove strong growth in per capita GDP and household incomes, boosting domestic demand.

By the 1980s, the sustained success of the Japanese economy and rising household wealth eventually gave rise to financial markets euphoria, with price to earnings ratios for Japanese companies soaring as investors convinced themselves that Japan's long-term success was assured. Property prices also followed a similar path, as banks and corporations created a speculative bubble based on rapidly rising values of collateral comprising equities and property.

As with most such episodes of financial euphoria, the bubble eventually burst in 1990, with the Japanese equity and property markets crashing as leveraged corporate and private investors saw the value of their collateral erode. This in turn triggered a banking sector crisis, as collateral held by banks evaporated, and large companies with massive real estate sector losses went bankrupt.

The stock market bubble reached its peak in December 1989, with the Nikkei 225 Index reaching a high of 38,916. In 1990, the Nikkei 225 Index fell below the 25,000 mark by in November, down 40 per cent from its peak. Between 1990 and 2014, the Nikkei 225 never reached its 1989 high again. Indeed, the stock market continued to trend downwards for many years. In 2001, despite the usual stock market cyclical movements and volatility in the intervening period that had often created false hopes of a more sustained stock market recovery, the Nikkei 225 fell below the 10,000 mark.

After the Great Tohoku earthquake of March 2011, the Nikkei 225 fell to a low of 8,605 in November 2011. By the eve of Abe's election as Prime Minister of Japan, the Nikkei 225 had again fallen to similar lows, at around the 9,500 mark by the end of November 2011. It was only after Abe became the Prime Minister and introduced his "Three Arrows" economic policy that the Japanese stock market staged a sustained rally that pushed it back above the 20,000 mark by mid-2015 for the first time since the year 2000.

Japanese land prices also collapsed after the bursting of the asset price bubble in 1990. Prior to the bubble bursting, Japanese land prices had been rising ever since the end of World War Two, creating the myth that Japanese land prices would not fall in the future, which is reminiscent of the popular misconceptions that prevailed in the US about real estate prices before the US sub-prime crisis and ensuing global financial crisis in 2008–09. By the mid-1980s, land prices in commercial districts in Tokyo and other major cities like Osaka began to rise rapidly, followed by soaring residential property prices in major cities.

The bursting of the bubble in 1990 resulted in the average annual increase in Japanese land prices tapering off to around a +0.6 per cent rise in 1991. However, research by Dr. Ben Bernanke while he was an economics professor at Princeton University showed that in the following years from 1992 until 1999, Japanese land prices fell by between −3.8 per cent and −5.7 per cent every single year during that period (Bernanke, 2000).

Japanese commercial property prices continued to decline until 2004, to a low of around one-third of their peak levels during the bubble. Commercial property prices posted a small positive gain in 2005, and residential property prices rose for the first time in 16 years in 2006. However the recovery in property prices was short-lived, as the global financial crisis in 2008–09 had transmission effects through slumping global trade and investment to Japanese growth, pushing Japan into yet another recession. Property prices entered another protracted slump that only ended in 2014, when prices again showed a small increase.

The decade after the bursting of the Japanese asset bubble became known as Japan's '*Ushinawareta Junen*' or lost decade, as government efforts to stimulate the economy failed to gain traction despite repeated fiscal stimulus packages. The Great Hanshin Earthquake of 1995 created yet another setback to economic recovery, although the reconstruction spending to rebuild Kobe did create some positive effects on the economy. Between 1990 and 2014, Japan recorded negative GDP growth in six calendar years and grew at a very low positive rate of below 1 per cent in another five years. Successive Japanese governments resorted to fiscal stimulus packages, without achieving a durable recovery.

Meanwhile the successive fiscal stimulus packages deployed by the Japanese government were steadily raising Japan's government debt to GDP ratio. In 1991, the Japanese government debt to GDP ratio had fallen to 65 per cent, after having risen as high as 76.5 per cent in 1987, as the Japanese government had managed to lower their debt levels after several years of fiscal consolidation. However in the aftermath of the bursting of the financial bubble, Japan's gross debt to GDP ratio soared to 142 per cent a decade later in 2001, as a result of the extensive fiscal stimulus measures and efforts to bailout the banking system. Since then, Japanese public debt levels have continued to escalate. According to IMF estimates, Japan's gross debt to GDP ratio had risen to 243 per cent by 2013, with the net debt to GDP ratio at 134 per cent.

The cost of addressing banking sector non-performing loans between 1992 and 2000 has been estimated at 17 per cent of Japanese GDP, including transfers by the Deposit Insurance Corporation, capital injections and bank provisioning (Nakaso, 2001). In 1999, the Japanese government provisioned 43 trillion yen for recapitalization of the Japanese banking sector, which was equivalent to 9 per cent of GDP (Dekle, and Kletzer, 2004).

The costs of the banking sector bailout and numerous fiscal stimulus packages have resulted in Japan confronting the risks of a future debt crisis. Japan's gross government debt to GDP ratio is by far the highest in the OECD, at around double the OECD average. Even the net debt to GDP ratio is extremely high by international standards, with Japan's 134 per cent net government debt to GDP ratio significantly higher than the estimated US net debt to GDP ratio of 87 per cent and the UK net debt to GDP ratio of 82 per cent.

Japan's rising debt burden

Japan's contracting population and low long-term potential growth rate, combined with the high existing level of government debt as a share of GDP, indicate that Japan is facing significant risks from the rising debt burden.

The Japanese government has responded to this increasing risk by raising the consumption tax from 5 per cent to 8 per cent in April 2014. A political agreement was reached on this tax hike under the previous DPJ government led by Prime Minister Noda, which managed to have the parliamentary bill passed in both houses of the Diet. The legislation was for a two-stage hike in the consumption tax, with the first step being an increase from 5 per cent to 8 per cent, which was implemented by the LDP government led by Prime Minister Abe as planned in April 2014. However the impact of the hike was to push the Japanese economy back into a mild recession, and Prime Minister Abe called a snap election in November 2014 in which one of his main platforms was to delay the second stage of the consumption tax hike lifting the consumption tax to 10 per cent until April 2017, to allow more time for the Japanese economy to adjust to the economic impact of the first hike. With PM Abe having won this snap election, the second stage of the tax hike was delayed until at least April 2017.

The increase in the consumption tax, when fully implemented after the second stage hike to 10 per cent, will provide a very substantial step forward towards stabilizing Japan's primary fiscal deficit. In 2014, the Japanese government released its medium-term fiscal plan aiming to reduce the primary fiscal deficit to 3.3 per cent of GDP, which was half the level of the fiscal deficit in 2010, when it had been 6.6 per cent of GDP. The medium-term fiscal plan also aims to reduce the fiscal deficit to zero by 2020.

The stability of Japan's domestic debt market despite the extremely high level of net government debt as a share of GDP reflects the important role that the Bank of Japan has been playing through its quantitative easing programs as a major buyer of new government debt issuance as well as the high level of domestic debt issuance held by domestic investors.

Japanese domestic investors hold around 95 per cent of the total Japanese government debt outstanding, reducing the vulnerability of Japan to international capital markets. In contrast, many other countries that have had debt crises have had a high share of foreign ownership of their domestic debt, which has increased vulnerability to capital flight triggering a debt crisis.

However the savings rate in Japan has been gradually declining since the mid-1990s, and impact of ageing demographics in Japan is a significant contributor to this decline. Japan's ageing demographics over the long term economic outlook will continue to play a role in gradually reducing the savings rate. This decline in the domestic savings rate will gradually require a higher share of Japanese debt to be financed from abroad. This will increase the vulnerability of Japan to international financial markets over the longer term horizon.

One of the key vulnerabilities for the Japanese government due to the high level of government debt is from any significant increase in bond yields. Since the bursting of the asset bubble in Japan, Japanese Government Bond (JGB) ten-year bond yields have trended downwards, from levels of around 6 to 7 per cent prior to the bubble bursting. The JGB ten-year bond yield has been below 2 per cent since the East Asian crisis, and has been below 1 per cent since the middle of 2011. Such low levels of JGB yields have significantly lowered the cost of servicing Japan's government debt, and these costs have declined to as low as 0.2 per cent by January 2015, albeit rebounding back up to around 0.5 per cent by the middle of 2015. At such low levels of interest, the Japanese government has been able to limit the cost of financing its debt mountain at around one-fifth of budget expenditure.

However if JGB yields were to rise significantly higher due to global debt market conditions or due to Japan's increasing vulnerability to needing financing from international financial markets, Japan's debt sustainability outlook could deteriorate very significantly.

Therefore the combination of ageing demographics, the related decline in the savings rate and potential vulnerability to rising JGB yields could all affect Japan's debt sustainability profile. The outlook for debt sustainability is very sensitive to the inflation and GDP growth outlook, with higher nominal GDP growth rates potentially allowing Japan to achieve stabilization of the government debt to GDP ratio with less severe further increases in taxation or expenditure cuts than in a very low GDP growth scenario.

Therefore the success of the Bank of Japan's objective of using monetary policy to move Japanese price conditions from a persistent deflation over the past 15 years to moderate positive inflation is one important plank of Japan's fiscal escape plan.

The second part of the Japanese government's strategy is to lift Japan's GDP growth rates, which has been a key focus of 'Abenomics' through Prime Minister Abe's "Three Arrows" policy framework for engineering Japan's economic recovery.

The three arrows of 'Abenomics'

Soon after being elected to office at the end of 2012, Prime Minister Abe launched his "Three Arrows" economic strategy of generating Japanese economic recovery and higher long-term growth. The three arrows of this strategy comprise:

- monetary policy stimulus;
- fiscal policy stimulus; and
- structural reforms.

The monetary policy stimulus that has subsequently been conducted by the Japanese central bank, the Bank of Japan, under Governor Haruhiko Kuroda, who became the new central bank governor in early 2013, has been a key factor underpinning Japanese economic growth during 2013–15. The Bank of Japan implemented a widening program of quantitative easing measures in order to support economic recovery and a 15-year period of deflation in Japan. One of the most important factors that has supported Japanese growth during this period has been the sharp depreciation of the Japanese yen against the US dollar.

At the end of November 2012, the yen exchange rate was 82.5 yen per USD. By the end of May 2015, the exchange rate was 124.2 per USD. This resulted in a substantial improvement in export competitiveness for Japanese industry, which had been complaining vociferously during 2011 and 2012 about the adverse impact that the strong yen had on their international competitiveness.

Although the positive impact of the sharp depreciation of the yen on exports of goods has been gradual, signs of an improving export performance were evident in the last four months of 2014, with positive year-on-year growth in exports in each of these months. By December 2014, exports of goods showed a 12.9 per cent year-on-year rise. By April 2015, Japanese exports of goods were still showing positive growth, up 8.0 per cent year-on-year.

One of the most impressive structural changes in Japanese trade has been in trade in services, where the deficit in overall trade in services has gradually trended downwards since 2012. The net balance on travel has seen a much longer term structural improvement, with the net trade deficit on travel having declined from a deficit of USD 28.5 billion in 2000 to a deficit of USD 13.3 billion in 2012, USD 6.8 billion in 2013 and close to zero by 2014, when the deficit for travel narrowed even further, to just USD 500 million.

One of the key drivers for this dramatic improvement in the deficit on travel is the sharp depreciation of the yen, which has boosted international tourism to Japan significantly. In the 2014 calendar year, the number of foreign visitors to Japan increased by +29.4 per cent, which represented a large boost for the overall tourism economy.

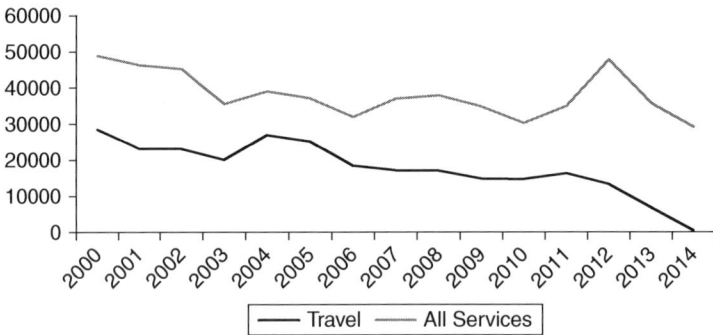

Figure 7.1 Japan's deficit on trade in services, 2000–14 (USD million)
Source: JETRO.

The second arrow of Abenomics consisted of initial fiscal stimulus measures that were introduced by the LDP government to help boost the economy in 2013, as well as to mitigate the impact of the consumption tax hike in 2014 for a transitional period.

However it is the third arrow of Abenomics, which focuses on structural economic reforms, that is the most crucial to the long-term growth outlook for Japan. Without structural reforms, the long-term potential growth rate in Japan is expected to be very weak, due to the impact of ageing demographics. The Bank of

Japan has estimated in 2014 that the potential growth rate of the Japanese economy was around 0.5 per cent annual GDP growth, which is extremely low compared to even the moderate growth pace of developed countries. While the Bank of Japan has indicated that it expected the potential rate to gradually rise, the outlook for the Japanese long term GDP growth rate is constrained by the impact of ageing demographics and the declining size of the Japanese workforce.

> *"Japan's potential growth rate – under a certain methodology – is estimated to be 'around 0.5 per cent' recently, and is expected to rise gradually toward the end of the projection period. However, it should be noted that estimates of the potential growth rate are subject to a considerable margin of error as they rely on the specific methodology employed and could change as more data for the relevant period become available."*
>
> Bank of Japan, "Outlook for Economic Activity and Prices",
> Tokyo, 30 April 2014.

By way of comparison, the IMF has estimated in 2015 that the average potential GDP growth rate for all developed countries is 1.6 per cent over the medium term outlook from 2015 to 2020 (IMF, "Where Are We Headed?", 2015).

The long-term GDP growth rate that Japan can achieve is critical for Japan's future debt dynamics, and a very low growth economy will have much greater difficulty in generating escape velocity from a future debt crisis. Therefore the "Third Arrow" of Abenomics is crucial to resolving Japan's debt problems.

If Abenomics is successful in generating significant structural reforms, then this could lift Japan's potential growth rate over the long-term.

I attended a conference at which Prime Minister Abe gave a speech about Abenomics in 2013, and I was very impressed by his determination to making critical structural reforms to lift Japan's long-term growth path. In his speech, Prime Minister Abe highlighted the importance of economic reforms and the urgent need to boost Japanese economic growth.

> *"Japan has lost as much as 500 billion U.S. dollars in gross national income during the deflationary period of the last few years. This is the same as a country the size of Norway simply disappearing from the face of the earth.*

Needless to say, our tax base has shrunk accordingly, and we have become unable to maintain our public finances without relying on government bonds.

Now you can see the picture. Without growth, there can be no fiscal reconstruction. Without growth, we can neither maintain nor enhance our social security system.

And without growth, a strengthening of our diplomacy or national security will also be simply impossible. I trust that from this, the situation has become clear to you. All of these are predicated on economic growth."

Japanese Prime Minister Shinzo Abe, 33rd ISEAS
Singapore Lecture, Singapore, 26 July 2013.

One of the most significant areas of focus for structural reforms is boosting the female participation rate in the labour force. Japan's female participation rate is relatively low compared to other OECD countries, and the "Third Arrow" reforms are aiming to improve this participation rate through various new programs such as significantly increasing the number of child care centres to encourage mothers with young children to rejoin the work force. The Japanese island culture has a strong preference for homogeneity and large-scale immigration is not considered a realistic policy politically, although the government is also trying to make some reforms to allow more foreign workers to work in Japan to mitigate the impact of the declining workforce.

Another high priority for Prime Minister Abe in delivering his "Third Arrow" reforms has been trade liberalization, which will not only help to boost Japanese exports, but could also be a mechanism to force internal change and competition. As a result, Japan joined the Trans-Pacific Partnership (TPP) trade negotiations as a member on 23 July 2013, after having received an invitation from the 11 existing members of the TPP to join the trade negotiations.

Japan is also in an advanced stage of negotiations with the EU for a bilateral free trade agreement that could also provide a significant boost to the Japanese economy, according to an impact study by the European Commission. The European Commission economic impact assessment based on economic modelling indicated that Japanese GDP would increase by 0.3 per cent by 2020 in the scenario of a conservative EU-Japan FTA deal while Japanese exports to the EU would increase by 17 per cent. If a more ambitious bilateral FTA is concluded, the economic impact could increase Japanese GDP by 0.7 per cent by 2020, with Japanese exports to the EU rising by 23 per cent. Consequently the gains from this bilateral FTA are expected to be significant (European Commission, "Impact Assessment Report", 2012).

The reduction in both tariff and non-tariff barriers would be expected to provide a particular boost to Japan's auto and electronics industries, by improving market access to the EU markets. However the EU-Japan FTA would also enable greater access for EU firms to tender for Japan's large public procurement market, which would also be an important structural reform for Japan.

If both the EU-Japan FTA and the TPP are concluded in the near future, the combined impact on the Japanese economy could be significant, and could provide an important boost to Japan's long-term potential GDP growth rate over the next decade.

Japanese multinationals and foreign direct investment flows

The large Japanese multinationals have built up well-diversified global production operations across the globe over the last three decades. In part, this reflects push factors in the Japanese economy, notably rising wage costs and the contracting domestic market, that have encouraged Japanese multinationals to establish plants abroad. However there are also important pull factors that are increasingly attracting foreign direct investment from Japanese multinationals, such as low wage costs in many emerging markets, as well as the large potential consumer market size in some of the large developing countries.

With the long-term outlook for Japanese consumer market growth constrained by the impact of ageing demographics as the total Japanese population continues to decline over the next two decades, Japanese multinationals continue to invest heavily in other Asian emerging markets that have strong long-term growth prospects and a better demographic profile.

The ASEAN region has become the most attractive global emerging markets region for Japanese multinationals in recent years, due to rapidly rising wages in coastal China as well as the souring in bilateral political relations since 2012, notably due to the anti-Japanese protests in China.

India has also resurfaced on the radar screen of Japanese multinationals, after they had become increasingly disenchanted with the poor economic performance of India and the difficult business

climate during the second term of office of the UPA coalition government led by Prime Minister Manmohan Singh. The election
victory of the BJP led by Narendra Singh Modi has brought a new
optimism into the bilateral relationship, helped by the very good
personal relations between Prime Minister Abe and India's new
leader.

Japanese multinationals are likely to continue to pursue their
global foreign direct investment strategies, as they try to position
their global business operations to benefit from a combination of
low labour costs and fast-growing consumer markets. The process
of hollowing-out of Japanese manufacturing has been underway
since the 1980s, but the trend is expected to continue, posing a
structural challenge to the Japanese economy.

While low-cost manufacturing operations have gradually left
Japan for other centres of manufacturing production, other
industries in Japan still offer growth potential. The international
tourism sector in Japan had been relatively underdeveloped until
the recent past, but the rapid growth of other Asian economies is
likely to make this a fast-growing sector of the economy for many
years. The upcoming Tokyo Olympics in 2020 will provide an
important opportunity for showcasing and branding Japan as an
international tourism destination.

Long-term prospects

The consequences of the bursting of Japan's speculative bubble
are still reverberating through the Japanese economy 25 years
after the bubble burst. The most severe impact of the bubble has
been on Japanese public sector debt, with the successive Japanese
governments having attempted to stabilize the debt level. The
structural reforms that Japan is attempting to implement offer
some prospects of improving the long-term potential growth rate
of Japan. If the Bank of Japan is also successful in implementing
sustained positive inflation rates, this could allow Japan to tame
its debt dragon.

While tackling the high level of government debt is a critical
challenge, the long-term implications of ageing demographics that
confront Japan will also require substantial economic reforms that
will improve competitiveness in key sectors of the services economy.
Trade liberalization offers some of the most promising opportunities for significantly boosting long-term growth prospects. One

major new free trade agreement that could be concluded quickly is a new bilateral free trade agreement with the EU. A second important boost to Japan's growth prospects could come from a successful conclusion of the Trans-Pacific Partnership negotiations. If Japan does find a workable solution to improve skilled worker inflows from abroad, this could also provide an important means of mitigating some of the skill shortages that are expected due to Japan's ageing demographics.

Chapter 8

Can India Become Asia's Next Growth Engine?

The Hindu rate of growth

"The Indians are too spiritual." This was the astonishing comment one senior minister from an OECD country made to me in 1991 when I asked him whether he thought India could emulate China's economic rise. Fast forwarding to the present day, he has to go knocking on Indian government ministers' and business leaders' doors seeking new market opportunities as Chinese growth cools. Not exactly instant karma, but quite close.

As another anecdote of the arrogant perceptions about India among some OECD countries in the recent past, a member of an Indian delegation told me the story about an Indian industry delegation he had been part of during a visit to Europe about a decade ago. He told me that the Indian delegation had asked during a meeting with a large European multilateral financial institution whether this European institution could lend to Indian companies. One of the European executives had responded by saying that he didn't see why India needed their funding, since he thought that the Indian economy mainly comprised of call centres and IT back offices which did not need much capital to set up. This response left the Indian delegation stunned, given India is one of the world's largest industrial economies, and also because many of the Indian delegation members were from various large Indian manufacturing corporations.

Of course, not all OECD multinationals were so complacent or ill-informed about India. A number of Western multinationals have had a long-standing and very successful presence in India, such as ABB, Unilever, and GE, to name just a few. HSBC's Indian roots trace back to 1853.

In the last decade, many US and EU multinationals have significantly increased their foreign direct investment into India, including auto manufacturers such as GM, Ford and VW. Asian auto manufacturers also have a strong presence in India, with Hyundai, Suzuki, Toyota and Honda all having auto manufacturing facilities in India, with Suzuki operating through a large joint venture that has been in place for many years with India's Maruti.

The concept of the Hindu rate of growth tainted global perceptions about India until the 1990s, as India had been growing at a pace of around 5.6 per cent per year in the decade prior to the 1991 economic reforms that began to liberalize the Indian economy. Compared to China's rapid double digit average annual GDP growth rate for three decades after economic liberalization, India had seemed rather lacklustre as a market for global multinationals.

As India gradually continued to liberalize its economy and reduce protectionist barriers, the performance of the Indian economy also improved. By the first term of the Congress-led UPA coalition government led by Prime Minister Manmohan Singh, India's economic performance surged, with real GDP growth rates averaging over 8 per cent per year.

However when the UPA coalition was elected for a second term of office, still under the leadership of Prime Minister Manmohan Singh, the government reform agenda stalled, partly due to lack of vision but also because the fragmented coalition government was made up of various political parties that were unable to agree on some key reforms. Furthermore, rising inflationary pressures in 2010 and 2011 resulted in the Indian central bank having to tighten monetary policy significantly, which resulted in a slowdown in economic growth.

By 2013, global investor confidence in India had waned considerably, with many multinationals becoming disenchanted with the lack of progress with economic reforms and the moderation in the pace of GDP growth. The manufacturing sector had stalled, partly due to the impact of monetary policy tightening, with industrial output showing zero growth in the 2013–14 financial year.

Meanwhile the impact of surging oil prices had resulted in a substantial deterioration in the Indian current account by the middle of 2013, triggering significant depreciation in the Indian rupee. The Indian central bank was forced to intervene to smooth rupee depreciation, resulting in some depletion of Indian foreign exchange reserves.

The UPA government had to take emergency measures to stave off an economic crisis, with tighter restrictions imposed on foreign currency remittances abroad by individuals, and restrictions on imports of gold, as part of the measures to stabilize the current account deficit.

India's economic recovery

With the Indian economy teetering on the brink of an economic crisis in August 2013, a new governor was appointed to the Indian central bank, the Reserve Bank of India (RBI). The RBI already had a strong reputation as a well-managed central bank and sound regulator. The incoming RBI governor, Raghuram Rajan, who took office in early September 2013, had stellar credentials that gave confidence to global financial markets, since he had recently served as IMF Chief Economist and then as Professor of Finance at the University of Chicago. Almost as soon as he took up his new appointment, the Indian rupee stabilized, as global and Indian financial markets cheered his appointment.

Every step he took in the next two years after his appointment signaled his extremely capable leadership, as he impressed financial markets with his skillful technical management of monetary policy. When he took office, the RBI's foreign exchange reserves had declined to USD 275 billion. By May 2015, the RBI foreign exchange reserves had reached a new record high of USD 354 billion, up USD 79 billion since the date he became central bank governor. Of course, macroeconomic factors supported him during this time, and the accretion of foreign exchange reserves was by no means solely attributable to his skill, but nevertheless he had presided over a period of very successful management of monetary policy and improving foreign exchange reserves.

Napoleon is reported to have said to his secretary Baron Fain, that "In war, luck is half of everything" (Jordan, 2012). In his first two years of office as RBI governor, Raghuram Rajan had luck firmly on his side.

The greatest good fortune that Rajan had was the collapse in global oil prices in late 2014. India is highly dependent on energy imports, and rising oil prices had played a major role in pushing up Indian inflation during 2010–11, forcing the RBI to tighten monetary policy.

As oil prices tumbled during the last quarter of 2014 and during early 2015, Indian inflation rates also moderated significantly. Wholesale price inflation fell to zero on a year-on-year basis by early 2015, and consumer price inflation fell within the range that Rajan had set out in his medium term inflation target. This allowed the RBI to begin easing monetary policy, with several small rate cuts to help stimulate economic recovery.

With Rajan at the helm of the RBI, financial markets perceptions about the Indian economic outlook began to stabilize in late 2013 and early 2014. However as the Indian general elections approached in 2014, financial markets began to anticipate the possibility of a victory by the BJP party led by Narendra Singh Modi, who had a strong track record of economic performance as Chief Minister of Gujarat.

I recall discussing the possibility of Modi becoming the next PM about a year prior to the elections with an Indian business leader. We discussed Modi's achievements in Gujarat. "Gujarat is not India," he said. He waxed lyrical about how Modi had created excellent infrastructure in Gujarat, and how Gujarat even had power surpluses in a nation famous for having chronic power shortages. Many other Indian business executives and even some foreign business executives with plants in Gujarat echoed these sentiments in the months leading up to the 2014 Indian general elections.

In the end, after the long process of the Indian elections which is spread out over many weeks due to the enormous task of polling in a nation of 1.3 billion people, Modi and the BJP won a stunning victory in the elections, with a strong majority in the lower house of the Indian parliament.

This triggered a euphoric response from financial markets, thrilled to see the back of the UPA coalition, and convinced that Modi would deliver substantial economic reforms and lead the way for Indian economic recovery. The stock market rallied strongly through 2014, resulting in strong net portfolio capital inflows into India as global investors piled back into Indian equities as well as Indian debt markets. This in turn strengthened the capital account on the balance of payments, helping RBI governor Rajan with his task of rebuilding Indian foreign exchange reserves.

There is still a long and challenging road ahead for the RBI in terms of tackling inflationary pressures and achieving a sustainable low inflation rate as well as grinding down inflation expectations as any respectable University of Chicago economics professor would feel honour-bound to do. Furthermore, despite the improved foreign exchange reserves of India, which reached USD 354 billion in July 2015, this is still just a small fraction of China's USD 3.65 trillion in reserves. Therefore the RBI still faces a difficult path ahead in order to reduce inflation and bring interest rates down to levels that are more accommodative for Indian economic growth.

Rebranding India

After taking office, incoming Prime Minister Modi took on the mantle of de facto CEO of India, as had been expected by his supporters, bringing a new sense of vision and enthusiasm to driving forward India's economic development. The mood in India had been despondent during the tail end of the UPA coalition government's rule, but this changed dramatically once Modi took office. Surveys of business confidence showed a sharp improvement in the months following the BJP victory. Anecdotes of PM Modi's new CEO style delighted the media and Indian general public, who took particular pleasure in his crackdown on the Indian bureaucracy, which was notorious for red tape and lack of action.

One Indian banker working abroad told me that he had visited India soon after the 2014 election, and had stayed with one of his cousins who was a senior civil servant in the Indian government in New Delhi. He was surprised to find the next morning that his cousin was up very early. He had never seen his cousin going to work so early, so he asked him the reason for the early start. "Well ever since Modi became PM we have to come to work on time as otherwise we have our names taken down and we will be subject to disciplinary action," said his cousin.

Golf courses in Delhi bemoaned the sudden drop in weekday activity, as senior public servants stopped frequenting golf courses for morning rounds of golf as they had to be at their desks at the start of the day. Even ministers stayed in their offices as PM Modi might suddenly call them at their desk phone to check whether they were in the office.

Endless anecdotes about the new broom sweeping through the Indian bureaucracy began to surface in the months following the BJP taking office.

Having galvanized a new sense of urgency in the Indian civil service, PM Modi embarked on a major program of international diplomacy, to meet with key global political and business leaders and convince them to boost their bilateral economic and investment ties with India. Japan, China, the US and Germany were among his top priorities, and his official visits, accompanied by large delegations of Indian business leaders, were heavily focused on discussions related to boosting foreign trade and investment with India. He also hosted state visits by global leaders within his first year in office, including Chinese President Xi and US President Obama. Within PM Modi's first year in office, the outcomes of these official visits were extremely positive. PM Modi not only had successful positive dialogue with the leaders of the world's largest economies, but he charmed business audiences as well as audiences of Indian diaspora with his focused messages about Indian economic development.

Foreign direct investment into India surged by 40% in the 2014–15 fiscal year, to reach USD 34.9 billion. The rebound in foreign direct investment inflows does reflect PM Modi's considerable success in his global investment promotion roadshows to rebrand India as an emerging markets' star economy. However despite this success, India needs to ramp up foreign direct investment to catalyze economic development. By way of comparison, foreign direct investment into China was USD 120 billion in 2014, which was more than three times larger than foreign direct investment inflows to India.

The messaging that he has delivered to foreign multinationals is built around the theme of 'Make in India', as part of an Indian government campaign to persuade foreign firms to establish manufacturing facilities in India to produce for the domestic Indian market or for export markets. As Chief Minister of Gujarat, Modi was extremely successful in attracting foreign firms into his state to build manufacturing plants, so this is a message he is extremely successful at communicating.

The BJP government announced a number of significant reforms in its first two budgets, including lifting foreign ownership limits in the insurance and defence industries to 49 per cent, and reducing corporate tax rates from 30 per cent to 25 per cent over a three year period. Long delayed Real Estate Investment Trusts (REITS) legislation has also been implemented, finally allowing a domestic REITS industry to be established, as well as establishing legislation for Infrastructure Investment Trusts.

The BJP government has also announced that the introduction of a Goods and Services Tax (GST) is a key priority, but this is dependent on negotiations with the state governments, so there is still uncertainty about when the GST can actually be implemented. If the BJP government is successful in implementing the GST, an initiative which the previous Congress-led coalition government had been unable to successfully conclude during its term, this would provide a significant positive boost to the Indian economy. The Indian corporate sector are keen to have such a national GST tax implemented as it would remove the complexity of having to deal with different state sales tax regimes across the country.

India's infrastructure crisis

For decades, inadequate investment in infrastructure in India has been a key bottleneck to economic development. Increased government expenditure on infrastructure has become a key area of focus for the BJP government, with significant increases in the national railway budget and the announcement of plans for a number of major new power megaprojects to be built.

The development of India's urban infrastructure has also been put to the forefront of the Indian government's priorities by PM Modi, who has announced plans for 100 smart cities to be built across India. The BJP government has also accelerated efforts to develop a number of industrial corridors in India, most notably the Delhi-Mumbai Industrial Corridor. Although the Delhi-Mumbai Industrial Corridor had already been underway for some years, the BJP government is revitalizing initiatives to bring in foreign government and private sector investment into these industrial corridors, which include rail and road links, industrial estates and office parks as well as smart cities and modern urban townships.

The BJP government has ambitious plans for the development of India's transport infrastructure, including building high speed rail networks linking up major cities and new airports. The government has established plans for semi high speed rail links in nine transport corridors, and has been negotiating with foreign firms to assist in these projects to bring leading-edge rail technology. Two new greenfield airports are planned for Navi Mumbai and Goa Mopa, as well as public private partnerships for existing government-owned airports in Chennai, Kolkata, Jaipur and Ahmedabad.

The agricultural economy is still a very important sector of the Indian economy, with around 60 per cent of the total work force employed in in rural regions. Therefore a critical area for development is agricultural infrastructure, which has suffered from underinvestment for decades. Significant ramping up of agricultural infrastructure is a high priority in order to boost agricultural productivity and crop yields, as well as to mitigate the extreme volatility in food prices in India. Volatile food prices have a significant impact on consumer price inflation and wholesale price inflation in India, since India is a low income country and food still accounts for a high share of total consumer spending. Therefore food prices have a high weight in the consumer price index weighting, and volatile food prices for key items can have a significant impact on headline inflation and potentially could impact the conduct of monetary policy. A key area where agricultural infrastructure needs to be boosted is in food cold storage, warehousing, and refrigerated logistics networks, since an estimated 25 to 30 per cent of fruit and vegetable production is lost due to lack of modern storage facilities.

Another key area where agricultural infrastructure needs to be boosted is in water storage and irrigation systems, to substantially improve the management of limited water resources and to mitigate the impact of droughts. The long term implications of climate change for weather patterns make this task even more of a priority. Heavy use of groundwater resources has resulted in depletion, creating risks of crises for water supply in some parts of India. Large-scale investment is needed in improving water storage systems to capture and store rainfall during the monsoon season, combined with efficient water management systems for irrigation.

Food security remains one of India's greatest economic and social challenges, with the United Nations Food and Agricultural Organisation having estimated that the number of undernourished people in India was 195 million in 2014, which equates to 15.2 per cent of India's total population (FAO, 2015).

The previous Congress-led coalition government did implement the National Food Security Act in 2013, which gives entitlements to low-income households to obtain rice or grains at highly subsidized prices, but due to the large number of people covered by these entitlements, the fiscal cost is extremely high to the government for funding these subsidies. With the BJP government giving a high policy focus to reducing the cost of agricultural subsidies, increasing the productivity and efficiency of the Indian agricultural system is an important priority. Improving agricultural infrastructure is a critical strategy for boosting Indian food production and national food security over the long-term, with India's population projected to grow significantly over the next two decades.

India's large and growing population is creating considerable pressure on agricultural and water resources. The long term outlook for Indian water consumption is for substantial increases in demand as India's population is projected to grow significantly over the next three decades, and urbanization is also driving water demand. At the same time, Indian food production will also need to increase substantially to meet the rising demand for food from a growing population. To add to India's challenges, there is also potential competition for water resources with China. China is also facing tremendous problems in managing its water resources, with many parts of inland China facing severe drought problems. China has been trying to harness water resources from the Himalayas, and there are fears that this could affect the flow of water from the Himalayas downstream to the Deccan plateau, which could result in political tensions between India and China on this issue. However due to the significant improvement in bilateral relations between China and India in recent years, this matter may be resolved through mutual co-operation and a negotiated solution. The issue was of such national importance that during his term of office, former Prime Minister Manmohan Singh did raise the issue with President Xi Jinping during a state visit to China.

Energy infrastructure

One of India's greatest shortcomings in infrastructure is the chronic shortage of power generation and transmission infrastructure. India's total electricity generating capacity at the beginning of 2015 was 261 gigawatts (GW) for a population of 1.3 billion people. This compared with China's electricity generating capacity of 1,360 GW at the beginning of 2015 for a population of 1.3 billion people. China therefore had slightly over five times the power generating infrastructure of India at the beginning of 2015, for a population size that was roughly equal.

Chinese power generating capacity has grown at around 12 per cent per year over the last decade, and is projected by the Chinese National Energy Administration to reach 2,000 GW by 2020. India is targeting the addition of 57 GW of power generating capacity by 2016–17, which would push its total electricity generating capacity to 318 GW. In the 2014–15 financial year Indian electricity output was up 8.4 per cent, according to industrial production data.

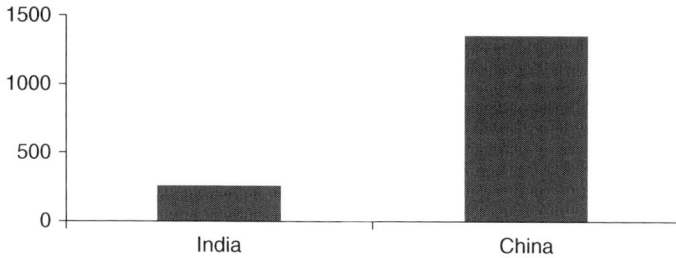

Figure 8.1 Indian power generating capacity compared to China (gigawatts, 2015)

Source: National statistics.

With India's power generation capacity being around 20 per cent that of China for a population of similar size, India continues to have chronic power shortages. For commercial and industrial businesses, this creates the need for additional capital expenditure to purchase alternative backup power systems that are also more costly per kilowatt hour than grid electricity.

If Indian economic growth can return to rates of between 8 and 9 per cent per year over the next five years, the minimum annual addition to power generating capacity would need to be around 40 GW per year between 2017 and 2020. This would require the addition of 120 GW between 2017 and 2020, which would be equivalent to the entire power generation capacity addition aimed for during the 12th Five Year Plan between 2012–17, for which the government is aiming to add a total of 118 GW capacity over five years. The additional power generating capacity increase planned under the 12th Five Year Plan target has been considerably increased by the BJP government since it took office, compared to the original five-year target set by the previous UPA coalition government. If indeed the Indian government meets its objective of adding a total 118 GW capacity over the 12th Five Year Plan, this would be quite an impressive outcome, since the previous 11th Five Year Plan only added 55 GW to total capacity.

The Modi government has given a high priority to accelerating power infrastructure development, and has a diversified strategy to achieve these goals. While coal will continue to play a central role in new power infrastructure, the BJP energy policy strategy also includes use of gas, nuclear power and renewable energy as key components of the overall strategy. The most dramatic shift in energy policy under the new Modi government has been a big shift towards solar energy, with the BJP having announced goals to lift solar energy generating capacity from 3 GW in 2015 to 100 GW by 2020.

Furthermore, a large share of the total population of India does not even have access to electricity yet. An estimated 300 million Indians still do not have access to electricity, and the electricity distribution system has been facing financial problems for decades, with many power utilities and distributors having accumulated losses due to government controls on electricity tariffs. A recent study by the World Bank has estimated that accumulated losses of the electricity distribution sector amount to 3 per cent of Indian GDP, with further losses expected to continue in future years unless the government reforms electricity tariffs to allow electricity generators and utilities to improve their balance sheets (Pargal and Banerjee, 2014).

The financial problems of the electricity distribution companies are a key constraint delaying the rollout of electricity connections to the remaining 300 million Indians without electricity, since these are predominantly low income households that will also be low electricity consumers. With distributors already suffering financial losses, there is little incentive for them to rollout electricity infrastructure that will most likely result in increasing losses for them. Therefore an overall reform of the electricity distribution sector is necessary in order to implement tariff structures that make the distributors profitable, while also finding a solution for incentive structures to allow distributors to connect the remaining 25 per cent of the Indian population that do not have access to electricity.

One of the potential solutions that may assist with providing electricity to rural households is the use of solar panels to power microgrids, with a number of such microgrids having already been established in rural India.

Overall, while the long-term challenges facing India in relation to energy infrastructure are still are enormous, the BJP government is pushing forward with more ambitious reforms that may gradually succeed in significantly boosting power generation capacity over the medium term outlook. This includes policy measures such as the substantial increase in power generating capacity targeted by the end of the 12th Five Year Plan and the large increase in new solar energy generating capacity planned by 2020. It will also be crucial to make major reforms to the electricity distribution system, so as to bring distributors back to long-term financial viability and reduce the cost of electricity subsidies.

Unleashing the Indian consumer

While the Indian economy compares unfavourably with China in many respects, one important advantage for India is that the structure of the Indian economy has an overall better balance towards domestic demand than the Chinese economy. Since the economic reforms commenced in China in 1980, the key drivers of Chinese economic growth have been investment and exports. This resulted in the gradual decline of household consumption as a share of total GDP, from around 50 per cent in the early 1980s to around 35 per cent by 2012. This has made the Chinese economy excessively dependent on exports and investment as growth drivers.

In contrast, the Indian economy is mainly driven by domestic demand rather than exports, with household consumption accounting for around 57 per cent of GDP in 2012–13. When government consumption is also included, Indian consumption as a share of GDP rises to 70 per cent of GDP in 2012–13, compared to 52 per cent in China.

This domestic consumption engine gives the Indian economy considerable underlying strength as it implies that India is less vulnerable to external shocks than many other emerging markets which are much more highly dependent on exports as a growth engine. Although India's trade and investment linkages with the world economy have increased over the last decade, India still has a relatively low share of exports and foreign investment when measured as a share of GDP compared to many East Asian economies.

Therefore if the Indian government and Indian central bank can get the domestic macroeconomic settings right, the Indian domestic demand engine should be able become a key driver for Indian economic growth over the long-term.

The BJP government's policy focus on substantially boosting infrastructure development could provide the trigger to stimulate Indian economic growth to rebound to above 8 per cent over the medium term. In addition, a second key factor that will be essential to allow sustained strong growth will be containing inflationary pressures, so that interest rates do not choke off the economic rebound.

With India's young demographic profile, the Indian economy has the potential for sustained long-term growth of at least 8 per cent per year over the next decade, which will support the rapid growth in the number of middle class households as well as household incomes, creating strong momentum for consumer spending growth.

Best of the BRICS?

By the Indian government's own admission in the Indian Budget for 2015–16, India's progress when benchmarked in terms of the United Nations human development indicators has been unsatisfactory. India was ranked 135th in the world, according to the 2014 Human Development Report published by the UNDP (UNDP, 2014).

When compared to China, the per capita GDP of India in 2014 was just a fraction of Chinese GDP. Indian per capita GDP measured in nominal USD terms was USD 1,640 in 2014, compared with Chinese per capita GDP of USD 7,550. Therefore Indian per capita GDP was only one-fifth of Chinese per capita GDP in 2014. Indian per capita GDP was also considerably lower than Indonesia, which had reached per capita GDP of USD 3,515 by 2014.

These very different trends in terms of per capita GDP increases between China and India are also reflected in the achievements in reducing extreme poverty in the two nations. The World Bank has estimated that the number of people living in extreme poverty in China had declined to 155 million by 2010, whereas in India the number of people living in extreme poverty was 394 million in 2010 (Olinto et al., 2013).

Yet when China commenced its economic liberalization process in 1978, Indian per capita GDP was slightly higher than Chinese per capita GDP. Since that time, Chinese economic growth has been considerably faster than India's, while Indian population growth has been faster than China's. The combination of these two factors has resulted in Indian per capita GDP lagging Chinese per capita GDP significantly. In addition, the CNY has appreciated against the USD over the last decade due to China's strong current account surpluses and burgeoning foreign exchange reserves, while the Indian rupee has depreciated against the USD due to India's chronic current account deficit and relatively modest foreign exchange reserves. This also acts as a drag on Indian per capita GDP relative to Chinese per capita GDP in USD terms.

The key message is that India remains a relatively low income nation compared to many East Asian industrial economies, even the most populous Asian emerging markets notably China and Indonesia.

However India may now be on the threshold of a period of sustained rapid growth, helped by accelerated infrastructure development by the BJP government and increased foreign direct investment inflows by foreign multinationals. If the planned boost to infrastructure development is implemented, this upturn in investment could increase India's GDP growth rate over the next decade by at least 1 per cent. Furthermore, by reducing bottle-necks to economic development, this could also lift India's long term potential growth rate. If India's average annual rate of GDP growth can reach between 8 per cent and 9 per cent over the next decade, this will also help to unleash growth in consumer spend-ing in the economy, helping to support rapid growth. India's long term potential growth rate is also supported by a relatively young demographic profile.

With Chinese economic growth projected to gradually moder-ate, India could grow faster than China for many years, which would gradually allow Indian GDP and per capita incomes to nar-row the gap with China. However the size of the gap is so great that it is unlikely India could actually catch up with China within the next three decades unless China had a period of protracted economic weakness and low growth.

The most likely scenario is that over the next three decades, Indian GDP and per capita GDP would gradually converge towards Chinese GDP. At present, Indian GDP accounts for only one-fifth of Chinese GDP. Over the next three decades, if India is able to sustain relatively rapid economic growth while Chinese growth rates gradually slow down, then the size of the Indian economy could converge to being around half the size of Chinese GDP.

This has significant geopolitical implications for the Asia-Pacific, as it would make India a large global political and economic power. From a geopolitical risk perspective, this would mean that India could act as a regional counterbalance to China's political, economic and military weight. This would increase the risks of a regional arms race in the Asia-Pacific region, with China and India at the forefront.

However both India and China have shown a willingness to build bilateral economic relations and set aside some of the frictions related to sovereign territorial claims along their common border areas. Both President Xi and Premier Li have made significant efforts to build ties with successive Indian governments, and new Indian Prime Minister Modi has reciprocated by giving a high level of priority to building bilateral economic ties and involving

Chinese companies in some key infrastructure and urban development projects. Bilateral trade between China and India has risen from just USD 3 billion in 2000 to USD 70 billion by 2014, reflecting the positive transformation of bilateral economic relations.

The rise of India as an economic power will also bring tremendous opportunities for future fast-growing trade and investment between China and India, creating large growth markets for both countries. As the size of Indian GDP eventually overtakes Japanese GDP in around a decade's time to become Asia's second largest economy, this would also help to reduce the vulnerability of other Asian nations to the risk of a recession in the Chinese economy. As India becomes one of Asia's largest growth engines, the structure of both the Asia-Pacific regional economy and the world economy will become more diversified and better balanced, particularly as the ASEAN region also becomes an increasingly important growth engine for the Asia-Pacific.

Chapter 9

ASEAN

Trade Liberalization and Economic Integration

ASEAN growth outlook

The implementation of the ASEAN Economic Community (AEC) by ASEAN leaders planned for the end of 2015 is one of a range of structural changes that will accelerate the economic development of ASEAN as a leading global growth hub for manufacturing and services. The ASEAN region is already experiencing rapid economic growth, and further economic liberalization and integration of the ASEAN economies is poised to trigger more rapid economic development.

Major strategic trends are supporting the rise of the ASEAN region, notably the impact of increasing wage costs in coastal Chinese provinces, which are forcing global multinationals to find new production hubs for low-cost manufactures. Accelerating infrastructure development in ASEAN, helped by China's new infrastructure financing initiatives such as the AIIB and the Silk Road Fund, will also improve the connectivity of regional transport infrastructure. The creation of better road and rail links between ASEAN and the southern provinces of China will help to boost trade and investment flows between ASEAN and southern China, accelerating regional development in Southeast Asia.

The size of ASEAN GDP had exceeded USD 2.4 trillion by 2013, making the combined GDP of the ten Southeast Asian member countries larger than Indian GDP. With a total population of around 600 million persons, the ASEAN region has become an important growth engine for the Asia-Pacific region as well as for global economic growth.

The origins of ASEAN as an organization were political, as an attempt to forge closer political co-operation amongst Southeast Asian governments following the serious conflicts that had taken place between Southeast Asian countries, notably Indonesian President Sukarno's *Konfrontasi* campaign to undermine the creation of the Federation of Malaysia during the early 1960s.

Following Indonesia's PKI coup plot and the political turmoil that ensued, President Suharto took office in 1967, and this change in leadership also brought about a new foreign policy stance that ended the period of *Konfrontasi*. ASEAN emerged as a valuable forum for political dialogue amongst the Southeast Asian nations, but for decades its further evolution as an institution was rather limited in scope. Initially comprising just six member states when it was formed in 1967, namely Indonesia, Malaysia, Singapore, Thailand, Philippines and Brunei, four other nations, Vietnam, Cambodia, Laos and Myanmar, joined subsequently.

The trade liberalization agenda of ASEAN gained momentum during the 1990s, with the ASEAN Free Trade Area (AFTA) having come into force in 1993, and the first six ASEAN members implementing the removal of tariffs on intra-ASEAN trade in goods. This represented a very significant step in trade liberalization, and resulted in substantial gains to some economies. Since the implementation of the ASEAN Free Trade Area in 2010, the Thai automotive industry has grown rapidly to become one of Asia's leading hubs for auto and parts production and is an important location for the production of cars for export. The Thai auto industry produced 1.9 million passenger cars and light commercial vehicles in 2014.

ASEAN has also been at the forefront of negotiating free trade agreements with other nations, notably the China-ASEAN Free Trade Area agreement, for which the initial agreement was signed in 2002 but came into force at the beginning of 2010. A network of other ASEAN FTA deals have also been signed with other major trade partners, including for India. The ASEAN-India Free Trade Area agreement came into effect in January 2010, with the Trade in Goods agreement forming the first pillar of this free trade agreement.

The network of free trade agreements that ASEAN has established with other major economies in the Asia-Pacific have helped to underpin the development of its export sector, with the China-ASEAN FTA being the most significant since China is the world's second largest economy and its rapid economic growth has provided a fast-growing market for ASEAN exports.

With China's industrial heartland in the coastal regions of the Pearl River Delta and Yangtze River Delta facing increasing pressures on competitiveness due to rising labour costs, Southeast Asia offers considerable potential as an alternative location for the establishment of low cost manufacturing. Average manufacturing wages in Vietnam, Myanmar, Cambodia and Laos are considerably below the average manufacturing wages in most Chinese provinces and considerably lower than industrial hubs such as Shanghai, Guangzhou, Tianjin and Beijing. However, a major competitive weakness of some parts of Southeast Asia is relatively poor infrastructure connectivity, which has been a constraint on economic development.

Consequently strengthening connectivity has become another key strategic priority for ASEAN governments, with efforts to co-ordinate regional initiatives to build intra-regional infrastructure. The creation of the ASEAN Single Aviation Market (ASAM) is one of the pillars that form part of the roadmap for the establishment of the ASEAN Economic Community in 2015. ASEAN has recognized the importance of air transport for the economic development of Southeast Asia, and has designated this sector as one of the 12 priority sectors for the establishment of the ASEAN Economic Community. The agreements implemented in 2015 will significantly liberalize the ASEAN aviation market for ASEAN airlines flying between designated international airports in the ASEAN member countries.

This rapid growth in ASEAN airline fleet size will drive a boom in the SE Asian maintenance, repair and overhaul (MRO) industry over the next two decades. Singapore is particularly well positioned to benefit from this trend. Singapore is currently the leading hub for MRO in Asia, accounting for an estimated 25 per cent of total Asian MRO market, and will be a key beneficiary of the rapid future growth of the ASEAN airline fleet. Singapore has become one of the centres-of-excellence globally for MRO for commercial aircraft engines. The decision by Rolls-Royce in February 2015 to establish a regional Customer Service Centre in Singapore will strengthen operational support to Asia-Pacific airlines and further build Singapore's role as a leading global aircraft MRO hub. The Rolls-Royce Customer Service Centre in Singapore will support 20 per cent of Rolls-Royce large civil aircraft engines worldwide. Rolls-Royce has already built a major aerospace facility at Seletar Aerospace Park for assembly and testing of Trent aero engines as well as the manufacture of fan blades for jet engines. Pratt & Whitney has also opened an MRO facility at Singapore's Seletar Aerospace Park in 2014, and is also building a manufacturing facility to manufacture jet engine fan blades and turbine disks. Over the next two decades, the ASEAN airline industry is poised for rapid growth, contributing a significant part of the overall expansion of the Asia-Pacific commercial airline fleet. This will underpin the rapid expansion of ASEAN's MRO industry, with Singapore, Malaysia and Indonesia likely to see substantial expansion in their MRO industries. In Indonesia, Lion Air has established its own MRO centre, Batam Aero Technic, at Hang Nadim International Airport in Batam. The new MRO facility commenced heavy maintenance operations in February 2014.

The development of ASEAN connectivity is also moving ahead rapidly in the area of rail transport, with China and Japan helping a number of ASEAN countries with plans for developing rail links within individual countries as well as projects connecting ASEAN countries. China has a long-term strategic plan to connect ASEAN countries to China's high speed rail network, which could accelerate economic development of ports and industrial zones in ASEAN that will link up with China. This could result in the development of ASEAN ports as transshipment hubs to send rail freight into southern and western provinces of China.

The planned implementation of the AEC at the end of 2015 by ASEAN leaders will provide another boost to the economic development of ASEAN, with significant liberalization of trade in services having been negotiated as part of the next phase of ASEAN trade liberalization.

The AEC will reduce barriers for trade in services and cross-border investment flows between ASEAN countries. Financial services integration are an important element of this upcoming agreement. In order to foster greater financial sector integration, ASEAN Finance Ministers and Central Bank governors concluded an agreement in March 2015 on a new ASEAN Banking Integration Framework (ABIF), in order to create a more integrated ASEAN financial services industry.

The ABIF is intended to create a new ASEAN banking system that will allow greater cross-border market access for Qualified ASEAN Banks (QABs). The intention of this new agreement is to allow ASEAN banks to undertake banking operations in other ASEAN countries, subject to these banks meeting appropriate regulatory and prudential guidelines in the other ASEAN country they are planning to enter. The new ABIF system will allow ASEAN banks to support their corporate clients that wish to expand their business operations into other ASEAN countries.

The determination of the necessary QAB criteria will be agreed bilaterally between ASEAN countries to agree on what standards the ASEAN banks will need to meet for reciprocal access to be granted. To that extent, the ASEAN framework is still built upon bilateral reciprocity, rather than a single standard across all ASEAN countries. Since there is no single central bank authority for the whole of ASEAN in the way that the EU has the ECB, it is necessary for national central banks and financial regulatory authorities to agree the standards for QAB status.

While the first phase of ASEAN trade liberalization has supported the ASEAN countries with strong manufacturing hubs by giving them tariff-free market access for goods to other ASEAN countries, the next phase of ASEAN trade liberalization will be the liberalization of trade in services.

Singapore is a global leader in exports of a wide range of services, and will benefit significantly from this next phase of liberalization. However Malaysia and the Philippines are also major exporters of services, and the growth of their service sector economies will be key drivers of their long-term economic growth.

The economic renaissance of the Philippines

One of the most populous nations of ASEAN, the Philippines, which had languished for decades, has shown rapid economic growth under President Aquino's administration, particularly in its exports of services.

Two key growth drivers for the Philippines economy are the rapidly growing Information Technology-Business Process Outsourcing (IT-BPO) industry and the strong flow of remittances from Filipino workers abroad. The export revenue from the IT-BPO sector has more than doubled between 2008 and 2014, reaching an estimated $13.3 billion. The competitiveness of the Philippines in this industry has been particularly helped by the large pool of university-educated workers as well as the strong English-language skills of the workforce. In the Philippines, the export revenue from the IT-BPO sector has more than doubled between 2008 and 2014, reaching an estimated $18 billion in revenues by 2014 with the total number of employees in the IT-BPO industry exceeding one million. By 2016, the Philippines IT-BPO industry is projected to have 1.3 million employees. The rapid growth of this industry is also driving economic development in a number of cities across the Philippines, with Manila and Cebu now ranked among the world's leading IT-BPO hubs.

Meanwhile remittances from Filipino workers abroad rose to a new record level of $26.9 billion in 2014, up 6.2 per cent on the 2013 level, providing a key source of strength for the Philippines balance of payments. Overseas worker remittances are a key driver of GDP growth in the Philippines, as they provide support consumer expenditure and also residential housing construction.

An estimated 35 per cent of annual worker remittances are flowing into new residential property purchases, which has created robust expansion in the residential construction sector in major cities in the Philippines in recent years, with momentum expected to remain strong in 2015–16. Meanwhile the rapid growth of the IT-BPO industry is also creating positive transmission effects for the rest of the economy, including for the commercial property sector, with rapid growth in demand for commercial floor space, underpinning the development of existing and new office parks in urban centres. The gross value of construction grew by an estimated 10 per cent in 2014, with continued rapid growth forecast for 2015.

While the current growth drivers of the Philippines are the IT-BPO industry and the strong and stable remittances of the overseas Filipino workers, the long-term outlook for the future development of the Philippines will be heavily dependent on the ability to make the manufacturing sector more competitive and to mobilize both foreign and domestic investment flows into the manufacturing sector. A key challenge for the Philippines is to improve the business climate for foreign investment. The Philippines is ranked 95 on the World Bank's global Ease of Doing Business Index for 2015, which surveys 189 countries worldwide. While the Aquino government has made efforts to improve this ranking, there is still a great deal of work to do to improve the overall competitiveness of the Philippines to attract large inflows of foreign direct investment (FDI).

However, the Philippines did make tremendous progress during 2014, with FDI investment surging by 66 per cent to $6.2 billion. A key priority for the Philippines must be to attract greater FDI into the manufacturing sector, in order to support employment growth and make the Philippines a competitive ASEAN manufacturing export hub. This will help to reduce poverty rates by boosting jobs growth and household incomes. Another key challenge for the Philippines is to increase infrastructure investment, in order to create high quality transport infrastructure for roads, ports and airports, as well as for power generation and transmission, essential for growth in manufacturing and services. Tackling urban crime must also be another key priority, in order to make the Philippines a more attractive environment for foreign investment and tourism.

The Philippines continues to face other economic development challenges. Poverty and unemployment remain very high in the Philippines with around 28 per cent of the population still living in poverty according to government estimates, while the total number of unemployed or underemployed workers exceeds ten million. Large numbers of new workers are also entering the workforce each year, with around one million new workers expected to join the labour force each year. In 2014, an estimated 962,000 workers joined the labour force. Underemployment is also a key issue, as an estimated 12 million workers are underemployed. Therefore creating a diversified economy with growth industries that can generate rapid jobs growth will be a key strategic imperative for the government.

Sustained rapid growth will require continued economic reforms to improve the business climate of the Philippines, making it more attractive for FDI into sectors such as manufacturing, the IT-BPO sector and tourism.

Malaysia's economic transformation program

The Malaysian economy is on the threshold of becoming a high income country within the next decade. Malaysia is currently classified as an upper middle income nation according to World Bank classifications. While the near-term growth outlook has been impacted by the sharp decline in world oil prices since mid-2014, the Malaysian economy is expected to be relatively resilient to the impact effects, due to the well-diversified structure of Malaysian exports, which include mineral and agricultural commodities, manufactured goods, as well as a range of service sector exports. Good macroeconomic policy management with recent economic reforms such as the removal of fuel subsidies in 2014 and the implementation of a GST (Goods and Services Tax) in April 2015 have also helped to mitigate the impact on the government's fiscal position.

Over the next decade, Malaysia is expected to be a beneficiary of the rapid growth of the ASEAN region, with Malaysian exports to other ASEAN countries likely to grow strongly, helped by ASEAN Economic Community trade and investment liberalization. By 2025, Indonesian GDP is projected to exceed USD two trillion, creating a very large market for Malaysian goods and services exports. Middle class consumer spending is expected to grow rapidly in Indonesia as well as other ASEAN emerging markets such as Vietnam, Philippines, Cambodia, Thailand and Myanmar, and this will underpin rapid growth in Malaysian service sector exports of tourism, financial services, education and medical services.

Malaysian multinationals are also expected to continue to expand their international operations across ASEAN as well as in other parts of Asia and the Middle East, with South-South trade becoming an increasingly important driver of Malaysian exports.

ASEAN is a rapidly growing global hub for the IT-BPO industry with Malaysia among the leading hubs. The competitiveness of Malaysia in this industry has been particularly helped by the large pool of university-educated workers as well as the English-language skills of its workforce. In Malaysia, the IT-BPO industry has shown rapid growth with major IT-BPO hubs having developed in Kuala Lumpur and Penang. A new IT-BPO Park is being built in Penang which is expected to create around 21,000 new IT-BPO jobs by 2020.

Malaysia is expected to grow rapidly over the next decade, with exports continuing to play an important role in economic growth, as ASEAN domestic demand becomes an increasingly important source of demand for Malaysian exports. The rapid growth in the number of ASEAN middle class households is expected to provide a sustained source of growth in ASEAN domestic demand. However, Malaysia will also benefit from strong growth of consumer demand in other emerging markets, notably China, whose share of world consumer spending is forecast to double by 2025. India and the Middle East are also expected to be fast-growing consumer markets for Malaysian exports.

However, to fully realize Malaysia's economic potential and to become a high-income nation, Malaysia will need to continue its economic reform initiatives, including pursuing the development of strategic growth industries identified under the Economic Transformation Programme, giving high priority to developing Malaysia's human capital through universities, technical colleges and vocational training programs, and continuing to develop key physical infrastructure such as urban transport systems, ports, airports and power infrastructure.

With Malaysia on the threshold of becoming one of Asia's high income nations, Malaysia will also have an increasingly important leadership role to play among Asian and global emerging markets in helping other countries with their long-term economic and social development.

The outlook for ASEAN

Over the next two decades, the ASEAN region is projected to be one of the most dynamic growth hubs in the global economy. The hollowing out of Chinese low-cost manufacturing will continue to drive investment in low cost manufacturing into ASEAN low-wage economies such as Vietnam and Cambodia.

Meanwhile the service sector economies of Singapore, Malaysia and the Philippines will benefit from the rapid growth of the ASEAN region, as well as growing demand from other Asian economies, notably South Asia.

ASEAN as an institution has made significant contributions to building peace and stability in Southeast Asia, as well as in creating a framework for trade liberalization in goods and services amongst the ASEAN nations as well as between ASEAN and other major Asia-Pacific economies, including China and India.

The success of ASEAN in forging closer economic co-operation and trade liberalization provides a role model to the rest of the Asia-Pacific about how regional institutions can reduce geopolitical tensions and accelerate trade liberalization and economic integration in Asia.

Chapter 10

Indonesia

Southeast Asia's Emerging Regional Power

The collapse of Suharto's New Order

On 13 May 1998, as the Indonesian economy was disintegrating during the depths of the East Asian financial crisis, anti-Chinese riots began in Jakarta. Over the next three days, ethnic Chinese Indonesians in major Indonesian cities, including Jakarta, Solo and Medan, became victims of an upsurge of racial attacks, with thousands assaulted, raped or killed. While estimates vary, some figures put the death toll as high as 1,200 people just in Jakarta during the riots. Thousands of properties were looted or burnt down in Jakarta, with 288 people estimated to have been killed when the Yogya Plaza shopping centre was set on fire. In Jakarta and other major cities, angry mobs had burnt down many bank branches, destroyed ATM machines and torched hundreds of vehicles.

As the US government arranged for chartered flights to evacuate their citizens from Jakarta, the IMF delegation that had been working on the IMF bailout package for Indonesia fled the country from Jakarta's military airport. The IMF staff had good reason to be particularly fearful of the angry mobs, since the IMF austerity measures that were being imposed on the nation as part of the conditionality for the release of various tranches of the IMF bailout funds had already triggered widespread protests from ordinary Indonesian citizens for several months.

With the nation in political and economic crisis and descending into widespread social unrest, President Suharto, who had ruled Indonesia since 1967, was forced to resign on 21 May 1998. The economy had been destroyed as a result of underlying economic imbalances that had been exposed during the East Asian crisis.

Political turmoil and the anti-Chinese riots triggered further capital flight out of Indonesia, as wealthy Indonesians sought safe havens, which put further downward pressure on the rupiah. The Indonesian rupiah had already plunged from 2,600 per USD in August 1997 to 14,800 by January 1998 as investors had reduced their exposure to rupiah. The deteriorating political and economic situation resulted in further currency depreciation, to 16,650 by June 1998.

The sharp depreciation of the rupiah exposed the foreign currency debt vulnerabilities of many large Indonesian corporations, which had borrowed in foreign currency loans at lower interest rates than domestic rupiah loans while the rupiah had been appreciating. The situation had been exacerbated by a decision by the Indonesian central bank to ban issuance of commercial paper by finance companies, leading to increased borrowings by Indonesian corporates in foreign currency loans. By 1998, Indonesian industrial corporations had foreign debt of USD 65 billion, with a large share being short-term debt (Pangestu and Habir, 2002). This created leverage that was vulnerable to foreign exchange rate volatility due to largely unhedged exposures, which eventually destroyed their balance sheets once the rupiah collapsed against the USD.

The transmission effects of the problems in the corporate sector related to foreign currency loans as well as the broader economic downturn unfolding in the Indonesian economy resulted in increasing problems in the Indonesian banking sector, with a first round of bank closures occurring in November 1997. Although a deposit protection scheme was introduced to protect depositors, this was not comprehensive, and instead of creating confidence among depositors, resulted in a capital flight and bank runs among many private banks, with 154 banks experiencing bank runs by the end of 1997. The banking crisis continued in the first half of 1998, with the Indonesian Bank Restructuring Agency (IBRA) forced to take over seven large banks; banking sector non-performing loans were estimated to have reached 75 per cent in 1998.

There ensued a long period of bank restructuring and recapitalization under IBRA, as the slow process of economic recovery began by 1999, following the 13 per cent contraction in Indonesian GDP in 1998.

President SBY's legacy

Between President Suharto's resignation in 1998 and the election of General Susilo Bambang Yudhoyono (SBY) in 2004, Indonesia went through a period of economic and social turmoil. Suharto's Vice President B.J. Habibe took over as the president when Suharto resigned in May 1998, but his term of office was very short. The Indonesian Democratic Party–Struggle (PDI-P) led by Sukarno's daughter Megawati Sukarnoputri won the largest number of seats in the 1999 legislative elections, which allowed her to run as the PDI-P candidate in the presidential elections in October 1999. Although she was defeated by Abdurrahman Wahid, leader of the National Awakening Party (PKB), she was selected as Vice President in a political compromise. President Wahid's period in office was also short, and he was ousted from office in July 2001 due to his perceived ineffectiveness in the face of the nation's economic and social turmoil. Megawati succeeded Wahid as President, but she also struggled to make significant progress with economic recovery, and she was eventually defeated in the 2004 presidential elections by SBY.

At the height of the East Asian crisis, the Indonesian economy went through a deep recession. In 1998 alone, Indonesian GDP contracted by 13 per cent, and there was virtually no growth in 1999. For a nation where a high proportion of the population lived in poverty, this created tremendous hardship for the most vulnerable segments of society. Between 2000 and 2004, moderate positive economic growth was again achieved, but living standards of ordinary Indonesians had barely been restored to pre-crisis levels by the time President SBY took office.

However, after President SBY was elected as president in 2004, Indonesia entered a period of economic and political stabilization, achieving steady macroeconomic progress during two terms of office under President SBY's leadership. Indonesia made significant economic strides during this period, with per capita GDP tripling from USD 1,160 in 2004 to USD 3,400 by 2014. This was a tremendous achievement given that per capita GDP in 1996 had been USD 1,150 and had subsequently fallen sharply during the East Asian crisis before gradually recovering to just about the same level as in 1996 by the time that President SBY took office in 2004. The East Asian crisis had resulted in almost a whole decade being lost in terms of economic progress.

Having inherited an economy that had seen no improvement in per capita living standards since 1996, the tripling in per capita GDP during SBY's ten years in office was a remarkable achievement, reflecting sound macroeconomic policy and economic reforms that helped to underpin economic growth momentum. The total GDP of Indonesia also showed a very significant increase, from USD 260 billion in 2004 to USD 860 billion by 2014, putting

Indonesia on the threshold of becoming one of the few Asian economies with a total GDP exceeding one trillion USD.

One of the major macroeconomic successes of the Indonesian government under President SBY was the single-minded reduction of government debt as a share of GDP, from 56 per cent in 2004 when he took office to just 26 per cent of GDP by 2014. This is extremely low by international standards, especially when compared with the very high government debt to GDP ratios currently for OECD countries. President SBY's economic frontbench during his first term of office showed very skillful macroeconomic policy management, led by Finance Minister Sri Mulyani Indrawati, who later became a Managing Director and Chief Operating Officer of the World Bank in 2010. A key test for President SBY and his economic ministers came in 2008–09, when the global financial crisis shock waves hit emerging markets.

Initially global financial markets feared that the Indonesian economy would again be vulnerable to an external shock, which resulted in sharp rupiah depreciation during the second half of 2008 and some depletion of Bank Indonesia's foreign exchange reserves as the central bank intervened to smooth the rupiah depreciation. Indonesian Credit Default Swap (CDS) spreads, which measure the likelihood of sovereign default, rose to 1,200 basis points by December 2008 as the global financial crisis peaked. The Indonesian CDS spreads were a strong indicator of perceptions that global financial markets expected an economic crisis similar to a decade earlier.

However Indonesia weathered the global economic and financial storm far better than financial markets had expected, with GDP growth showing a resilient performance in 2009, recording positive GDP growth of 4.6 per cent. The Indonesian government and Bank Indonesia also bolstered Indonesia's foreign exchange reserves with a World Bank sovereign bond issue as well as currency swap agreements with the Bank of Japan. By the second half of 2009, Indonesian CDS spreads were consistently below 200 basis points, reflecting the substantial change in perception in global financial markets about the outlook for the Indonesian economy.

The resilience of the Indonesian economy during 2009 convinced financial markets that the macroeconomic vulnerabilities of the Indonesian economy had been significantly reduced since the East Asian crisis. From 2010 onwards, Indonesia began to attract stronger portfolio equity inflows as well as net inflows into the local government debt markets, and achieved steady sovereign credit rating upgrades from the major international credit rating agencies.

On the external account, the performance of the SBY government has also been very positive, with Indonesian foreign exchange reserves increasing from USD 36 billion in 2004 to USD 112 billion by 2014, and total external debt declining from 53.3 per cent of GDP in 2004 to 30.5 per cent of GDP by 2014. While the accumulation of foreign exchange reserves was temporarily disrupted during the global financial crisis when Bank Indonesia had to use some of its reserves to smooth the sharp depreciation of the rupiah, Indonesia's foreign exchange reserves rose steadily during the second term of President SBY's administration, helped by strong foreign capital inflows.

One of the most impressive indicators of the changed perception amongst international investors of Indonesia after a decade of President SBY's governance is shown in the performance of foreign direct investment inflows. Total foreign direct investment inflows into Indonesia had been close to zero in both 2002 and 2003 and had only managed to reach USD one billion by 2004. By 2012 and for 2013, total foreign direct investment inflows were around USD 19 billion in each year, and by 2014, foreign direct investment inflows reached a new peak of USD 37 billion, up 16 per cent on the previous year. Unlike foreign portfolio capital inflows, which can be quite volatile, foreign direct investment inflows reflect long term investor sentiment as these figures represent investment by multinationals building new factories, developing new mining projects or infrastructure development. This therefore indicates a much more positive perception by foreign investors about the Indonesian medium to long-term economic outlook than had been the case a decade ago.

However one area where there have been increasing concerns about Indonesian investment policy is in the resources sector, where the Indonesian government and parliament have implemented new legislation that they believe is necessary to protect their national sovereignty over their natural resources. A new mining law passed by the Indonesian parliament in 2009 requires majority Indonesian shareholding for the local ownership structures of mining companies conducting mining operations in Indonesia. Since some foreign mining firms with long-standing operations in Indonesia were affected by this rule, a ten year transition period was granted for the transition of ownership to majority

Indonesian ownership. A second rule that came into effect in January 2014 was a ban on exports of unprocessed mineral ores, with the ban taking effect from that date for nickel, copper and bauxite, and for certain other ores by 2017. The immediate impact of the implementation of the ban was a disruption of ore exports. While some temporary relief measures were given for copper ore exports, the main objective of the new requirement is to force mining companies to process their ores in Indonesia before exporting them, thereby creating higher value-added exports for Indonesia. The Indonesian government has reported in 2015 that 11 nickel refineries were being built in Indonesia, with a combined total investment of USD 1.4 billion, with three new alumina refineries also under construction to process bauxite ore, although the government was considering lifting the ban on bauxite exports to allow companies to improve their revenues to fund construction of the refineries.

Despite international investor concerns about increased resource nationalism in Indonesia, foreign direct investment inflows have been rising rapidly between 2011 and 2015. A large share of foreign direct investment flows in the last three years have come into the auto sector, with major new investments in auto plants by Japanese automakers, including Nissan, which opened its second manufacturing plant in Indonesia in 2014, lifting its annual Indonesian production capacity to 250,000 vehicles. Suzuki Motor Corporation's Indonesian unit Suzuki Indomobil Motor opened its fourth auto plant in Indonesia in May 2015, with the capacity to assemble 106,000 vehicles per year, as well as having engine and transmission production lines. In 2014, Suzuki already had achieved auto exports of 25,000 vehicles to other ASEAN markets.

Isuzu's Indonesian subsidiary Isuzu Astra Motor Indonesia has also opened a new truck manufacturing plant in Indonesia during 2015, in a joint venture with PT PPI (Perusahaan Perdagangan Indonesia Trading Company). Meanwhile the Mitsubishi Motors joint venture with local partner PT Krama Yudha has announced that it will build a new vehicle assembly plant in near Jakarta, with the new plant expected to be completed in 2017. The new plant will have an annual auto production capacity of 160,000 vehicles. Japan's automakers are consolidating their strong market share of the Indonesian auto market, with expectations of rapid long-term growth in Indonesian auto demand.

Therefore the scorecard for President SBY's two terms of office can be summarized as having delivered an impressive transformation of the Indonesian economy as well as maintaining a stable democracy in one of the world's most populous emerging markets. Hardly any other major emerging market worldwide has performed so consistently over the last decade.

The political transition after two terms of office under President SBY was also a model of democratic due process. President SBY stood down as required under the Indonesian Constitution after two terms of office, and the next presidential elections were conducted on schedule. While the losing presidential candidate Prabowo Subianto did challenge the election result alleging electoral fraud and other irregularities, he followed the due legal process and when the Indonesian Constitutional Court rejected his pleas, he did eventually step aside to allow the leading candidate Joko Widodo, known as Jokowi, to take office.

Key challenges facing Indonesia

With Indonesia facing significant economic hurdles in the medium term, President Jokowi entered office facing a difficult economic management task to try to deliver the same kind of economic growth performance that President SBY had achieved during his ten years in office.

Indonesia will face tremendous challenges in trying to sustain this remarkable economic performance over the next decade, for a number of reasons.

Firstly, Jokowi entered the national presidential race from his previous post as Governor of Jakarta, a post he was elected to in November 2012. Although his candidacy was based on the widespread grassroots support for him from the Indonesian electorate, his political candidacy for the presidential elections was made possible when the Chairperson of Indonesia's PDI-P Party, Megawati Sukarnoputri, former Indonesian president and daughter of Sukarno, invited Jokowi to run as the PDI-P candidate with the broad national backing of the PDI-P party infrastructure for the presidential election. For PDI-P, Jokowi was seen as the best opportunity for PDI-P to win the presidential election, which was an astute political decision.

However this meant that Jokowi was not himself the true leader of the PDI-P party, and has needed to continuously court the political backing and support of key PDI-P politicians. This has meant that his political position within his own party was relatively weak compared to other recently elected political leaders of major Asian economies such as Prime Minister Shinzo Abe of Japan, who had led the LDP party to a resounding electoral victory in 2012, or Indian Prime Minister Narendra Singh Modi, who led the BJP party to a decisive victory in the Indian national elections in 2014, winning a clear majority in the lower house of parliament. The implications for Indonesia are that Jokowi has faced struggles to implement ambitious reforms due to the need to continuously win backing from within the PDI-P leadership for his policies, as well as the added complexity because the PDI-P itself did not win a majority in parliament, and legislative reforms therefore need the support of a broader political coalition.

Secondly, the Indonesian economy is facing structural changes that are undermining its traditional reliance on commodity exports. Historically, Indonesia has been heavily reliant on commodities exports, particularly oil and gas. During the 1960s and 1970s, it had been oil and gas exports that had been a key driver of Indonesian economic growth and development, boosted further by the world oil price shocks of 1973 and 1979. While Indonesia's manufacturing sector showed rapid economic growth during the 1980s until the East Asian crisis, since the late 1990s commodities exports have again emerged as the most important driver of export growth.

Already by the time of the East Asian crisis, Indonesian oil exports had been falling rapidly as oil reserves in existing oil fields were depleting and new oil fields had not been developed rapidly enough. By 2004, when SBY took office, Indonesia had become a net oil importing nation, and by 2009, it decided to leave OPEC since it was no longer a net oil exporting nation. Indonesia is still a large exporter of liquefied natural gas, but due to rapidly rising domestic energy demand, Indonesia will gradually need to reduce its LNG exports and also increase its LNG imports in order to meet domestic consumption needs.

As oil exports were fading as a source of export revenue, Indonesian commodity exports were boosted by the boom in demand from China and India for Indonesian thermal coal exports, as well as demand from other Asian coal importing nations. The rapid growth in Chinese thermal coal imports from Indonesia and other international sources since 2005 created a sense of euphoria in global coal exporting nations such as Indonesia and Australia, with large-scale new investments in coal projects based on expectations that the good times would carry on due to further strong growth in Chinese coal demand.

However coal exports are facing headwinds, firstly due to the slump in world traded thermal coal prices between 2011 and 2015, and more recently due to weakening Chinese demand for Indonesian thermal coal. The rise and fall in internationally traded thermal coal prices has been dramatic, with rapidly rising Chinese demand for coal imports pushing thermal coal prices up from around USD 40 per ton in late 2005 to a peak of around USD 190 per ton just before the onset of the global financial crisis in 2008. Coal, like other commodities, fell sharply during the global financial crisis, but as China's stimulus package boosted Chinese GDP growth in 2009–2010, traded thermal coal prices recovered to USD 140 per ton by early 2011.

Those were heady days for global coal producers, and anecdotes of truck drivers in Australian coal mines being paid salaries of USD 150,000 or even more became commonplace. I sat next to the CEO of a large coal mining company at a coal industry dinner in Indonesia in late 2010, and I asked him if these legendary inflated salaries were actually true. He said they were, and wrote for me on a piece of paper some rough calculations showing me why at such high coal prices, the impact on company profitability per ton of coal mined of such high wages was not significant, due to the capital-intensive nature of their coal mining operations. However, the coal miners' party was shortly about to end.

From 2011 onwards, increasing global exports of thermal coal as a result of rising production in major coal-producing nations, including the from the US due the switch from coal to gas by US electricity generators due to falling domestic US gas prices, led to a protracted decline in thermal coal prices which fell to around USD 60 per ton by April 2015.

The long-term outlook for Chinese traded coal imports has also weakened due to the construction of long-distance power transmission grids in China linking inland coal producing provinces with the coastal provinces, allowing inland coal mines to supply coal to nearby power stations which then transmit electricity by transmission grids to the coastal industrial hubs. Indonesian coal exports to China fell from 130 million tonnes in 2013 to 100 million tonnes in 2014, although the impact on the Indonesian coal industry was mitigated by an additional 18 million tonnes of exports to India. However, in the first half of 2015 total Chinese coal imports from the rest of the world fell by 38 per cent compared to the first half of 2014, resulting in a further large decline in Indonesian coal exports to China.

While the slump in Chinese demand for Indonesian coal exports has been mitigated by rising Indian demand for coal in 2014, India also has large domestic deposits of thermal coal, and if its coal mining industry becomes more efficient, this could also reduce the future growth in India's import requirements for thermal coal from Indonesia.

The combination of weakening exports of oil and gas together with the new headwinds for Indonesian exports of thermal coal have resulted in a significant deterioration of Indonesia's current account position since 2011, which has also resulted in a substantial depreciation of the Indonesian rupiah against the USD, as financial markets have factored in a structural deterioration of Indonesia's current account position. Weaker commodity exports have also flowed into softening GDP growth momentum, with some deterioration in the contribution of net exports to GDP growth.

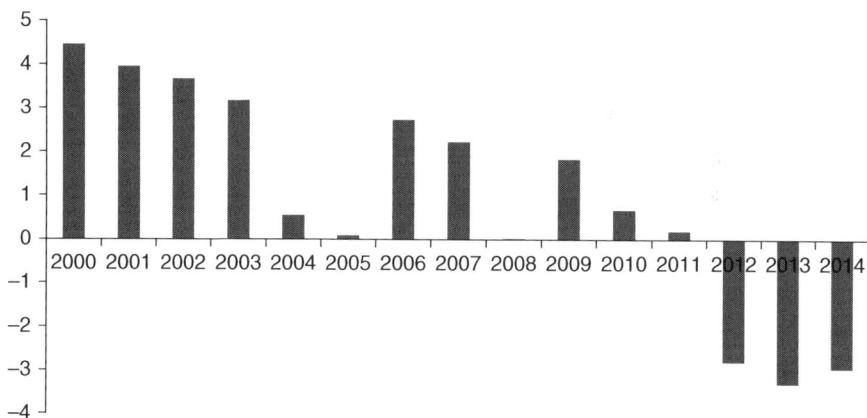

Figure 10.1   Indonesian current account balance (as share of GDP)
Source: IMF.

Indonesia's infrastructure challenges

Among the most important factors constraining Indonesia's economic development is the poor quality of infrastructure. To improve the business environment, Indonesia will need to overcome some of the major hurdles that have deterred foreign multinationals from establishing manufacturing operations in the past. This will require building better essential infrastructure for manufacturing, including adequate power infrastructure, modern highways and efficient port terminals to reduce shipment costs.

In the UK, it is polite to talk about the weather when starting a business meeting. In India or Australia, one could talk about cricket to break the ice. Similarly in Jakarta, it is only good manners to open the conversation if you are a foreigner visiting the country by inquiring how many hours it will take to get to Soekarno-Hatta International Airport so that you won't miss your flight back home. Indonesians are among the most polite and friendly hosts, but this will generate an animated and lively start to the meeting, as everyone commiserates with each other about the travails of Indonesian infrastructure deficiencies. By the way, if you want an answer to this question, my own experience in recent months is that it takes an hour on a good day when traffic is flowing well to get from the airport to Plaza Indonesia in central Jakarta, and also the same time to go in the other direction if traffic is flowing smoothly.

During a recent trip to Jakarta, I arrived at the airport in the early afternoon and reached central Jakarta in somewhat less than one hour. However when going in the other direction a couple of days later on my return journey, I left my hotel later in the afternoon, and was trapped in traffic moving at a crawl for much of the journey to the airport on exactly the same road. The trip to the airport ended up taking almost three hours. It wasn't even raining, which would have made the travel time even longer.

President Jokowi has fully recognized the need to address the infrastructure challenge, which is one of Indonesia's most significant hurdles to economic development, and this was a key platform of his election manifesto. President Jokowi had already placed a high priority on infrastructure development when he was the Mayor of Solo from 2005 until 2012 and as the Governor of Jakarta from 2012 until 2014. At a national level, he has continued to press ahead with making infrastructure a top economic priority.

The first step towards this was the substantial reduction in fuel subsidies that were implemented soon after he became President, significantly reducing the cost of subsidies in the total budget and allowing a large boost to government investment in infrastructure development. With the total cost of fuel subsidies estimated to decline from 2.5 per cent of GDP in 2014 to around 0.5 per cent of GDP in 2015, this has created significant fiscal savings that can be reallocated for government infrastructure spending equivalent to at least 1 per cent of GDP per year, allowing for some reduction in the annual budget deficit as a share of GDP. Moreover with the government debt to GDP ratio very low by international standards at just 26 per cent of GDP, the Indonesian government has considerable scope to increase government infrastructure spending. The Jokowi administration's first budget in 2015 did announce a 60 per cent increase in infrastructure spending, with a USD 22 billion allocation for infrastructure projects.

One of the major infrastructure bottlenecks facing Indonesia is insufficient power generation and transmission infrastructure. The Jokowi government has set a target of building 35,000 megawatts of new electricity generating capacity over the next five years, which if achieved, will represent very substantial progress towards improving Indonesia's power infrastructure. However Indonesia faces many challenges in delivering such large increases in generating capacity.

Another major area of infrastructure development expenditure by the Jokowi administration will be on urban development, to provide better infrastructure for the large cities of Indonesia. For 2015, the Indonesian government has announced plans to build one million affordable homes, at a total cost of USD 6.2 billion. The Indonesian government will fund a share of the total cost of this housing program from the national budget, but other organizations will also contribute to the construction program, including Indonesia's state-owned housing developer, the national social security fund as well as plans to get development finance support for the program from multilateral development finance institutions such as the World Bank and Asian Development Bank. While this may be a very ambitious goal to achieve within one year, even if substantial progress is made towards this first year target by commencing construction starts for significant proportion of this total it will be a very positive step towards boosting affordable housing for low-income households.

Improving transportation infrastructure is also a central platform of the Indonesian government's medium-term infrastructure development policy. Given Indonesia is an archipelago with over 17,000 islands, port infrastructure is critical to the Indonesian economy. Over the medium term outlook to 2020, 24 seaports are planned to be built or upgraded.

At present, Indonesia's port infrastructure creates a bottleneck for the economy, with only two international ports at Jakarta and Surabaya handling international container shipping. The port of Tanjong Priok in Jakarta currently handles an estimated two-thirds of total international shipping. A major expansion of Tanjong Priok is underway with the construction of New Priok port, which is expected to triple Jakarta's total port capacity by 2023 from five million 20-foot equivalent units (TEU) to 18 million TEU. State-owned port operator Pelindo 2, which is responsible for ports in Jakarta as well as some other major regions of Indonesia, is planning to build five new ports, with construction expected to commence in 2015–16.

In addition to the need for expansion of container port shipping capacity, Indonesia also is planning to increase the number of coal terminals handling thermal coal exports. At present around 20 coal terminals exist across the nation, including a number of private coal export terminals in Kalimantan and Sumatra. The government is planning to add additional coal terminals as part of its infrastructure upgrading.

Another important part of the development of future port infrastructure will be the construction of more LNG import terminals. As domestic demand for energy is projected to grow rapidly over the next two decades, Indonesia will need to use both coal and gas as feedstock for domestic power plants, and building additional LNG import terminals will allow greater use of gas feedstock in Indonesia's future energy mix.

The Arun LNG export terminal shipped its last LNG export cargo in October 2014 after 36 years of operation, and was converted into an LNG import terminal that began operations in March 2015. The LNG import terminal will supply gas to Aceh and North Sumatra provinces, with a gas transmission pipeline to Medan to allow gas to be used for industrial uses as well as gas feedstock for electricity generation.

The combined impact of the large new government initiatives to boost infrastructure development started slowly in the initial months since Jokowi's election; however there have been signs of greater momentum as the government attempts to accelerate infrastructure spending. The Indonesian government does have a long track record of underspending on its infrastructure budget, so one of the key challenges facing the government will be to improve the implementation of planned infrastructure development programs. If the government's ambition for rapid infrastructure development is realized over the next couple of years, it could provide a boost to Indonesian GDP growth over the medium-term outlook, with the potential to add at least one percentage point to real GDP growth rates over the next decade. Although the reduction in fuel subsidies will allow the Indonesian government to allocate more spending for infrastructure, the private sector will also have an important role to play through public-private partnerships as well as investing in new privately-owned and operated infrastructure projects.

Employment growth

Another key economic challenge will be to generate sufficient employment growth to provide jobs for the large number of youth entering the Indonesian workforce each year. With an estimated 1.5 million people joining the Indonesian workforce annually, the formal sector of the economy is unable to create sufficient jobs for such a large number of workers. A large proportion of the Indonesian workforce is estimated to be employed in the informal sector in the shadow economy, as low-paid workers in agriculture or retail service industries. The youth unemployment rate in Indonesia is estimated to be in the range of around 25–30 percent.

Tackling the high level of unemployment and underemployment in Indonesia will need to be a key priority for the Indonesian government over the next decade, in order to prevent the risk of social unrest. Long before the Arab Spring occurred in 2011, the demographic profiles of many Middle East countries were flashing danger signals for country risk analysts. I recall writing country reports in 2005 about a number of Middle East countries highlighting the demographic time bomb that was building due to the large numbers of youth that would be entering the labour force in many Middle Eastern countries, which would put tremendous pressures on their governments to reform their economies and create more dynamic economic growth that would generate employment. However for various reasons most of these countries were unable to make sufficient reforms and eventually suffered an explosion of social unrest.

While the Indonesian economy has performed very well over the last decade and averted social unrest similar to the Arab Spring, the fundamental demographic profile of Indonesia does signal that rapid employment growth will be needed over the next decade. Not only will Indonesia need to generate sufficient employment growth for the cohort of youth joining the labour force each year, but there will also need to be progress towards reducing the high levels of underemployment and unemployment.

Therefore Indonesia will need to deliver sustained rapid economic growth rates of between 6 to 7 per cent per year in order to achieve sufficient growth in employment and sustained improvement in living standards.

Poverty reduction

Sustained economic growth over the last decade has resulted in significant reductions in poverty levels in Indonesia in recent years, with the share of the population living in poverty having declined from around 24 per cent during the East Asian crisis to 11 per cent by 2014. However poverty remains a major economic and social problem for Indonesia, with an estimated 28 million Indonesians still living below the poverty line, according to World Bank data. Furthermore the World Bank estimates that around half of Indonesian households remain close to the national poverty line, which is set at USD 24 per month.

Therefore a large share of Indonesia's total population still remain highly vulnerable, living just above the poverty line and at risk of falling back into poverty very rapidly if they lose their job or if other factors such as sickness prevent them from working. With half the population still close to poverty and having little if any savings, much of the population remains highly vulnerable to any large macroeconomic shocks.

Moreover poverty rates remain higher in rural provinces when compared with urban poverty. Although rural poverty has declined significantly during the decade of President SBY's governance, from 20 per cent of the rural population when he took office to 13.8 per cent by the time he stepped down, rural poverty still remains high compared to urban poverty, which was 8.2 per cent in 2014. Poverty rates also vary significantly among the Indonesian provinces, with Papua having the highest poverty rate of 27.8 per cent, far above the national average.

Therefore despite the significant progress that Indonesia has made in improving national per capita GDP levels, a large share of the Indonesian population still have incomes that are close to the poverty line, and sustained strong economic growth is needed over the medium term to further reduce poverty levels and reduce the vulnerability of a large share of the population.

Governance

Among the major hurdles to economic development that Indonesia faces, governance remains one of the most important challenges. Like many other large developing countries, Indonesia is perceived to have relatively high levels of corruption, as reflected in Transparency International's Corruption Perceptions Index. In the 2014 Corruption Perceptions Index, Indonesia was ranked 107th out of 174 countries, well below other some other large Asian developing countries, including India, Philippines, Thailand and China.

There are also many other governance challenges, such as lengthy approvals processes and government red tape related to doing business in Indonesia. In 2015, Indonesia was ranked 114th on the World Bank's Ease of Doing Business Index, with the survey indicating that Indonesia still ranked low on indicators relating to government regulations for getting building permits, registering property as well as enforcing contracts.

As if these governance challenges were not enough to deter investors, from time to time the Indonesian government creates new forms of red tape. A recent initiative of the Jokowi government announced in early 2015 was to introduce tests of language proficiency in the Bahasa Indonesia language for foreigners in order to obtain a work permit. After some months of confusion and consternation amongst the expatriate community in Indonesia, the plans for this language test were withdrawn. Had the regulation been introduced, it could have become a significant barrier for multinationals with large operations in Indonesia, since it would have made it difficult for global executives with specialist knowledge to take up assignments in Indonesia.

Diversification of exports

The diversification of Indonesia's exports is another key challenge facing the Indonesian government. Commodity exports accounted for around 68 per cent of total Indonesian exports in 2011, although this had declined to 62 per cent of exports by 2014, mainly due to the slump in commodity export prices.

Unlike many other East Asian economies which have achieved rapid economic development through industrialization and exports of low-cost manufactures, Indonesian exports have remained heavily dominated by commodities.

If Indonesia is able to accelerate the growth of its manufacturing export sector, this would address several macroeconomic challenges, by diversifying Indonesia's export structure and reducing vulnerability to commodity price shocks, as well as by generating stronger growth in formal employment for Indonesia's rapidly growing labour force.

Improving human capital

The Indonesian vocational and tertiary education system has suffered from decades of underinvestment since Indonesian independence, as a result of which Indonesia suffers from relatively weak human capital compared to other large Asian emerging markets such as China and India. Unlike some other East Asian developing countries such as South Korea, China, Hong Kong and Singapore, which have invested heavily in their tertiary educational infrastructure as key expenditure priorities, Indonesia has performed relatively poorly in developing its tertiary education system.

One indicator of the weak quality of the Indonesian university system is that no Indonesian universities appear in the Times Higher Education World University Rankings for 2014–15 of the top 500 universities. There were also no Indonesian universities in the list of the Top 100 Asian Universities produced by the Times Higher Education Asia University Rankings 2014. In contrast, many other Asia-Pacific economies did have some of their universities on this list, including China, Japan, South Korea, Taiwan, India, Hong Kong, Singapore and Thailand.

Another measure of the Indonesian higher education system compared to other nations worldwide is the "U21 Ranking of National Higher Education Systems 2013", a project sponsored by Universities 21, with the research undertaken by the Institute of Applied Economic and Social Research at the University of Melbourne published in May 2013 (Williams et al., 2013). This study compared the higher education systems of 50 countries, including both developed and developing countries worldwide. The report concluded in their overall ranking of higher education systems for the 50 countries assessed that Indonesia was ranked the lowest among all the countries analysed.

Although the Indonesian government has responded to these deficiencies in the Indonesian educational system by significantly increasing government expenditure on tertiary education and vocational training, it will take many years to significantly change the educational system.

Meanwhile the Indonesian government can undertake a range of other measures to accelerate the development of human capital, such as establishing centres of excellence in key disciplines, through provision of special funding for specialist research institutes and R&D centres in leading Indonesian universities.

These initiatives can be further strengthened by establishing more strategic alliances and partnerships with leading universities in other countries, to reinforce the development of these centres of excellence in Indonesian universities.

The Indonesian tertiary education system could also be strengthened by attracting more international universities to establish campuses in Indonesia, which will help to bring international best practice standards in education into key disciplines of the Indonesian educational system.

In addition to strengthening the tertiary education system, another priority for Indonesia is to improve the vocational education system, to provide a skilled workforce for growth sectors of the Indonesian economy. In order for the Indonesian manufacturing sector to become more competitive internationally, greater vocational training opportunities for the Indonesian workforce will be necessary.

One example of the pressing need for skilled vocational training in Indonesia is the maintenance, repair and overhaul (MRO) industry for commercial aviation. The Indonesian commercial aviation industry is growing rapidly, with very strong growth in the number of airline passengers over the past decade. This has resulted in significant expansion in the fleet size of Indonesian airlines. As a result of this rapid growth in airline fleet size, the demand for MRO services is also growing quickly. However due to shortages in skilled MRO personnel and lack of sufficient MRO training capacity, the Indonesian domestic MRO industry is unable to cope with the rapid growth in demand for MRO services. As a result, a significant share of total Indonesian MRO requirements have to be met by MRO service centres in other nearby countries, such as Singapore.

Indonesia: the next BRICS economy

Despite the considerable economic challenges that Indonesia is facing, it is one of the largest emerging market economies and offers considerable potential growth opportunities in future if economic reforms continue to improve the business climate. With a population of around 250 million, rapid economic growth over the last decade, a fast-growing domestic consumer market and strong inflows of foreign direct investment, the Indonesian economy has become one of the world's leading emerging markets.

At present, Indonesia is still not a member of the BRICS economic club of emerging markets, which comprise Brazil, Russia, India, China and South Africa. However given its economic performance and the size of its economy and population, the merits of the case for Indonesia to be included amongst the BRICS economies seems quite compelling.

The size of Indonesia's GDP in 2014 had reached an estimated USD 890 billion, on the threshold of crossing the USD 1 trillion mark that would make Indonesia one of only a handful of Asian economies to have a trillion dollar GDP. However Indonesia has been trapped just below trillion dollar status for several years, due to the depreciation of the rupiah since 2011, with further sharp depreciation in 2014–15 pushing the rupiah to its lowest levels since the 1998 East Asian crisis. Rupiah weakness has resulted from the combination of Indonesia's deteriorating current account position as global traded thermal coal prices slumped, as well as the general depreciation of many emerging market currencies against the USD on expectations of Fed rate rises and some rebalancing of investor portfolios away from emerging markets assets towards US asset classes since 2013.

Despite these short-term hurdles, Indonesian GDP should soon exceed one trillion US dollars, making Indonesia one of Asia's largest economies. With Indonesia having the potential to sustain GDP growth at around 6 per cent for the next decade, the size of the Indonesian economy could exceed USD 2 trillion by 2025, which could push Indonesian GDP above Australian GDP by that time. Indeed Indonesia's GDP has already become larger than the Netherlands, Indonesia's former colonial ruler.

The rise of Indonesia's economy in the global rankings would have significant implications for Indonesia's geopolitical influence. Indonesia's increasing importance in global geopolitics would likely result in it being invited to become a BRICS economy, as well as playing a more important role in many international organizations, including the UN, G-20, IMF, World Bank and ADB.

As one of the largest emerging markets in the world and Asia's third BRICS economy, Indonesia will also play an increasingly important role within the ASEAN region as a driver for ASEAN economic growth as well as for boosting intra-ASEAN trade and investment flows.

After sustained economic growth over the last decade and with Indonesia's fiscal position having become quite strong by international standards, the Indonesian government has recognized the need for modernization of the Indonesian armed forces, after many years of very constrained defence budgets in the aftermath of the East Asian crisis. As Indonesia's economy continues to grow over the next decade, Indonesia will not only become a major Asian regional power, but this will also be reflected in continued modernization and strengthening of the Indonesian armed forces.

The Indonesian defence budget has increased from USD 1.7 billion when President SBY took office and announced his first budget in 2004, to USD 8.1 billion in his final budget for 2015 announced before he stepped down. In 2015, this level of defence expenditure is estimated to account for around 0.8 per cent of GDP. President Jokowi has announced that he plans to raise this level of spending to 1.5 per cent of GDP by 2020, and the Indonesian legislature made a commitment in April 2015 to raising defence spending to USD 15 billion by 2020, which is in line with President Jokowi's pledge. Even if moderating economic growth rates constrain these ambitions to boost defence spending, it is nevertheless likely that defence spending will rise to at least 1.0 per cent of GDP by 2020, which still represents a significant boost to defence expenditure.

In his election manifesto and during his early months in office, President Jokowi has set out a vision to make Indonesia a 'Global Maritime Axis', which has a strong economic component to the strategic vision, as well as a maritime security architecture perspective.

Therefore the rise of the Indonesian economy over the next two decades will significantly alter Indonesia's geopolitical influence, particularly in terms of its role as a leader amongst emerging market nations as well as a regional economic and military power in the Asia-Pacific region.

Chapter 11

Majulah Singapura

The Next 50 Years

'A poor little market in a dark corner of Asia'

When Singapore became an independent sovereign state in 1965, its GDP per capita was only USD 516 in nominal terms. By the time that Singapore celebrated its 50th birthday as an independent nation in 2015, its per capita GDP had reached USD 53,000. This placed Singapore above Japan in terms of per capita GDP. Singapore has established itself as the Asia-Pacific's leading international financial centre, as well as a leading global shipping and commercial aviation hub.

Given the lack of any natural resources such as oil or other key minerals in Singapore, such a dramatic economic ascent is one of the most remarkable economic development stories amongst the former colonies that became independent after the end of World War Two.

At the time of independence, Singapore was a developing nation that was highly dependent on its port and its role as a British military base, which were mainstays of its economy. However within a few years of independence, British foreign policy changed significantly, and Britain decided to close down its military bases in Singapore by 1971. This was a tremendous economic blow for the fledgling nation, with the military bases accounting for a significant share of Singapore's GDP as well as tens of thousands of jobs.

However the next five decades were a remarkable period of economic development that has transformed Singapore into Asia's leading high income nation with an extremely well-diversified, leading edge economy.

Singapore's greatest fortune was to have a visionary statesman as its first prime minister. Under the leadership of Prime Minister Lee Kuan Yew, the Singapore government created the framework for modern Singapore's success, building upon Singapore's historical role as an entrepot and making Singapore a leading Asian hub for multinationals to develop their manufacturing operations. He remained Singapore's prime minister until 1990, leading the People's Action Party which he had co-founded to successive election victories. Under his leadership, Singapore was transformed into one of Asia's leading economies and a nation globally reputed for good governance and fighting corruption.

The strategic planning for the development of the Singapore economy began in 1960, when a United Nations Survey Mission visited Singapore to assess the future economic prospects for the economy. The UN mission was led by Dr Albert Winsemius, a Dutch economist whose experience had included working in the Dutch Ministry of Finance. The UN Mission's initial impressions of Singapore were pessimistic, with Dr Winsemius reported to have said that Singapore 'is a poor little market in a dark corner of Asia'.

Clearly undeterred by this minor obstacle, Dr Winsemius played a significant role in building a strategic development plan for Singapore, with a strong focus on making Singapore a hub for low value-added manufacturing industries such as garments as a first step in the development process. This was followed by the establishment of Singapore as a hub for the oil refining industry in the mid-1960s, and then by initiatives to make Singapore a centre for low value added electronics assembly.

Dr Winsemius served as the economic advisor to the Singapore government until 1984, working closely with the Singapore economic frontbench to create a long-term economic development plan that would transform Singapore's economy during the time he served as Singapore's economic adviser. Singapore's Economic Development Board was established in 1961 to lead the implementation of the economic development strategic plan.

In addition to establishing Singapore's role as an industrial hub, the economic development strategy built upon Singapore's traditional success as a shipping transportation hub. Singapore Airlines and Changi Airport helped to make Singapore a leading Asian centre for commercial aviation.

The strategic approach to Singapore's economic development remains a dynamic process and the Singapore government has never been complacent or rested on its laurels. The Singapore government continues to encourage the development of new industries that allow the economy to evolve in the face of competitive pressures from other Asian countries and rising wage costs that have eroded Singapore's competitiveness in low value added industries.

The success of Singapore has attracted increasing attention from other countries as its economy has continued to prosper. Many developed countries as well as developing countries now study the Singapore economic model to see how they can emulate Singapore's success.

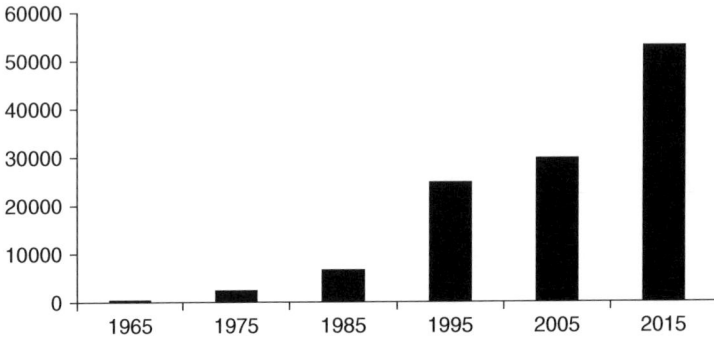

Figure 11.1 Singapore GDP per person, 1965–2015 (Nominal USD)

Source: World Bank Data.

However Singapore's magic economic development formula does not come in an instant packet, and few countries have managed to emulate Singapore's tremendous success. Dubai may be one of the few economies that managed to achieve similar stellar economic progress thanks to a creating a long-term economic vision along comparable lines to Singapore, albeit following their own distinctive development path.

Yet most other developing countries, including Singapore's closest neighbours, have not managed to achieve anything like the same extent of progress in terms of their economic development and key human development indicators. What is this magic economic development formula that endless government delegations from all over the world come to Singapore to search for?

Singapore's growth formula

There are many factors that have combined to make Singapore a global leader in economic development.

One of the most important lessons that other governments observe from Singapore is the importance of good governance, although few are able to implement similar standards in their own nations. From the outset, Singapore's first prime minister, Lee Kuan Yew, was determined to establish a high standard of governance in Singapore, and the principles of integrity and anti-corruption became hallmarks of the Singapore government. Key ingredients of this high standard of governance were the establishment of a meritocracy and also a system of remuneration that was designed to attract talent to the public service.

For many reasons, most developing countries continue to struggle with this first fundamental ingredient of success. While Singapore is a global leader in maintain high anti-corruption standards according to the Transparency International Corruption Perceptions Index, most other developing countries rank poorly, including many Asian emerging markets.

A second important factor that helped to make Singapore a very attractive hub for foreign investment by multinationals was political stability. The stable political climate created an oasis of calm in a politically volatile region, especially in the 1960s and 1970s. In Indonesia, there had been an attempted communist coup in October 1965, followed by months of purges and extreme violence in much of Indonesia as the military and pro-government parties reacted to defeat the communists.

In Indochina, the Vietnam War devastated not only Vietnam, but also Cambodia and Laos. An estimated two million tons of bombs were dropped on Laos by the US Air Force between 1964 and 1973. Cambodia suffered one of the world's worst genocides under the Khmer Rouge regime between 1975 and 1979 when they were ousted by the Vietnamese military.

A third important factor was the reliable regulatory environment, as Singapore has consistently aimed to maintain high standards of governance by international standards. The Singapore legal system is based on the English legal system, which was one important competitive advantage that Singapore inherited from the period of British administration. The Singapore government has also consistently sought to maintain high international standards across many different sectors, by closely monitoring international standards and being a leader in implementing changes to maintain global best practice. The regulatory environment has also been designed to be efficient and minimize regulatory burden and red tape, in order to create a favourable business climate that is attractive to multinationals. Regulatory certainty has also been a competitive advantage for Singapore, as successive governments maintain a broadly predictable regulatory regime, albeit with necessary reforms to maintain competitiveness and international best practice.

This is another area where many other nations admire the Singaporean system, but are unable to implement similar reforms in their own nations due to lack of political will or because some governments pursue different economic models, such as socialism or communism. During the 1960s and 1970s, Asia's largest emerging markets, China, India and Indonesia, were pursuing various economic models based on either communist or socialist principles. With much of Asia still subject to significant protectionist barriers and regulatory restrictions such as capital controls, Singapore continues to maintain a strong competitive advantage due to its advanced, world class regulatory system.

All of these factors played a role in making Singapore an attractive location for foreign direct investment by multinationals. However these factors have been reinforced by other strategies which have helped to make Singapore a highly competitive economy globally.

The Singapore government has from the outset understood the critical importance of developing its human capital through the establishment of a world class educational system at the secondary and tertiary levels. However unlike many other Asian countries, they also understood that to become a host for multinationals, it was important to allow companies to bring their global management executives to take up some positions in their Singapore subsidiaries. Singapore has also allowed global talent to move to Singapore to provide advanced skills in many key sectors of the economy. This has provided an important competitive advantage for Singapore as an Asia-Pacific headquartering hub compared to many other Asian locations where foreign executives face more significant barriers, therefore making these unsuitable locations for establishing an Asia-Pacific headquarters.

Another key advantage that has helped Singapore is its first class infrastructure, with one of the world's leading airports, high quality roads, a reliable power system and a well-designed, modern city. With a population of 5.5 million, Singapore is by no means a small city, so the high quality infrastructure plays an important role in ensuring the efficiency of the economy.

However the exception proves the rule. I was once asked to do a TV interview by the BBC in their Singapore studio about the new Indian government's plan to build 100 smart cities across India.

Planning to talk about the derelict infrastructure and decaying urban landscape in most of India's large cities, I arrived at the BBC office in Singapore to find that their building had some internal failures with their electrical system, and there was no elevator or air-conditioning operating. The studio had managed to hook up some backup power cables so the interview could still be conducted. The BBC TV interviewer and I were sweltering in the afternoon heat in a not so smart Singapore office tower with the windows open and an old fashioned desk fan on, as we tried to discuss India's need for smart cities. We tried to keep straight faces in the circumstances. The fact that it was so exceptional a situation in Singapore proves the point about Singapore's modern infrastructure though. The BBC have moved their Singapore office to a brand new building since then, no doubt to the considerable delight of their staff.

Singapore's highly efficient infrastructure is an important competitive advantage for a multinational headquartering hub, since global senior executives prefer to be located in Singapore rather than in many other Asian cities, where the infrastructure is often considerably worse. As a small example, one of the biggest challenges at Singapore's leading edge Changi Airport is to get to the luggage belt before the luggage arrives. I have often walked to the luggage area too slowly, only to find all the passengers have already taken their luggage and gone, with the baggage handler in the process of offloading my suitcase as they assumed that the passenger has not showed up.

Safe city

Singapore's reputation as a very safe city is also important for its competitive advantage. I have heard many anecdotes from senior executives who have moved from Kuala Lumpur to Singapore, and while the reasons for moving vary, most cite Kuala Lumpur's poor reputation for law and order as one factor, with many petty crimes and house burglaries. The inability of the Malaysian government to effectively tackle the high levels of crime has damaged Malaysia's reputation. The Malaysian government needs to give a much higher level of priority to tackling this issue in order to improve the business climate in Malaysia. Similarly the development of Iskandar, which is a very promising long-term megaproject for Malaysia's economy, is suffering due to its reputation for high levels of crime, which the Malaysian government has been unable to effectively tackle. One of my own relatives refused outright to consider buying a property in Iskandar due to the high crime rate.

Expatriates feel much safer locating their families in Singapore than in many other cities in Southeast Asia, due to the low crime rates in Singapore compared to other major cities such as Kuala Lumpur, Jakarta or Manila. Northeast Asia also has a good reputation for security though, with Japan and South Korea generally regarded as very safe by international standards.

By way of contrast with Singapore, the Philippines has an appalling record for crime, being more comparable with Latin America than Asia. Kidnappings of both local people and foreigners are commonplace, with the main objective being to obtain ransom money from their families. One recent anecdote I heard was about an American citizen who took a taxi from Manila airport to go to his hotel, but ended up being kidnapped by the taxi driver and held for ransom. I have heard an identical tale from a colleague who had a similar terrifying experience in Venezuela, where kidnappings are also rampant. Obviously being in the same peer group as Venezuela for crime does little to enhance the reputation of the Philippines as a good location to live and work.

India has its own set of problems with law and order, and there has been a great deal of media publicity in recent years about horrific rape incidents in many Indian cities, with women travelling alone being particularly vulnerable. The Indian government has reformed its legal system, toughened penalties for such crimes, and attempted to improve its policing. However, major changes in the effectiveness of the Indian police force across many Indian cities will take years even if the government continues to give a high priority to tackling this issue. In a nation struggling with high fiscal deficits and lack of sufficient government funds for many different competing needs, the pace of improvement may only be gradual. In the meantime, the nation is suffering from an extremely bad image globally in regard to these ugly crimes.

Against this backdrop of crime in Southeast Asian and South Asian cities, Singapore maintains its strong competitive advantage as a hub of safety and security for the many multinationals that need to locate their global staff in the region. This is yet another factor that helps to make Singapore a preferred headquartering hub for the world's multinationals.

However, as the Singaporean government is at pains to highlight, low crime does not mean no crime, and security is maintained through a relatively high degree of vigilance and the assurance that the legal system will severely punish violent crimes.

One of the greatest successes of Singapore's tough approach to crime was in the ruthless suppression of organized crime. The success of the government in tackling gangs began with the reform of the criminal law with the Criminal Law (Temporary Provision) Ordinance of 1958 (Ganapathy and Lian, 2002). This reform of the criminal law allowed the detention of criminal gang members without trial.

Due to Singapore's history of large immigration flows from China since its foundation as a port by the British colonial government under Sir Thomas Stamford Raffles, there had been a significant culture of secret societies that had evolved in Singapore, similar to mainland China and Hong Kong. Some of these secret societies became involved in criminal activities since the 1850s, in areas such as the opium trade, gambling and prostitution. Although the British colonial government did prohibit these criminal activities, the criminal gangs were still in existence in the 1950s.

The number of gang crimes reported in 1959 was 416, but by 1977, this had declined to just 13 reported crimes. While gang members were being detained under the 1958 ordinance following its introduction, a very powerful deterrent was the police supervision of thousands of gang members, who were confronted with the option of ending their gang-related activities or facing unlimited periods of detention. The outcome was a collapse in the activities of criminal gangs in Singapore by the 1970s.

The success of the 1958 ordinance has resulted in its continued extension, with the Criminal Law (Temporary Provision) Ordinance being extended by the Singaporean parliament for the 13th time in 2013, for another period of five years. The continued extension of this ordinance reflects its ongoing success in preventing the development of gang cultures and organized crime in Singapore. However the success of this ordinance is also closely linked to the high standards of governance in Singapore, which has ensured that the ordinance is correctly utilized and targeted.

Another great strength of Singapore is its commitment to multiculturalism, which has helped to build a peaceful society comprising ethnic communities that have their roots in China, India and the Malayan peninsula. Singapore has become a melting pot where foreigners from all different parts of the world are accepted and integrated into Singapore society. One way that Singapore builds multiculturalism is to have public holidays that recognize important celebrations for key religions, including Christianity, Buddhism, Islam and Hinduism.

Future Singapore: opportunities and challenges

As Singapore celebrated its first fifty years as an independent nation in 2015, there were many successes to be proud of for this small nation-state. Despite its small size in terms of geography and population, Singapore has become an Asian leader from many perspectives. As Asia's richest nation, Singapore is looked up to by many other Asian developing countries as setting the benchmark in many areas, such as public service standards, economic development planning, the efficiency of its infrastructure and the cohesive multicultural society that has been created.

However looking forward, there is a strong recognition that Singapore will face many challenges over the next fifty years.

One of the most important challenges that Singapore faces is tackling the impact of demographic ageing, which will become an increasingly significant factor over the next two decades. Demographic ageing can be expected to drag down Singapore's long-term growth rate over the coming decades, unless the size of the work force is stabilized through immigration. However given that Singapore already has a large share of foreign workers in its work force and considerable expertise in managing foreign worker immigration in order to support the Singaporean economy, the impact of demographic ageing in Singapore is likely to be mitigated by the carefully managed use of foreign worker flows.

Singapore's total fertility rate in 1975 was approximately at the replacement rate of 2.1, but ever since then the total fertility rate has been on a gradual downtrend and reached a low of 1.2 in 2011. This declining trend in the fertility rate is similar to trends in other advanced economies such as Japan, South Korea and many Western European nations. However Singapore has a very carefully developed immigration policy which has managed the inflows of foreign workers to ensure an adequate supply of labour for the Singapore economy.

Nevertheless like many other advanced nations, Singapore is facing the challenge of significantly increased life expectancy, which has risen from 66 years in 1970 to 82 years by 2010, while birth rates have been trending downwards. Population projections by Singapore's government indicate that without immigration inflows, the total population of Singapore citizens would begin to contract from 2025 onwards. At the same time, the structure of the population would be ageing, which will put an increasing burden on social services and health care services for senior citizens. At present, the ratio of working age citizens to senior citizens aged 65 and over is around six, but by 2030 this ratio is projected to decline to two, implying a very significant ageing of the population.

While the topic of foreign immigration has become more contentious in recent years and has resulted in some stricter controls being implemented to reduce the influx of immigrants, the imperative of ageing demographics will likely require continued use of immigration to mitigate the impact of ageing demographics. In particular, as the ratio of senior citizens to the working population rises, the use of foreign workers as nurses, social workers and other types of care givers may be necessary to provide essential care services for senior citizens. Another challenge facing Singapore in coming decades is sustaining productivity. While the manufacturing sector has been able to boost productivity by use of technology and advanced equipment, it is more difficult to achieve similar productivity gains in some sectors of service industries. Given that the size of the service sector accounts for the largest share of Singapore's GDP, this creates a significant constraint to sustaining high productivity growth rates.

The implications of low productivity growth rates over the long term would be that wage rises that were not offset by productivity gains would be directly reflected in rising unit labour costs, which would impact on the competitiveness of Singaporean industries with low productivity growth rates.

Singapore's geographic size is also a constraint, as the limited supply of land has created rising pressure on available land. When Thomas Stamford Raffles established a British colonial settlement in Singapore in 1819, the estimated population by the end of that year, after the influx of the first wave of settlers, was just 5,000 persons. By 2015, the population of Singapore had reached an estimated 5.5 million.

The considerable growth in the population of Singapore has put ever-increasing demands on the available land on the island. For example, Orchard Road, which is now part of central Singapore and is a highly urbanized district packed with office towers, shopping malls and hotels, used to literally be lined with fruit orchards and nutmeg plantations in the 1830s, during the early years of Singapore's settlement.

Tigers were a menace in the area during the 1840s, with many plantation workers reported to have been killed by tigers between the 1840s until the 1860s. The colonial government placed a bounty on tigers, giving a financial reward for every tiger killed. Even in 1890, a man was killed by a tiger along Thomson Road, about three kilometres away from Orchard, and in 1904, a tiger was shot at Goodwood House in Orchard. By the 1850s the plantations began to disappear as Singapore continued to develop and the district began to become filled with private bungalows. By the early 1900s, the commercial development of Orchard Road gathered momentum, and intensified during the early period of industrialization of Singapore after independence. As a result of the rapid development of Singapore, sadly the last wild tiger was killed in the 1930's. The magnificent Malayan tiger species that used to inhabit Singapore now can only be found in some parts of Malaysia and Thailand, and is an endangered species with only 350 to 400 of this species of tiger remaining. Perhaps Singapore, as the most advanced nation in Asia, can play a key role in future conservation efforts to preserve the Malayan wild tiger species which is an important part of its heritage.

The pressure on available land became more severe after the Second World War, particularly since the period of rapid industrialization in the 1960s. This rapid growth has resulted in significant increases in the cost of residential properties in Singapore, which as in other major international cities such as London, New York and Hong Kong, make purchasing a home increasingly prohibitive for young workers entering the labour market. The limited availability of land also acts as a constraint on industrial development, such as the need to continue to expand Changi Airport due to the rapid growth of Asia-Pacific commercial aviation passenger traffic. Reclaiming land from the sea has provided an important solution for the expansion of the central business district, but this solution has its limits.

While Singapore faces important challenges to the long-term economic outlook, there are also tremendous opportunities that give reason for considerable optimism about the future.

Many of the factors that helped Singapore's development in its early years as a nation will still remain important drivers of competitive advantage for decades to come. These include a wide range of factors, including Singapore's high standards of governance, its first class regulatory system, political stability, a high quality legal system based on English law, and Singapore's reputation for being a peaceful, low crime society.

One of the most important factors that will support the future success of Singapore is the commitment of the Singapore government to continuously upgrade the competitiveness of its economy, building clusters of competitive advantage. The skill with which the government has succeeded in transforming Singapore's economy from low value added industries to high value added sectors has already demonstrated the ability of the government to support economic transformation and change.

The new growth industries

Like other industrialized Asian economies, Singapore's economy has experienced hollowing out of its low value-added manufacturing industries that had been the original growth industries for Singapore's manufacturing sector during the 1960s and 1970s. The structure of the Singapore economy has also gradually shifted, with the service sector accounting for a higher share of total GDP. Although manufacturing was a small share of total GDP prior to independence, accounting for around 11 per cent of GDP in 1960, its share of the economy rose during the 1970s and 1980s. Manufacturing accounted for around 29 per cent of Singapore's GDP in 1980, but its share of GDP declined to 19 per cent by 2014.

Despite the decline in manufacturing's share of total Singaporean GDP, there has been a significant transformation of the manufacturing sector since 1980. Although there has been continued hollowing-out of low value-added segments of manufacturing production as rising wage costs make these segments uncompetitive, meanwhile new higher value-added manufacturing segments have expanded.

One of the growth sectors has been biomedical manufacturing, which accounted for around 7 per cent of total manufacturing output in 2014, with 50 manufacturing plants. The size of the biomedical manufacturing sector has grown significantly since 2000, when the total output of the sector was SGD 5 billion, to reach an estimated SGD 22 billion in total output by 2014, with

17,000 jobs. The range of products made in Singapore's biomedical manufacturing sector includes pharmaceuticals, vaccines, medical devices, contact lenses and surgical products. Some of the world's largest pharmaceuticals companies have established their regional headquarters for the Asia-Pacific in Singapore, including Roche, Johnson & Johnson and GSK. Singapore has also become a regional headquartering hub for global medical device companies, including for Philips, Siemens and Medtronic.

The aerospace engineering sector has also become an important growth segment of the manufacturing industry in Singapore, with total output estimated at SGD 8.5 billion in 2014, with around 20,000 jobs in the sector. A large segment of the aerospace engineering industry comprises aerospace maintenance, repair and overhaul (MRO), given Singapore's role as an Asia-Pacific commercial aviation hub. The Singapore government has developed an aerospace park at the former air force base at Seletar, and this has created a cluster of significant aerospace firms including Rolls Royce and Pratt & Whitney. Rolls Royce has an Advanced Technology Centre as well as an aero engine assembly and test facility that is well established in Seletar Aerospace Park. Rolls Royce has also invested in a Wide Chord Blade Fan manufacturing facility to manufacture turbine blades for the Rolls Royce Trent Aero Engine series, the first such facility to be built outside the UK. When the facility reaches full capacity, it will be able to manufacture 7,600 blades per year.

The largest segment of the manufacturing sector is still the electronics industry, which accounted for 27 per cent of manufacturing output and around 71,000 jobs in 2014. The continued importance of the sector reflects considerable transformation of the industry that has taken place since the 1960s, when Singapore was attracting low cost electronics assembly plants to drive the development of its industrial sector.

The lowest value added segments of Singapore's electronics sector have gradually been hollowed out, and the electronics sector has continued to move into higher value added segments. A key strategy of the Singapore government is to make Singapore a leader in some of the most advanced electronics segments, such as R&D and design. Singapore has already established itself as a hub for integrated circuit design, and the Singapore government is boosting its talent pool in this segment by funding research programs at several universities in Singapore to attract more talent into advanced degree programs in integrated circuit design.

Although the Singapore manufacturing sector has continued to benefit from new growth segments such as aerospace engineering and biomedical manufacturing, the overall share of manufacturing in GDP has still nevertheless declined, with the share of service sector industries increasing.

Singapore's service sector economy has also been helped by the development of new growth segments, as well as the expansion of well-established industries.

One of the most important service industries continues to be Singapore's port, which was the historic reason for the original establishment of Singapore as a British colonial settlement by Sir Thomas Stamford Raffles. The original success of Singapore was as an entrepot for shipping, with the port rapidly growing in importance due to the decision by Raffles to make it a free port that was exempt from customs duties and taxes.

By the time of independence in 1965, Singapore had remained an important port for shipping on key trade route from Europe to Northeast Asia, as well as being a key naval base for the British military forces in the Far East. Following the closure of the naval base in 1971, Singapore was facing a significant shock to its economy due to the importance of this base for the overall economy. However the economic impact was mitigated by the decision to build a container port at Tanjong Pagar, with operations starting in 1972. Within a decade, by 1982, Singapore had become the world's busiest port based on tonnage. By 1990, Singapore had become the world's largest container port. Further expansion of Singapore's port capacity with the Pasir Panjang terminal will increase port capacity to 50 million TEU by 2017.

Singapore's maritime industry including its ports accounted for around 7 per cent of GDP by 2013, employing an estimated 170,000 persons. Total container traffic in 2014 reached 34 million TEU, and cargo tonnage reached 580 million tonnes.

One of the important factors underpinning the success of the Singapore economic model is the long-term strategic planning undertaken by the Singapore government authorities. In 2012, the Singapore government announced that a new mega port would be built at Tuas, to provide a consolidated container port for Singapore with an annual capacity of 65 million TEUs. The Tuas mega port project is planned for completion by 2030, indicating the very long forward planning horizon used by the Singapore government to ensure that infrastructure capacity is sufficient to meet future demand growth.

Singapore's role as an Asia-Pacific commercial aviation hub has also become an important part of the economy, with Changi Airport employing an estimated 32,000 employees by 2015. By 2014, Changi Airport had become the world's sixth largest airport in terms of annual international passenger traffic, with 54 million passengers (Changi Airport Group Media Release, "AirAsia Group, Korean Air and Vietnam Airlines to operate at Changi Airport's new Terminal 4 in 2017", 9 July 2015).

Advanced planning for the future expansion of Changi Airport to provide sufficient capacity for the rapid growth of air passenger traffic has been undertaken, with a fourth terminal due to be completed by 2017 to provide an additional annual capacity for 16 million passenger movements. This will substantially increase the current capacity of the three existing terminals, which is around 66 million passenger movements per year.

The development of Singapore's financial services industry has been another important strategic growth driver, as Singapore expanded its role as a commercial banking hub to become a financial services cluster, including foreign exchange and commodities trading, investment banking, wealth management, funds management and insurance.

The Singapore financial centre is now the international banking hub for ASEAN, providing a range of financial services for the Southeast Asian region, including investment banking, trade finance, asset management and insurance services. The growth of Singapore's international financial centre has also been accompanied by the development of major clusters of accountancy and legal services.

The success of Singapore as an international financial centre has been underpinned by high quality financial sector regulation and supervision by the Monetary Authority of Singapore, the nation's central bank. Singapore has a well-capitalized banking sector that meets international best practice capital adequacy standards. Total assets under management in the Singapore financial centre by the fund management industry are estimated to have reached SGD 2.4 trillion by 2014.

In some ASEAN economies such as Vietnam, Cambodia, Laos and Myanmar, the banking sector is still relatively underdeveloped. For such nations, the Singapore financial centre can perform an important role in the provision of financial services such as investment banking and trade finance. Singapore's banks are amongst the best capitalized in Asia, and can contribute to the development of modern banking sectors in other ASEAN countries with relatively less advanced banking sectors. The presence of a large asset management industry and major stock exchange in Singapore also allows significant capital raising to be conducted in Singapore for investments into other ASEAN countries, including through listed equities, real estate investment trusts, private equity and fixed income products such as sovereign bonds and corporate debt.

Singapore has also been successfully developing its position as a headquartering hub for global multinationals to base their APAC or SE Asian headquarters. Tourism remains a key industry segment, benefiting from Changi's position as a leading international airport and transit hub. In 2014, there were an estimated 15 million international tourism visits to Singapore, with total tourism spending estimated at USD 17.5 billion, with annual tourism spending having increased by 117 per cent compared to a decade ago.

Looking to the future, the Singapore government is also continuing to develop new clusters of excellence in services, including encouraging the development of Singapore as a knowledge hub for think tanks, research institutes and international universities to establish their Asian regional operations.

As other Southeast Asian economies continue to grow rapidly, they will increasingly turn to Singapore as the leading regional hub for services, including education services, medical services and a wide array of specialist skills such as legal services, accounting services and urban planning services.

Although Singapore does face challenges from demographic ageing, its continuous efforts to maintain industry competitiveness through developing new clusters of excellence will continue to support a dynamic economy and will also help to underpin its long-term growth rate. The fundamental principles of good governance, political stability, best practice regulatory standards and a highly skilled workforce should continue to ensure that Singapore has a bright future as a leading international services hub for the Asia-Pacific region.

Chapter 12

The Environmental Crises Confronting Asia

Environmental challenges in the Asia-Pacific

When I stayed in the Four Seasons Hotel in Jakarta a few years ago, one of the very friendly and helpful staff working in that hotel happened to mention to me that the hotel had been flooded a few years previously, when Jakarta had been disrupted by major flooding. The flooding had occurred in 2002, when the hotel was called the Regent Hotel, and due to the extensive flood damage it took 18 months to complete the repair and redevelopment work before the hotel could be reopened. With heightened awareness of this recent history of major floods in Jakarta, I attended an environmental conference in Jakarta about a year later. During the conference, one of the speakers spoke in detail about the severe environmental risks facing Jakarta from flooding over the long-term.

The vulnerability of Jakarta to flooding has been increasing due to the effects of depletion of groundwater resources, which have resulted in gradual subsidence of the city. The environmental challenges facing Jakarta due to its vulnerability to flooding are severe, and require large-scale expenditure on flood prevention infrastructure in a nation with many competing and urgent requirements for infrastructure spending.

In 2011, Thailand suffered the impact of devastating floods which lasted for months, and Bangkok also was flooded in some districts as the military and volunteers struggled to build barricades to prevent widespread flooding of the city. Like Venice, Bangkok is also slowly sinking each year, increasing the vulnerability of the city to major flooding. The city was built on a swampy floodplain of clay soil, and due to heavy use of groundwater the aquifers are depleting, causing the city to gradually sink. The widespread flooding across many provinces of Thailand was devastating for the Thai economy, as major industrial estates for the auto and electronics sectors were also affected by the flooding, with many factories having their production disrupted due to the floods. Although the Thai government invested heavily in flood prevention infrastructure subsequently, the widespread scale of the flooding highlighted the vulnerability of the Thai economy to such flooding disasters.

In 2013, the Philippines was hit by a series of typhoons, the most serious of which was Typhoon Haiyan, also known as Typhoon Yolanda, which struck the Philippines in November 2013. The typhoon was reported to have reached wind speeds of up to 285 kilometres per hour creating widespread destruction, with an estimated 6,300 people killed. At his speech to the UN Climate Change Summit in September 2014, the President of the Philippines discussed the impact of Typhoon Haiyan in his call for global action on climate change.

"Typhoon Haiyan struck in November of 2013. It was, according to many, the strongest typhoon to ever make landfall in recorded history. Since then, this is the largest meeting of world leaders that I have had the privilege of attending. That we are gathered here is a recognition of the stark reality we face as a collective. Climate change does not recognize national boundaries, or political or economic affiliations. The choice before us, then, is clear. Together we must face these challenges and surmount them, or together we will suffer the consequences of inaction."

President Benigno S. Aquino III, President of the Philippines,
Speech to the United Nations Climate Change Summit 2014,
New York, USA, 23rd September 2014.

Several years previously, in 2008, Cyclone Nargis hit the Irrawaddy delta in Myanmar, creating devastating flooding that resulted in an estimated death toll of over 130,000 people and causing severe economic destruction to property and agricultural production.

South Asia is also vulnerable to cyclones and flooding, with Bangladesh having had a long history of devastating floods when cyclones in the Bay of Bengal have created storm tides that have submerged vast tracts of the low-lying coastline on the Ganges delta. The scale of devastation that could occur in Bangladesh in future due to the impact of climate change can be understood by studying the impact of the 1970 Bhola cyclone. The cyclone generated wind speeds that reached 185 kilometres per hour, and created wind-driven tidal waves that swept over heavily popu-lated coastal areas. Due to the scale of the devastation and lack of records about the number of people living in each community, the estimated death toll ranges from 300,000 to 500,000 people. The Bay of Bengal is highly vulnerable to such powerful cyclones, and in April 1991, another cyclone with wind speeds of up to 250 kilometres per hour hit the coastline near the port of Chittagong, with the death toll estimated at 138,000.

In India, the nation's commercial capital, Mumbai, was flooded during heavy rains that hit the Indian state of Maharashtra in 2005. An estimated 5,000 people were killed in flooding in Maharashtra, while Mumbai was brought to a halt for days, creating economic disruption and chaos given Mumbai's crucial role as the main financial centre and commercial hub for the nation.

The vulnerability of Southeast Asia and South Asia to such flooding events is therefore a key policy challenge for regional governments to address, in terms of flood prevention, as well as disaster management when such devastating floods occur. The region's governments are concerned about the impact of climate change on weather patterns, with some experts, including the United Nations Inter-Governmental Panel on Climate Change (IPCC), expecting increased intensity of such flooding disasters due to the impact of climate change.

> *"Low lying, densely populated coastal areas in South Asia, including India and Bangladesh, will be at increased risk of storm surges, putting many millions of people at risk."*
>
> "IPCC Fifth Assessment Report: What's in it for South Asia",
> IPCC, 2013, (Cambridge University Press, Cambridge, UK.

According to the IPCC Fifth Assessment Report, the Asian region had the highest share of weather-related disasters between 2000 and 2008, and accounted for an estimated 27.5 per cent of total global economic losses from such disasters (CDKN, 2014, 11). While global warming increases the risk of extreme rainfall when typhoons or cyclones make landfall, the impact of climate change and its effect on weather patterns also increases the risk of droughts, with consequences likely to be more water and food shortages related to such drought events.

Responses to climate change

The IPCC has made a series of recommendations about policy actions that governments can take in order to mitigate the impact of climate change. One of their key messages is that the implementation of such policy changes will take decades, and therefore governments must plan to also tackle the increasing impact of climate change on food and water resources as well as planning for more extreme weather events.

While global initiatives to tackle climate change have been underway for many years, notably through the United Nations Framework Convention on Climate Change (UNFCCC), which provides a non-binding framework for governments to co-operate on measures and strategies to address climate change, the main responsibility for implementable actions continues to depend on national government responses.

The international negotiations did result in the Kyoto Protocol agreed in December 1997, whereby many developed countries did agree to binding commitments on reducing greenhouse gas emissions between 2008 and 2012. The US was not party to the Kyoto Protocol binding commitments, since although US President Clinton did sign the Kyoto Protocol treaty, the US Congress did not ratify it.

While progress at the international level on creating a binding set of international rules on reducing carbon emissions has been tortuous, nevertheless there have been signs of significant recent progress.

A key focus of the IPCC recommendations for policy action is on reducing greenhouse gas emissions from the energy sector.

China's policy responses on carbon emissions

China has made reducing carbon emissions a national priority, and is investing heavily in the use of renewable energy as one strategy towards this objective. China is estimated to have spent around USD 83 billion on investment in renewable energy in 2014, which represents a 39 per cent increase in spending compared to 2013. China has renewable energy generating capacity of 430 GW already installed, which accounts for around one-third of the nation's power generating capacity. The main source of renewable energy in China is hydroelectric power, which accounts for around 70 per cent of total renewable energy installed capacity.

At a bilateral US-China meeting at the APEC Summit held in Beijing in November 2014, President Xi Jinping met with President Obama and both made various pledges on carbon emissions.

President Xi pledged that Chinese carbon emissions would peak by 2030 if not earlier, while President Obama pledged that the US would reduce carbon emissions in 2025 by around 27 per cent below 2005 levels. President Xi also stated that China would achieve 20 per cent of its power generation from renewables and nuclear energy by 2030.

The Chinese State Council has announced as part of a national energy strategy that Chinese coal consumption will be capped at 4.2 billion tonnes by 2020. This is already resulting in a significant change in fuel mix in some provinces, with some of the most industrialized areas having committed to reducing coal consumption. Beijing, Tianjin, Hebei and Shandong will cut annual coal consumption by 83 million tonnes by 2017. Other industrialized regions of China are also expected to begin to reduce coal consumption over the medium-term.

The Chinese government imposed new restrictions in 2013 preventing the construction of new coal-fired power stations in Beijing, and in 2014, a coal-fired power station in Beijing was closed down. Two more coal-fired power stations in Beijing were closed in 2015, and a fourth will be shut down in 2016. The new replacement power stations are being fuelled by natural gas, which will reduce carbon emissions and also help reduce local air pollution loads.

China already reported a decline in coal consumption for 2014, with China's National Bureau of Statistics data showing that Chinese coal consumption fell by 2.9 per cent in 2014. This marks a major shift in the past trend of rapid growth in Chinese coal consumption, with China estimated to have accounted for around 80 per cent of the increase in global coal consumption between 2002 and 2012. If Chinese coal consumption levels peak by 2020 or possibly even earlier, this will represent a significant step towards controlling global growth in carbon emissions.

A number of driving forces are creating this shift in energy policy in China.

Firstly, the Chinese government recognizes the important role that China must play in reducing global greenhouse gas emissions if international efforts to manage climate change are to succeed.

Secondly, the extent of air pollution in some of the largest Chinese cities has created a tremendous public backlash, as urban residents suffer from the health consequences of persistent high levels of pollution generated by the Chinese coal-fired power stations.

In response to both international pressures and domestic discontent about urban air pollution levels, at the beginning of 2014, all Chinese provinces agreed to cut their air pollution levels by significant proportions by 2017.

India's policy responses on carbon emissions

The future energy policy of India will also be a key factor in determining the trajectory of global carbon emissions. Although Indian energy consumption is still very low compared to China, the projected rapid growth of the Indian economy is expected to result in a high rate of growth in power consumption. India's fuel mix is still heavily dependent on coal as a low-cost feedstock for power production.

Unlike China, previous Indian governments put less policy focus on renewable energy, with their main investments in power generation being based on coal and gas power stations as well as nuclear energy. India's total renewable energy installed capacity at the beginning of 2015 was 36 GW, compared to 430 GW of renewable energy installed capacity in China.

Prime Minister Modi has significantly changed the direction of India's energy policy towards renewable energy, setting a very ambitious target of reaching a level of 15 per cent renewable energy contribution to India's total power generation by 2020. The BJP government has set a target of reaching 175 GW of renewable energy production by 2022, which is four times larger than current renewable energy generation of 36 GW. The target for solar energy production by 2022 has been set at 100 GW, compared with current solar energy production of just 4 GW.

The target for wind energy installed capacity by 2022 is 60 GW. India has been more successful in developing its wind energy than other forms of renewable energy, with existing installed capacity of around 23 GW at the beginning of 2015, or approximately two-thirds of India's total renewable energy capacity. The strategic thrust of the BJP government's massive push to boost renewable energy is focused on solar energy, where the government also anticipates significant employment creation in the solar manufacturing industry in India.

The next major challenge facing the Indian government in achieving these ambitious renewable energy goals is to raise the necessary financing for such large-scale development of solar and wind energy projects. An estimated US 160 billion of renewable energy infrastructure financing will be needed to achieve the 2022 renewable energy goals. The Indian government held a green energy financing summit in early 2015 at which Indian state-owned and private sector banks pledged to lend USD 57 billion for renewable energy projects over the next five years, although these pledges obviously have caveats about the suitability and bankability of projects applying for such financing.

The Indian government is also seeking infrastructure financing from international development banks, including the World Bank, Asian Development Bank and the Japan Bank for International Co-operation. During President Obama's visit to India in January 2015, one of the issues that was discussed during his bilateral talks with Prime Minister Modi was US co-operation to support India's renewable energy program. Large scale financing assistance from US government agencies is expected as a result of these negotiations, with the US Trade and Development Agency, the US Export-Import Bank and the US Overseas Private Investment Corporation all expected to provide significant funding to support India's renewable energy program.

However India's future power capacity expansion will still rely heavily on coal-fired power stations based on current medium term plans, since coal remains a low-cost feedstock and is still essential for the rapid capacity expansions needed in India's power sector.

Therefore Indian cities are expected to face increasing problems from air pollution due to carbon emissions, with some major Indian cities already suffering from very high levels of pollution. According to a World Health Organisation assessment, an estimated 3.7 million premature deaths of people aged below 60 were caused globally in 2012 due to exposure to small particle matter of ten microns (PM10) or less in polluted air (WHO, "Air Quality Deteriorating", 2014).

The WHO guidelines indicate a guideline annual mean for PM10 of 20 particles per cubic metre. In the WHO latest available statistics on PM10 readings in cities worldwide, Delhi had an annual mean reading for PM10 of 286 particles, far higher than Beijing, which had an annual mean reading for PM10 of 121 particles. By comparison, London had an annual mean reading for PM10 of 22 particles, and Paris had a reading of 24. The WHO measured pollution levels in many Indian cities, and although Delhi was much higher than most other Indian cities, nevertheless the readings for many Indian cities exceeded 100 (WHO, "Ambient (Outdoor) Air Pollution", 2014).

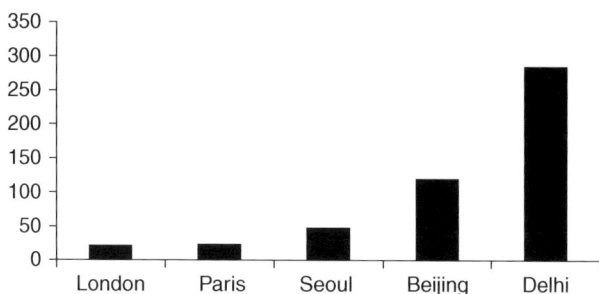

Figure 12.1 Air pollution in major cities. PM10 measure (per cubic metre)
Source: WHO data.

ASEAN energy policies

Although China is significantly changing its energy policy to stabilize its use of coal, other parts of Asia are likely to increase their use of coal as an energy feedstock. Malaysia, Thailand, Indonesia and Myanmar are all facing challenges from reduced domestic supplies of gas. Malaysia, Indonesia and Myanmar are exporters of gas, but the projected growth of domestic demand for gas is forcing changes in policies regarding gas exports. Therefore increased use of coal as a feedstock is expected, given abundant supplies of cheap Indonesian thermal coal.

Indonesia is planning to install an additional 35 GW of power generation capacity over the next five years, and around 60 per cent of this new capacity is expected to be from coal-fired power stations, requiring an additional coal supply of around 80 million tonnes per year.

Thailand has existing installed power generating capacity that is heavily dependent on natural gas, accounting for around two-thirds of electricity generation, and coal accounting for around 20 per cent of power generation. This high share of electricity production from natural gas has reflects the availability of natural gas in Thailand and neighbouring countries. Thailand has its own domestic gas reserves, as well as access to imported gas through pipelines from Myanmar and Malaysia. However Thailand's existing proven domestic gas reserves are rapidly running down, with around six years of domestic gas reserves estimated to be remaining. This reflects large increases in demand for gas, which have risen from four billion cubic feet per day two years ago to over five billion cubic feet per day. Therefore large increases in LNG imports are expected over the next two decades (Bangkok Post, 28 May 2015).

While Myanmar currently supplies natural gas to Thailand by pipeline from the Zawtika and Yetagun gas fields, the Myanmar government is intending to use future gas discoveries for its own domestic energy needs, as it is rapidly developing its own power infrastructure to support the rapidly growing economy.

Although the Thai government is planning a long-term power strategy based on increased use of coal and nuclear power, there has been a public backlash to plans for a coal-fired power station in the Krabi area, as some local residents are concerned about the health implications, and the fishing industry are worried about the impact of the coal importing terminal on the local ecosystem.

Water resources

In addition to the challenges Asia is facing with regard to energy resources and carbon emissions, water resources are also becoming a major policy concern. While flooding is a key risk factor for many countries, lack of water is also a major long-term concern.

In part, the problem of scarce water resources reflects past water management practices by governments, such as lack of controls over use of groundwater resources. There has also been inadequate investment by Asian governments in groundwater storage and irrigation schemes.

China has been facing a growing water crisis in northern China, due to the rapid urbanization of the region and the industrial development in major Chinese cities including Beijing. The northern region has an estimated one-fifth of China's water resources but has two-thirds of China's farmland. Use of groundwater resources has resulted in depletion of these underground aquifers in many areas of northern China. The Chinese government has responded to this water crisis by developing an infrastructure megaproject that is diverting water from southern China to the north, called the South-North Water Diversion Project.

The scale of the project is vast, with three major canals planned as part of this project, at a total estimated cost of USD 67 billion, although this figure could escalate depending upon the construction costs of the third canal along the western route. The three canals are designed to divert water from the Yangtze River in the south to supply northern China. Two of these canals have been completed, with one still under development. The total amount of water that will be diverted each year once all three canals are completed is estimated to be 45 billion cubic metres of water annually.

Of the three canals, the eastern canal, which follows the route of the historic Grand Canal, was completed at the end of 2013, supplying 9.5 billion cubic metres of water from the Yangtze River to Tianjin and other areas of the north including Shandong. The original Grand Canal was built in the 13th century to link Beijing with Hangzhou for the transportation of grains.

The middle route canal was completed in 2014 and covers a distance of 1,423 kilometres. One of the most controversial environmental impact effects of this canal was that it required major water reservoir infrastructure to be built to increase the water storage capacity of the Danjiangkou Reservoir, resulting in the displacement of the population of many villages. In addition, around 350,000 people were displaced due to this expansion of the size of the reservoir, resulting in considerable social problems despite government rehousing programs and compensation packages for households that had to be resettled.

The western route canal is the most costly of the three, with a total estimated cost of around USD 40 billion. It has also created considerable concerns in India, as some of the water that would feed the western route canal would involve using water from rivers on the Tibetan Plateau, which are also the source of major rivers flowing into India. Of particular concern is the intended diversion of waters from the Brahmaputra River, which flows downstream into India and Bangladesh.

This issue has been a priority at the highest levels of Indian government, with past Indian Prime Minister Manmohan Singh having raised this matter with President Xi Jinping when he visited China on a state visit while he was still the prime minister of India.

India's water crisis

India is also facing a growing water crisis due to depletion of its groundwater resources and inadequate investment in water infrastructure for decades.

"If current trends continue, in 20 years about 60 per cent of all India's aquifers will be in a critical condition. ... aquifers are depleting in the

most populated and economically productive areas. Climate change will further strain groundwater resources."

The World Bank, "India Groundwater: A Valuable but Diminishing Resource",
6th March 2012. Washington D.C., 2012.

The depletion of Indian groundwater resources in the northern Indian states of Rajasthan, Punjab and Haryana has been measured by NASA using satellites, and the results of their analysis highlighted the risks of an escalating groundwater crisis in northern India.

"If measures are not taken to ensure sustainable groundwater usage, consequences for the 114 million residents of the region may include a collapse of agricultural output and severe shortages of potable water."

Matt Rodell, NASA Hydrologist, "NASA Unlocks Secrets of
Vanishing Water", NASA, 12th August 2009.

The Indian government will therefore need to refocus its infrastructure priorities in order to ramp up investment in addressing India's water infrastructure. Key areas of increased investment will need to be in water storage systems in areas with the greatest water shortages, as well as advanced irrigation systems to manage water use in the agricultural sector more efficiently. Use of new technologies can significantly improve the efficiency of water use in irrigation systems.

Pollution of Indian rivers is another facet of India's environmental crisis, with much of India's sewage remaining untreated when it flows into national waterways. According to the World Bank, one of India's most important rivers, the Ganges, flows through around 50 major Indian cities, and the World Bank estimates that these cities generate around three billion litres of sewage every day, with only a small proportion being treated before it enters the river. The situation is similar for many of India's other major rivers.

In Francis Ford Coppola's iconic movie "Apocalypse Now" about the Vietnam War, General Corman says to Captain Willard (the hero, acted by Martin Sheen), *"Captain, I don't know how you feel about this shrimp, but if you'll eat it, you never have to prove your courage in any other way"*. The same can be said about drinking water from taps in India.

A number of surveys of water quality conducted in Delhi by the Municipal Corporation of Delhi found that many water samples tested contained contaminated water that was not suitable for drinking, with the majority of the contaminated samples found to contain faecal material (Hindustan Times, 25 March 2011). This is also true in many other developing countries. I once accidentally drank contaminated water in Indonesia by having ice in my drink at an outdoor reception, and spent the next six months repenting for my foolishness. The horror, the horror!

In order to address the severe pollution of the Ganges River, which has a particular importance to India as it is considered a sacred river by Hindus, Prime Minister Modi has launched a high priority initiative to clean up the river. The project has already been launched and is called the National Mission for Clean Ganga. India has obtained a USD one billion development assistance financing package to assist with this project. Around USD 800 million will be allocated from this funding for infrastructure investment in wastewater treatment and management, controlling industrial pollution and developing the riverfront (World Bank News, 23 March 2015).

The Japan International Co-operation Agency is also providing funding for projects to clean up the Ganges River, and VA Tech Wabag Ltd, an Indian multinational specializing in construction of wastewater treatment plants, has won a contract for the design and construction of a sewage treatment plant to be built at Dinapur, Varanasi as part of a co-ordinated action plan by the Indian government with the help of international donors to clean up the Ganges River.

Tackling Asia's environmental crises

The scale of environmental challenges facing Asia is extremely large in terms of their potential economic and social impact on many Asian countries. While China has taken a strategic approach in implementing responses to carbon emissions and water shortages, many other countries in developing Asia have not yet implemented effective national strategies in response to the environmental problems they are facing. China also still faces tremendous challenges in reducing air pollution in its major cities and also reducing pollution of its waterways.

"In China, energy and mineral depletion (3.1 per cent), air and water pollution damages (3.8 per cent), soil nutrient depletion (1 per cent),

and carbon dioxide damages (1 per cent) amount to 9 per cent of GDP."

World Bank and DRC (Development Research Center of the State Council, China). "Seizing the Opportunity for Green Development in China". Supporting Report 3 for China 2030: Building a Modern Harmonious and Creative High Income Society. World Bank (Washington D.C., 2012).

In India, the BJP government that was elected in 2014 has announced a major shift in its energy policy towards renewable energy, which is a very important strategic response to tackling carbon emissions. However India continues to face considerable environmental challenges due very high levels of air pollution in some major cities, as well as due to the poor quality of water infrastructure and depletion of underground water resources in some parts of India, amongst other environmental challenges. The World Bank has estimated that the annual cost of environmental degradation in India is USD 80 billion, or around 5.7 per cent of annual GDP (World Bank Press Release, 17 July 2013).

Some of Asia's largest cities, including Mumbai, Jakarta and Bangkok, are also facing long-term threats from flooding, which will require large-scale infrastructure investment to mitigate their vulnerability to floods.

The impact of climate change is also changing weather patterns, and may intensify extreme weather conditions, resulting in more frequent and severe floods, typhoons and also droughts. The impact of rising sea levels over the long-term also will increase the vulnerability of large parts of Asia, including low-lying river deltas in Vietnam, Myanmar and Bangladesh.

While accelerated infrastructure development will help to combat these risks, governments in the Asia-Pacific will need to plan for an increased frequency of disasters in the region as a result of more severe weather events such as floods and typhoons. With much of the Asia-Pacific already vulnerable to major earthquakes and the risk of tsunamis, this increases the need for strengthening the disaster prevention and management capability of individual nations in the Asia-Pacific, as well as improving the regional capacity for co-ordinated responses to such disasters.

ASEAN has already established a co-ordination mechanism in response to disasters as part of the action plan following the ratification of the ASEAN Agreement on Disaster Management and Emergency Response in 2009. An ASEAN Co-ordinating Centre for Humanitarian Assistance has been created, which is intended to help co-ordinate a response to disasters among ASEAN member states as well as with key international partners. ASEAN's capability for responding to disasters has also been enhanced by the decision of the Singapore government to establish the Changi Regional Humanitarian Assistance and Disaster Relief (HADR) Coordination Centre. The mission of the Centre, known as the Changi RHCC Centre, which has become fully operational in 2015, is to provide military-to-military co-ordination in responses to a disaster. Teams from the RHCC were deployed to Nepal in April 2015 to assist with disaster rescue operations following the Nepal earthquake. The Changi RHCC Centre will work with partner militaries to assist the military in the disaster-impacted state with its disaster response.

> *"Enhancing our collective HADR capacity requires advanced countries to share technologies and platforms with countries that are willing to play a positive role in this regard. This can be a force multiplier and enable a stronger coalition to emerge in dealing with natural disasters and maritime threats."*
>
> "New Forms of Security Collaboration in Asia", Rao Inderjit Singh, Indian Minister of State for Defence, IISS Shangri-La Dialogue, Singapore, 29 May 2015.

Despite important positive progress towards tackling Asia's environmental crises, the Asia-Pacific region continues to face large-scale challenges that will require urgent government strategies to address these in a co-ordinated way. Major infrastructure investment spending is required as part of these responses, although the capacity of many low income Asian nations to fund such infrastructure spending is constrained by high government debt and fiscal deficits. Meanwhile the cost of addressing Asia's environmental problems continues to escalate with every passing year, as the impact of climate change, air pollution, water pollution and depletion of groundwater resources continues to rise.

Chapter 13

Combating Terrorism and Organized Crime in Asia

The dark side of globalization

The Asia-Pacific region has been a major beneficiary of globalization over the last 50 years, as trade liberalization and globalization of supply chains in manufacturing have become a major positive force driving economic growth. Rapidly growing exports have been a locomotive of economic growth for many Asian countries, and cross-border people flows for tourism, commerce or employment abroad have been an important contributor to the rapid growth of the economies of many Asia-Pacific countries.

However Asia-Pacific nations are increasingly confronting challenges from the dark side of globalization, including terrorism and organized crime. Both terrorist groups and organized crime gangs are exploiting the rapid growth in people movements and cross-border trade flows.

One of the greatest threats to Asia is from the rise of Islamic terrorist groups operating globally and radicalizing sympathizers in countries worldwide. Another major threat to Asian nations comes from transnational organized crime, as criminal networks undermine governance and the rule of law with the proceeds of crime from a vast range of illegal activities, including the narcotics trade, counterfeiting and human trafficking. Indeed, a key risk relates to the inter-relationship between terrorist groups and organized crime, as terrorists utilize organized crime networks to move people and money to conduct their terror attacks.

The evolving terrorist threats in Asia

As the proliferation of terrorist groups is occurring in parallel with the rapid increase of Asia-Pacific cross-border people flows for commerce and tourism as well as fast growth in merchandise trade flows through airports, ports, road and rail transport, Asian governments are confronting rapidly growing security challenges in containing the threat from terrorism. The nature of the terrorist threat is also becoming increasingly complex, as governments face the challenge of preventing proliferation of weapons of mass destruction by non-state actors, including nuclear and biological weapons, as well as the increasing sophistication of terrorist groups in using modern information technology for cybercrime as well as exploiting social media to recruit sympathisers.

Political turmoil and conflict in Pakistan, Afghanistan, the Middle East and North Africa combined with extreme poverty and high levels of youth unemployment have generated hotbeds for the proliferation of terrorist groups driven by radical Islamic ideology. The withdrawal of US and other international peacekeeping forces from Iraq created a military vacuum that the Iraqi security forces were unable to effectively fill in the face of the sudden rise of the ISIS insurgency in Iraq and Syria. This has created a stronghold for radical Islamic terrorist groups in large parts of Syria and Iraq, utilizing porous borders between Syria and Turkey.

These threats from radical Islamist terror groups are also increasingly evident in some Sub-Saharan African nations, most notably with escalating terrorism in Nigeria, Africa's most populous nation, with a population of 173 million. The escalating attacks within Nigeria by Boko Haram and its attempts to create an Islamic caliphate in Nigeria pose a major threat of destabilization in Sub-Saharan Africa and the creation of safe havens for terrorist groups in the region.

This proliferation of terrorist groups driven by radical Islamic ideology in the Middle East and Africa also poses significant long-term threats to South and Southeast Asia, due the interlinkages between terrorist groups operating in these different regions.

Terrorism in South Asia

In South Asia, Pakistan and Afghanistan have long been in the front line of the escalating global threat from terrorism. The substantial downgrading of the International Security Assistance Force (ISAF) presence in Afghanistan that has been underway will almost inevitably create a security vacuum in Afghanistan that will result in the renewed ascendancy of Taliban forces and destabilize Afghanistan.

NATO combat operations in Afghanistan ceased in December 2014 after 13 years, although the number of attacks by insurgents escalated during 2014, with over 5,000 Afghan security forces killed during that year. If Afghanistan again descends into civil war and large tracts of the nation fall under the control of Taliban forces – which is a likely scenario following the withdrawal of most ISAF forces – this will again make Afghanistan a stronghold for terrorist groups.

While this may be well understood from a strategic and military perspective by NATO military forces, the political and economic costs of the peacekeeping operations by the US, UK and other allies in both Iraq and Afghanistan had become too onerous, particularly in the aftermath of the global financial crisis, and the human cost in terms of armed forces personnel being killed and wounded was increasingly difficult to accept politically. The prospect of keeping large peacekeeping forces on the ground in Iraq or Afghanistan for many more years, perhaps decades, had become increasingly unpalatable politically and economically.

Meanwhile Pakistan has long been a major hub for terrorist group operations, particularly in the regions adjacent to Afghanistan. Despite large-scale offensives by the Pakistani armed forces to suppress terrorist groups in these areas, there is little sign of any positive progress, with many terrorist attacks occurring within Pakistan on a frequent basis.

> *"Portions of Pakistan's Federally Administered Tribal Areas, Khyber Pakhtunkhwa province, and Balochistan province remained a safe haven for terrorist groups seeking to conduct domestic, regional, and global attacks. Al-Qa'ida, the Haqqani Network, Tehrik-e Taliban Pakistan, Lashkar i Jhangvi, Lashkar e-Tayyiba, and other terrorist groups, as well as the Afghan Taliban, took advantage of this safe haven to plan operations in Pakistan and throughout the region."*
>
> US Department of State, Country Reports on Terrorism 2013, Chapter 5,
> "Terrorist Safe Havens".

The widespread presence of terrorist groups in Pakistan has also been a major security threat for India, as was demonstrated by the 2008 attack on Mumbai by Pakistani terrorists. The terrorists who mounted this attack came by boat from Pakistan and were being controlled by Pakistani handlers by mobile telephone during their attacks. These calls were intercepted and recorded by the Indian government while the attacks were being carried out. The Mumbai attacks were planned by an American national of Pakistani origin, Daood Sayed Gilani, who later changed his name to David Headley as part of his attempts to cover his Pakistani origins so that he could undertake planning visits to India for the Lashkar e-Tayyiba (LeT) terrorist attacks. He used his American passport to frequently enter India to plan the terrorist attacks.

Almost a year after the Mumbai attacks, Gilani was arrested in the US and interrogated. In his statements under interrogation made in June 2010 *(Statement of Accused David Coleman Headley.* Transcript, National Investigation Agency, Government of India (30 May 2011)), he stated that his handler was Major Iqbal of the Pakistani intelligence agency, the Internal Services Intelligence (ISI). Gilani admitted in his statements that he had briefed Major Iqbal and Iqbal's boss, Lt Colonel Hamza of the ISI, about his plans for staging terrorist attacks in India. In his statements Gilani said that Major Iqbal paid him USD 25,000 in 2006 to fund his travel to India to undertake further detailed planning for the attacks. He also said that to his knowledge, every operative of the Lashkar e-Tayyiba terrorist group, of which he was a member, had an ISI handler. Gilani's statements named a number of other ISI officers who were handlers for other LeT terrorists, including Major Sameer Ali and Brigadier Riyaz.

Gilani also confessed that he had been instructed by LeT to undertake planning for a similar terrorist attack on Delhi, and that he had visited Delhi to conduct surveillance on potential targets, including the National Defence College, which his handlers later decided was a priority target. He had also undertaken reconnaissance on the Bhabha Atomic Research Centre in Mumbai at the request of his handler. Gilani also undertook planning trips to Copenhagen for an attack on the Danish newspaper *Morgenavisen Jyllands-Posten* as LeT reprisals for satirical cartoons published, but this attack was not carried out at the time, although the January 2015 terrorist attack on *Charlie Hebdo* in Paris seemed to be very similar to the terrorist attack Gilani had been planning in Copenhagen.

The role of Pakistan's intelligence agency, the Internal Services Intelligence agency (ISI), in colluding with terrorist groups has been heavily criticized by the Indian government as well as by US government officials.

"A second, but no less worrisome, challenge we face is the impunity with which certain extremist groups are allowed to operate from Pakistani

soil. The Haqqani network for one acts as a veritable arm of Pakistan's Internal Services Intelligence agency. With ISI support, Haqqani operatives planned and conducted that truck bomb attack as well as the assault on our embassy. We also have credible intelligence that they were behind the June 28 attack on the Intercontinental Hotel in Kabul and a host of other smaller, but effective operations.

In choosing to use violent extremism as an instrument of policy, the government of Pakistan and most especially the Pakistani army and ISI jeopardizes not only the prospect of our strategic partnership, but Pakistan's opportunity to be a respected nation with legitimate regional influence."

Testimony by Admiral Michael Mullen, Chairman of the Joint Chiefs of Staff, US Department of Defense before the US Senate Armed Services Committee on September 22, 2011, Washington D.C., Hearing to Receive Testimony on the US Strategy in Afghanistan.

The links between Pakistan's intelligence agency and terrorist groups operating against India remains one of the key risks for conflict in the Asia-Pacific region. With Pakistan-based terrorist groups having a long history of conducting terrorist attacks in India, including the LeT attack on the Indian parliament in 2001 and the Mumbai bombings in 2008, the Indian government is under considerable pressure to show a resolute response to future attacks. Moreover the BJP government led by PM Modi has portrayed itself as taking a tougher stand against external threats. Consequently a trigger for an escalating Indo-Pakistan conflict could come from a significant terrorist attack on India which shows any evidence of Pakistani intelligence agency involvement.

Southeast Asian terrorism and the links to ISIS

In Southeast Asia, the rapid rise of ISIS in Syria and Iraq has highlighted the potential risks of domestic terrorism threats, due to the number of Southeast Asian recruits who have gone to Syria and Iraq to join ISIS. Hundreds of recruits from Malaysia, Indonesia and the Philippines are estimated to have gone to join ISIS, raising fears that these people will become hardened terrorists who will eventually return to their countries and become the nucleus for a new wave of terrorist activities in their home countries.

The Southeast Asian members of ISIS have also proclaimed an objective of creating an Islamic caliphate in Southeast Asia, which would include Indonesia, Malaysia, Singapore, Brunei, Philippines and Thailand.

The potential destabilizing impact of such extremists has already been demonstrated, following the arrests of 19 terrorists in Malaysia between April and June 2014 for plotting a series of terrorist attacks on bars and a brewery in Kuala Lumpur. The discovery of this plot by Malaysian police highlights the risks to national security and stability posed by even small numbers of hard-line extremists. A few terrorist attacks could be devastating for Malaysia's international image as a safe, moderate Islamic nation that has attracted large investment inflows from multinationals as well as large international tourism inflows.

In addition to these arrests of Malaysian terrorists, a further 36 persons planning to join ISIS were arrested in Malaysia during 2014, although dozens of Malaysians are believed to have successfully managed to reach Syria to join ISIS. This upsurge in radical Islamists and their terrorist attack plans in Malaysia created shock waves within a nation that had a reputation for being a moderate and tolerant society. In April 2015, a further 17 persons were arrested in Malaysia on suspicion of planning terrorist attacks in Kuala Lumpur, and further arrests were made by Malaysian police in July 2015 of two Malaysians with links to ISIS who were believed to be planning similar attacks.

For Indonesia, the potential risk from this latest upsurge in terrorism linked to the rise of ISIS is an even greater threat, since Indonesia has a population of 250 million people, and is still a low income country with large segments of the population living in extreme poverty.

Moreover Indonesia has suffered from a number of major terrorist attacks in recent years, including the Bali bombings in 2002, which resulted in 202 people being killed, with a further 209 injured, and the co-ordinated suicide bombings of the Ritz-Carlton Hotel and the JW Marriott Hotel in Jakarta in 2009, which *Jemaah Islamiyah* (JI), an Indonesian Islamic terrorist group affiliated with Al Qaeda, were responsible for. However there were also many other terrorist attacks by Islamic terrorists, including the bombing of the Australian Embassy in Jakarta in 2004, and another bombing outrage in Bali in 2005. These attacks resulted in a major crackdown by Indonesian police and security forces on Indonesian terrorist groups, notably JI and *Jemaah Anshorut Tauhid* (JAT).

The Indonesian security crackdown stabilized the situation during the second term of office of President Yudhoyono.

While JI terrorists continued to attempt major terrorist attacks in Indonesia, including a plot to blow up the Indonesian parliament in 2012 while parliament was in session and also to attack the US Embassy in Jakarta, the Indonesian security forces were very successful in containing the threat and disrupting major terrorist plots. Indonesia's National Counter Terrorism Agency was established in 2010 to co-ordinate the Indonesian anti-terrorism response. The creation of Densus 88, an elite special forces anti-terrorism force, after the Bali bombings has been highly successful. Densus 88 has established a strong reputation as a very capable anti-terrorism force during this period, foiling many terrorist plots and eliminating many key terrorist cells and their leaders.

President Yudhoyono had a long and successful career in the Indonesian military, rising to the rank of general before his retirement and entry in politics. Therefore he retained very good links to the military during his term of office as President, with a close understanding of how the capabilities of the Indonesian military could be used to suppress terrorism, and was able to successfully mobilize a strong anti-terrorist response during his presidency. However Indonesia's new leader, President Jokowi, is from a civilian background, and his anti-terrorism policies are still not clearly defined.

With Indonesia expected to face a renewed upsurge in terrorist activity as Indonesian terrorists fighting in Syria and Iraq return to their country, the national anti-terrorism response capability will likely be strongly tested during President Jokowi's term of office.

Although the Philippines is a predominantly Christian nation, with over 90 per cent of the population being of the Christian faith, there are significant Muslim communities in the southern Philippines. A number of Islamic terrorist and insurgents have become well-established in the southern Philippines, of which the most notorious is the *Abu Sayyaf* group. The group has the objective of creating an Islamic state in Western Mindanao and the Sulu archipelago. The group has links to Al Qaeda and has also linked itself with ISIS in order to try to leverage the publicity that ISIS has received following its rapid rise in Iraq and Syria.

In 2014, the Aquino government signed a peace treaty with another Islamic insurgent group, the Moro Islamic Liberation Front (MILF), which had waged an insurgency for decades in Mindanao. However in January 2015, President Aquino's negotiations with the MILF to establish regional self rule were derailed by the massacre of 44 police commandos attempting to capture a terrorist suspected in relation to the 2002 Bali bombings in Indonesia. The police commandos had attempted to capture the suspect in a terrorist camp of the Bangsamoro Islamic Freedom Fighters, a group which had also linked itself to ISIS. The police commandos were pushed back in the fighting and entered the adjacent MILF camp, which resulted in a heavy battle in which the 44 commandos and many MILF insurgents were killed.

The death of so many police in the incident resulted in a strong public and parliamentary backlash in the Philippines against the idea of a deal with the MILF for establishing a region with Islamic self-rule, given the obvious strong links with global Islamic terrorism that the insurgent groups have. These links to international terrorism were apparent, given that the reason for the police raid was to apprehend a notorious terrorist believed to be responsible for one of the worst terrorist bombings in Southeast Asia.

China's war on terrorism

One of the major emerging threats to China's internal security over the last two decades has been from the Uighur Islamic population in the northwestern Chinese autonomous province of Xinjiang, which shares borders with a number of Central Asian nations that are Islamic. Xinjiang has had a long history of civil unrest, with Uighur separatist groups having been backed by the Soviet Union against China since China became a communist nation.

During the last two decades, there have been a number of major terrorist attacks within China by Uighur terrorist groups. Tensions between Uighurs in Xinjiang and immigrant ethnic Han Chinese who had moved into Xinjiang turned into violent riots in 2009, with the deaths of an estimated 200 Han Chinese and Uighurs during the riots, followed by a military clampdown in Xinjiang. The tough suppression of Uighur separatists has subsequently resulted in an upsurge in Uigher terrorist acts within China in the last five years. The threat from these terrorist groups has also escalated due to the involvement of Uighurs in international terrorist groups operating in Afghanistan, Pakistan and more recently with the ISIS group in Syria and Iraq.

Uighurs had been able to travel across the Chinese land border to Central Asia in order to join the Taliban insurgents in Afghanistan or Pakistan, but due to much closer co-operation between China and a number of Central Asian governments, this route has become increasingly difficult for terrorist groups to utilize. Uighurs have increasingly been crossing illegally into Thailand, Vietnam and Myanmar, from where they have relatively easily been able to obtain false documents and travel to Turkey. Turkey has provided asylum for Uighurs on the basis that they are ethnically Turks, and thousands of Uighurs have fled through Central Asia to Turkey since the 1950s, with the intent of establishing new lives in Turkey. A large proportion of these Uighurs have genuinely sought asylum to build new lives in peace in Turkey, but during the last two years there have also been a significant number of Uighurs who have crossed over the relatively porous borders between Turkey and Syria to join various rebel groups fighting the Assad regime, including ISIS and allied Islamic insurgent groups.

In January 2015, the Shanghai police arrested ten Turkish citizens who were alleged to be selling falsified Turkish passports to Uighurs, with nine Uighur terrorist suspects also arrested as part of the operation.

In March 2014, around 300 Uighurs were discovered in a human trafficking camp in southern Thailand, with the group claiming they were Turkish. Turkey offered to accept them, but the Chinese government worked with the Thai authorities to try to establish whether they were Chinese Uighurs. In October 2014, a further 144 Uighurs were arrested in Malaysia hiding in several apartments. The group claimed that they were Turkish. This upsurge in Uighur Muslims fleeing to Southeast Asia has generated fears that Muslim Uighur terrorists are also mingling with genuine refugees and being transferred through by human trafficking groups to Turkey and then joining ISIS in Syria.

Turkish Prime Minister Erdogan had described the Chinese government's actions to control the Xinjiang Uighurs as "a kind of genocide" in 2009 (BBC News, "Turkey Attacks China 'Genocide'", 10 July 2009). Since then, China's trade ties with Turkey have rapidly strengthened, forcing the Turkish government to adopt a more diplomatic face in its relations with China, although it continues to maintain an open-door policy towards Uighur immigration to Turkey.

Meanwhile despite Chinese government efforts to boost economic development in Xinjiang province, this does not appear to have made much impact on Uighur separatist sentiment. There have been many attacks by Uighur terrorists within Xinjiang, but also a significant number of attacks in other Chinese cities, which have resulted in much increased police and military resources being deployed to try to control this threat.

The terrorist attack on passengers in a railway station in Kunming in Yunnan Province in China in March 2014 resulted in the deaths of 29 passengers, with four of the eight terrorists also killed by police during the attack. The attack was widely attributed to Islamic Uighurs.

Future challenges

Over the last two decades, one of the dark faces of globalization has been the globalization of terrorist groups. The proliferation of new Islamic terrorist groups globally that are aligned to similar objectives of using terror to achieve their objective of creating Muslim fundamentalist societies has become a major threat to sovereign states and governments globally. Many Asian countries are also in the front line of this terrorist threat.

At a national level, government responses have been to significantly increase resources devoted to internal security, including police forces, specialized counter-terrorist groups and intelligence capabilities. This will continue to be a major focus for increased government resources for the foreseeable future.

Increased co-operation between Asian governments in co-operation with other governments worldwide to combat the rising threat of terrorism will be a key focus given the increasingly global nature of terrorist groups and their international cells.

The growing sophistication of global terrorist networks is also creating alarming new dimensions to the scope of the terrorist threat, as terrorists attempt to gain capabilities to use nuclear weapons as well as biological weapons.

The links between terrorist groups and organized crime in Asia is also an increasing concern, as the criminal networks that have been established by organized crime groups can become conduits that facilitate the operations of international terrorist groups. For example, Afghanistan is an important source of illegal opium and heroin production, with Xinjiang province in China having become a key distribution hub for Afghan heroin in western China, facilitated by Uighur groups. The heroin trade therefore has become a funding source for Islamic terrorist groups operating in Afghanistan and in China.

Organized crime in Asia

"One of the most serious unintended consequences of the globalization that we have been experiencing for the last few years has been the rapid rise of transnational organized crime groups."

Bruce G. Ohr, Chief, Organised Crime and Racketeering Section, Criminal Division, United States Department of Justice, "Effective Methods to Combat Transnational Organised Crime in Criminal Justice Processes", 116th International Training Course, Asia and Far East Institute for the Prevention of Crime and Treatment of Offenders, November 2000.

Transnational organized crime is vast in scale, with the United Nations Office on Drugs and Crime (UNODC) having estimated that transnational organized crime groups globally generated annual earnings of around 1.5 per cent of world GDP. According to their estimate, in 2009 transnational organized crime earned an estimated USD 870 billion, of which around 36 per cent was earned from drug trafficking.

Weak governance and high levels of corruption in many Asian countries have facilitated the growth of organized crime in many Asian regions. Even in the developed countries of the Asia-Pacific, organized crime remains a threat to governance, as reflected in the continuing power of the Yakuza crime organizations in Japan.

In mainland China, organized crime has also been on the rise since the 1980s, after having been severely curtailed by Chairman Mao after the Communist Revolution.

The scale of illegal revenues for organized crime groups in Asia is extremely large. The United Nations Office on Drugs and Crime has estimated that in East Asia, the total illicit revenue for organized crime groups from the drug trade for heroin and methamphetamines was around USD 31 billion in 2011. Revenue for criminal groups from counterfeit goods in Asia was estimated at USD 24 billion for the same year. Together, this amounted to USD 55 billion in earnings for organized crime groups in East Asia in 2011.

Taking into account other estimated revenues for organized crime groups from smuggling of wood products, human trafficking and counterfeit medicines, as well as revenues for other organized crime groups in other parts of Asia, including South Asia, the total revenue for East Asian transnational organized crime groups was estimated by UNODC to be around USD 90 billion in 2011 UNODC (United Nations Office on Drugs and Crime),

Transnational Organised Crime in East Asia and the Pacific: A Threat Assessment. [UNODC] (Bangkok, April 2013).

This is a large amount of annual cash inflow into the organized crime groups of East Asia. By way of comparison, this amount far exceeds the estimated GDP of Myanmar in 2014, which was around USD 64 billion, or Sri Lanka, which had an estimated GDP of USD 75 billion in 2014.

However even this vast sum of annual estimated earnings for Asian organized crime groups only considers transnational organized crime in East Asia, mainly focusing on illegal flows relating to China and Southeast Asia.

When the Yakuza organized crime groups in Japan are taken into account, the estimated annual earnings of the Yakuza are considerably greater. An estimate for earnings by the Yakuza done by the Japanese National Police Agency in 1989 put their annual earnings at Yen 1.3 trillion (see Hill, 2003), which was equivalent to around USD 9 billion at the time, although other estimates are considerably higher, in the range of USD 30 billion to USD 50 billion per year. Moreover, since the Yakuza have been very well established for decades, their financial assets have likely grown in parallel with the rapid growth of the Japanese economy between the 1960s and the 1990s, as they have had many decades to establish legitimate business empires and transfer their illegal earnings into legal business structures.

For Australia, the Australian Crime Commission has estimated conservatively that the total annual earnings of organized crime groups are in the order of 15 billion Australian dollars each year.

If one takes the UNODC estimate that transnational crime group earnings are around 1.5 per cent of world GDP, an estimate for the size of Asian transnational crime earnings can be deduced by applying the same percentage share to Asian GDP. In 2014, the total GDP of the Asia-Pacific economies, including China, Japan, Australia, East Asia and South Asia, was around USD 24 trillion in nominal USD terms. Therefore using the UNODC global estimate, this would translate into an estimated USD 360 billion of annual revenue for Asian transnational crime organizations.

Such large amounts of illegal earnings give considerable power to organized crime groups to undermine the rule of law and good governance in Asia. With corruption already a severe problem in many Asian countries, a significant proportion of these vast amounts of criminal funds will inevitably be used to buy the allegiance of corrupt officials in key government roles to allow the organized crime groups to pursue their illegal activities.

Business activities of organized crime groups

Organized crime groups have become increasingly sophisticated in laundering the proceeds of crime into legitimate businesses. This helps to conceal the illegal source of their funds and to give legitimacy to the wealth of key figures in organized crime, by establishing front companies which are operating legal businesses and can be used to purchase property or hold financial assets.

Highly complex legal structures can be created, which are then used for conducting legal commercial operations, helping to disguise the illegal activities that are being carried out under the cover of legal businesses.

The legitimization of the criminal assets of organized crime groups through legal businesses also facilitates their international expansion, as they establish apparently legal business structures across Asia and in other nations worldwide which help to camouflage and disguise their cross-border international activities.

Having large international business operations conducting legal business activities also helps to provide a sophisticated system for circumventing money laundering controls in the financial system. To illustrate the point, I was once questioned by a young and probably very inexperienced bank teller in London about the source of my cash deposit, which was the grand sum of only ten pounds sterling, which left me rather astonished. At the same time, an Asian restaurant employee (I could tell his profession from his waiter's uniform complete with food stains) at the next bank teller window was depositing a sackful of cash comprising large bundles of sterling notes, presumably into his restaurant's bank account, with no questions asked!

Organized crime groups use a wide range of methods to conceal their illegal financial transactions, through the use of retail businesses to launder money, as well as techniques such as misinvoicing of trade in goods and services.

A senior customs official of an OECD country once explained to me how organized crime groups acquire restaurants and other similar retail businesses to launder the proceeds of their narcotics trade, mixing their illegal cash earnings from the drugs trade into the legal cash flow from the normal restaurant or other retail operations.

The organized crime groups with large accumulated assets are therefore usually part of the normal business landscape of most Asia-Pacific nations, hiding in plain sight through their network of legal businesses such as restaurants, nightclubs and trading companies.

Once the illegal cash has been placed into the financial system, the organized crime groups can acquire a wide range of assets such as real estate, bank deposits, bonds or equities, as well as fund the expansion of legal business activities.

Combating organized crime

"Transnational Organised Crime is an abiding threat to US economic and national security. Criminals can play a significant role in weakening stability and undermining the rule of law in some emerging democracies and areas of strategic importance to the United States."

> James Clapper, Director of National Intelligence,
> "Worldwide Threat Assessment of the US Intelligence Community",
> US Senate Armed Services Committee, 11 February 2014.

One of the key priorities for Asian governments to be able to effectively tackle transnational crime organizations is to have more effective co-ordination and regional response capabilities in order to deal with criminal organizations that are operating across many nations.

The ASEAN regional grouping of ten Southeast Asian nations has established a framework for regional co-operation amongst East Asian governments on tackling organized crime, with regular biennial ASEAN Ministerial Meetings on Transnational Crime together with Japan, China and South Korea (AMMTC+3). The eight priority areas of transnational crime that the AMMTC+3 focus on are terrorism, drug trafficking, human trafficking, money laundering, sea piracy, arms smuggling, economic crime and cybercrime.

ASEAN and Japan have also established a framework for co-operation on transnational crime, with the first ASEAN Plus Japan Ministerial Meeting on Transnational Crime held in September 2013 in Laos. The scope of the discussions included counter-terrorism as well as cybercrime. Similarly ASEAN also has established a ministerial dialogue with China, with a regular AMMTC+China meeting.

While the establishment of such regular dialogue between East Asian countries on transnational crime is clearly helpful, the focus identified in the ministerial discussions has been on terrorism and cybercrime. In order to tackle organized crime, a separate East Asian task force on transnational organized crime would be able to work in parallel with initiatives to combat terrorism. At present, unless there is a fully resourced East Asian government initiative focused on tackling transnational organized crime, the risk is that the escalating war against terrorism will divert attention away from organized crime, allowing criminal groups to continue to expand their networks and revenues.

ASEAN has already created the necessary infrastructure for regional police co-operation through the establishment of ASEANAPOL, a forum for ASEAN police force co-operation. A permanent secretariat was established for ASEANAPOL in 2010, with a permanent headquarters in Kuala Lumpur. The mandate of the ASEANAPOL Secretariat is to implement the resolutions and plan of action adopted by ASEAN Chiefs of Police at the ASEANAPOL conferences.

With sufficient additional resourcing, the scope of ASEANAPOL capabilities could be significantly expanded to combat terrorism and organized crime in Southeast Asia. Similar co-ordinated capabilities could also be created for the ASEAN+3 countries, to strengthen co-ordinated police actions against terrorism and organized crime across East Asia.

The outlook

Despite efforts by many Asia-Pacific countries to combat organized crime both domestically and through regional and global co-operation amongst police forces, the current situation is hardly encouraging. Using the relatively conservative UNODC estimate that 1.5 per cent of global GDP is attributable to organized crime, this indicates an estimate of around USD 360 billion in revenue for organized crime groups in the Asia-Pacific each year. Such large amounts of illegal revenue each year provide considerable financial resources for transnational organized crime groups to buy influence over corrupt government officials. With Asia-Pacific economies still suffering from high levels of corruption in many countries, these large volumes of illegal proceeds from organized crime undermine governance and rule of law in many Asian nations.

With even the most developed Asia-Pacific nations of Japan and Australia, which are among the most advanced economies in the world, having organized crime groups operating on a vast scale, the ability of low income developing nations in Asia to tackle organized crime is considerably lower due to lack of law enforcement resources and high levels of corruption.

An important concern is also the extent to which criminal organizations and their leaders are building legal business operations, which are then used as fronts for large-scale international organized crime activities.

An evolving threat is from the linkages between organized crime and terrorist networks, which creates a wide range of risks to national security. These threats include the use of organized crime smuggling operations to transfer terrorists and their weapons worldwide, as well as co-operation between organized crime networks and terrorist groups for funding terrorism through illegal activities such as drug trafficking of opium from Afghanistan.

Therefore one of the greatest challenges for the Asia-Pacific region over the next two decades comes from terrorism and organized crime, which has already destabilized a number of Asian countries. Unless comprehensively tackled by Asia-Pacific wide government co-operation, these threats will pose a continuing threat to the rule of law and national security across the APAC region.

Chapter 14

Asia's Future Wars

Geopolitical Risks in the Asia-Pacific

The Asian geopolitical risk landscape

The Asian geopolitical landscape has many fault lines that could become flashpoints and triggers for future conflicts. The Korean peninsula, the India-Pakistan border, and competing territorial claims in the South China Sea and East China Sea are the most significant potential flashpoints that could threaten peace and stability in the Asia-Pacific region. Of greatest concern to many Asia-Pacific nations is that China's military actions in relation to territorial disputes in the South China Sea, which some nations consider as aggressive, have created rising risks of conflict.

Amongst the major potential geopolitical flashpoints in the Asia-Pacific, it is China's ascendance as a global superpower that is increasingly causing the most regional tensions. Over the last decade, China's rapidly increasing military capability has been accompanied by escalating regional tensions with some of China's neighbours over China's territorial claims in the South China Sea and East China Sea.

As China's military power continues to grow, some other Asia-Pacific countries fear that China's growing regional military dominance could increase the risk of future conflicts. China's official defence budget for 2015 was announced by the Chinese government to be around USD 140 billion. With the Chinese economy still expected to grow at around six per cent per year over the medium term in real terms, the annual growth in the military budget would still be able to be increased at least in line with economic growth. This would result in significant increases in the size of the Chinese military budget over the next decade. However if China's growth rate slows to around 5 per cent per year after 2025, this would imply a significantly reduced pace of annual increase in military budgets compared to the double digit annual growth rates in military spending in past decades.

Nevertheless, with China's defence budget already very large compared with other Asian nations, this would still allow significant further modernization of the Chinese armed forces as well as substantial ongoing investment into military research and development that would significantly improve the technological capability of the Chinese military compared to the military forces of other Asian nations.

The induction of China's first aircraft carrier, *Liaoning*, into service with the People's Liberation Army Navy (PLAN) in 2012 reflected the growing strategic ambitions of the Chinese military. China also has a second aircraft carrier under construction which is expected to be completed by around 2018. At present, the *Liaoning* is being used to train Chinese fighter pilots, who have had no previous experience of operating from an aircraft carrier. However, eventually it is expected that China's aircraft carriers will be used to project Chinese military capability to more distant naval operations, most likely in the Pacific and Indian Oceans.

Territorial disputes in the South China Sea

China's growing military capability has increased fears amongst many other Asia-Pacific nations that China may use its military strength to assert its claims in territorial disputes in the region. At the forefront of regional concerns are China's territorial claims in the South China Sea as proclaimed by China on maps by the depiction of the Nine Dash Line, a crudely portrayed dotted line that lays claim by China to most of the South China Sea (Submission by People's Republic of China to the UN Commission on the Limits of the Continental Shelf, CML/17/2009, New York, 7 May 2009). China claims Scarborough Reef and Second Thomas Shoal in the South China Sea, both of which are also claimed by the Philippines as being within its sovereign territorial waters. China has used military force to assert its claim to these shoals (BBC News, "Philippines says China 'Fired Water Cannon' on Filipino Fishermen", 24 February 2014).

The Philippines has filed a case with the UN Permanent Court of Arbitration, arguing that China's territorial claims in the South China Sea are illegal under the UN Convention on the Law of the Sea. Although China has refused to take part in the UN Court hearing, the UN Court of Arbitration has commenced hearings to consider its jurisdiction on this case (Reuters, "Court Begins

Hearing Philippines, China Dispute over South China Sea", 8 July 2015).

A key focus of the territorial disputes in the South China Sea is the Spratly Islands, which both China and the Philippines claim. During 2014–15, China constructed an airstrip and port facilities on Fiery Cross Reef in the Spratlys; construction of a second airstrip was commenced in early 2015 on Subi Reef, also in the Spratlys. Once completed, these could become military airstrips and forward bases for Chinese military operations, helping to assert their territorial claims in the South China Sea.

While the US has warned that these actions increase the risk of instability and potential conflict in the Asia-Pacific, the US has so far been cautious in the extent to which it has become involved in the dispute. The US and Philippines do have a Mutual Defence Treaty in force that was signed in 1951, and has recently been strengthened by the signing of a bilateral ten-year Enhanced Defence Co-operation Agreement in 2014. This agreement allows US military forces to have access to a number of Philippines military bases without establishing their own permanent military base in the Philippines.

Ironically the Philippines is now keen to welcome US military forces back after having forced the US military to leave its former Subic Bay naval base and Clark Air Base in the Philippines in 1992. However it remains unclear what the extent of US treaty obligations to the Philippines would be in relation to the increasingly unpredictable Chinese military actions in the South China Sea.

In response to the construction of Chinese military structures in the Spratly Islands, the Philippines government has also announced its intention to build a naval base at Oyster Bay on the island of Palawan, which would be opposite some of the new Chinese facilities in the Spratly Islands. To build up its regional military co-operation, the Philippines and Japan signed a Memorandum on Defence Co-operation and Exchanges in January 2015. This Memorandum is intended to strengthen their bilateral military ties. In May 2015, the Japanese Navy held joint naval exercises in the South China Sea with the Philippines Navy for the first time, and the Japanese government has signaled that it may provide funding support for infrastructure development around the new naval base planned for Oyster Bay, though not for the base itself.

However the Philippines is unable to project any type of credible military deterrence to China, having failed to invest anything in building its naval or air force capabilities for decades. The Aquino government has begun the process of modernizing the Phillipines armed forces, but this will be a long process that will take many years. The Philippines still does not have a single front line fighter aircraft, and its extremely limited naval capability was only recently boosted by the US providing two former US Coast Guard cutters to bolster the Philippines navy. In early 2015, the Australian government also decided to gift two decommissioned heavy landing craft that had been in service with the Royal Australian Navy to the Philippines navy, mainly to help with tasks such as humanitarian assistance and disaster relief. The Philippines government has also ordered two strategic support ships from an Indonesian shipbuilder, which will be built from the same design as the Indonesian Navy's Makassar class. The first of these two ships is due to be delivered by 2016. The Philippines has also ordered 12 FA-50 Golden Eagle advanced fighter jet trainer aircraft from South Korea, which will be delivered by 2017, as one of its initial steps to modernize its air force.

Despite the recent gifts of retired naval vessels to assist the Philippines navy as well as recent naval orders by the Philippines government, the lack of any effort by the Philippines in recent decades to build up its military deterrence capacity, combined with the actions of past Philippines governments in ejecting the US military from its Philippines bases in 1992, have left the Philippines extremely vulnerable to external military threats. Any form of strategic vision about regional geopolitics seems to have been entirely absent from the past conduct of Philippines foreign policy and defence policy until the Aquino government took office and began to respond to the assertive actions of the Chinese military in the Spratlys.

China also has territorial disputes with Vietnam in the South China Sea, and there have been a series of incidents in recent years in which Chinese naval vessels have disrupted Vietnamese offshore drilling exploration in disputed territorial waters. In 2011, a seismic vessel undertaking surveys for the Vietnamese state-owned oil company *PetroVietnam* had its cable cut by Chinese vessels.

When China brought its own offshore drilling rig into territorial waters claimed by Vietnam in 2014, there were repeated clashes at sea between Chinese and Vietnamese vessels, with Vietnam having accused the Chinese ships of aggressive tactics such as use of water cannon. These provocative actions by China in disputed territorial waters triggered widespread anti-Chinese riots in Vietnam during May 2014. These riots were also directed against manufacturing plants believed to be owned by Chinese companies, with a number of factories burnt down and an estimated 21 persons killed during the riots, mainly Chinese workers. As violence escalated during the riots, China was forced to evacuate its citizens from Vietnam using chartered aircraft and ships.

While the Vietnamese government acted quickly to suppress these riots, the underlying resentment and anger in Vietnam against China's provocative acts in the disputed offshore territorial waters was deep-seated. The strong backlash in Vietnam to China's territorial claims also reflects Vietnamese memories of China's invasion of Vietnam in 1979.

The Sino-Vietnamese War resulted in a very high number of casualties and caused considerable destruction in northern Vietnam in the border regions with China. The invasion began on 17 February 1979, when Chinese troops supported by tanks attacked Vietnam all along its Chinese border, as retaliation for Vietnam's intervention to oust the genocidal Pol Pot regime in Cambodia. After early territorial gains, the Chinese army suffered heavy casualties in bitter fighting with Vietnamese militia and border guard forces. While no official figures exist for the total number of casualties during this war, some estimates put the number of Chinese soldiers killed as high as 25,000 during the 17-day war. An estimated 10,000 Vietnamese military personnel were also killed, with a high number of casualties among Vietnamese civilians caught in the fighting.

By 6 March 1979, the Chinese army retreated back into China, having sustained such large numbers of casualties. They had not yet been fully engaged by the Vietnamese regular army, and they may have feared suffering an even heavier defeat had they not withdrawn. The Chinese invasion also had no impact upon Vietnam's Cambodia intervention, with Vietnamese troops remaining in Cambodia for many more years to ensure peace and stability and to prevent the Khmer Rouge from regaining power.

The Chinese military attack on Vietnam in 1979 has created a deep mistrust of China among much of the Vietnamese population, with fears that China's growing military power may eventually result in an escalation of tensions over disputed territorial claims, with the risk that this could result in open conflict.

Since the 1979 Chinese invasion of Vietnam, there was also a naval clash between China and Vietnam in the Spratly Islands, when Chinese forces attacked Vietnamese navy personnel at Johnson South Reef in the Spratly Islands in March 1988, killing 64 Vietnamese navy personnel. The Chinese military have been building large structures on Johnson South Reef during 2014–15, including a multi-storey building and other defensive fortifications on this reef.

Vietnam has responded to the territorial disputes with China by accelerating efforts to modernize its armed forces, which had suffered for many years to Vietnam's fiscal problems and broader macroeconomic difficulties, which had constrained resources available for defence. However with tensions with China having escalated significantly in recent years, Vietnam has taken initial measures to modernize its air force and navy. The Vietnamese Air Force has acquired a modest capability with around 35 SU-30 Mk2 fighters. A key priority is also the modernization of the Vietnamese navy, with the Vietnamese government having signed a deal in 2009 with Russia for the purchase of six Kilo class submarines at a cost of around USD 3.2 billion. The first four of these submarines had been delivered by mid-2015. In addition Vietnam bought two guided missile stealth frigates from Russia in 2011, with a further four frigates to be brought into service by 2017. Vietnam has also ordered four Dutch Sigma corvettes to further build up its naval capabilities.

To reinforce its territorial claims in the South China Sea, Vietnam has also built structures in the Spratly Islands, with reclamation of land at West London Reef and at Sand Cay. This reclaimed land has been built up with new military structures.

Territorial disputes in the East China Sea

In addition to its territorial claims in the South China Sea, China is also involved in a territorial dispute with Japan over the *Senkaku* (as named by Japan) or *Diaoyu* (as named by China) islets. Although these islets have long been administered by Japan, China has claimed that these islets belong to China. Tensions between the two countries escalated after the Japanese government decided to buy the islets from a private owner in September 2012, thereby triggering official Chinese protests that Japan had absorbed the islets into its sovereign territory.

The Chinese government escalated its confrontation with Japan over the sovereignty of these islets during 2012, with use of coast guard vessels and military aircraft in the proximity of the disputed islets. Meanwhile in mainland China the general public were stirring themselves into a nationalistic fervor in a backlash against Japan, with anti-Japanese protests in some mainland Chinese cities. Some protests turned ugly, with Japanese restaurant windows smashed and Japanese brand cars being vandalized. A boycott of Japanese branded goods also took effect, with auto sales of Japanese auto models plunging.

I had my own experience of the anti-Japanese boycott when I arrived in Beijing at an international chain hotel soon after the peak of the anti-Japanese fervor. At the time I had not realized the extent to which the anti-Japanese sentiment had escalated throughout China, and I rather innocently ordered a Japanese brand beer from the restaurant menu with my dinner. I was politely told that this well-known global brand was out of stock, which seemed peculiar in such a large global hotel chain. No matter, I ordered another Japanese brand beer shown on the menu, only to be told that was also out of stock. This had started to become very annoying. I thought I had finally stumbled across the legendary "Pub with no beer" as celebrated by the famous Country and Western singer Slim Dusty in a popular song. However all it took was to order any non-Japanese beer and they were suddenly able to provide ample quantities.

Not all the Chinese protests and boycotts were quite so subtle as declining to serve Japanese beer. Angry protestors damaged Japanese brand cars, sometimes tearing off the car emblem from the cars. On one occasion a TV crew filming the riots interviewed a rioter who proudly showed off the many auto emblems he had torn off from Japanese cars, opening his palms to show a fistful of Mercedes Benz emblems. Of course the victims of these acts of vandalism were their own fellow Chinese citizens who had bought Japanese cars, or for an unlucky few, even German cars.

Eventually the Chinese government tired of seeing unruly mobs of anti-Japanese protestors on the streets of major cities, and gradually clamped down on these protests, perhaps fearing that the mobs might eventually decide to protest about other issues, and that these anti-Japanese protests might become a trigger for more widespread social unrest.

The economic consequences of these anti-Japanese protests were quite severe, as not only did Chinese consumers stop buying Japanese brand name products such as autos, but Chinese tourists also stopped travelling to Japan, while Japanese tourists cancelled their holidays to China for fear of being attacked or persecuted.

While the political relationship between China and Japan soured for a protracted period of time, and military tensions also escalated due to frequent flights by Chinese military aircraft in the vicinity of the islets, eventually the impact on bilateral trade began to normalize, and tourism visits started to recover. The depreciation of the Japanese yen after 2012 proved irresistible to the Chinese, and by 2014 and early 2015, Chinese tourism visits to Japan were again surging.

However Japanese multinationals were shocked by these anti-Japanese protests in 2012, and realized that the exposure of their corporate supply chains to mainland Chinese production had become a source of vulnerability. For decades, Japanese firms had made China their preferred investment location for establishing factories, but this all changed following the anti-Japanese riots. During 2013 and 2014, it became apparent that Japanese corporate boardrooms had begun to gradually react to the anti-Japanese sentiment in mainland China, and Japanese foreign direct investment flows to China declined while Japanese investment flows into ASEAN surged.

The transmission effects of the dispute between China and Japan over the sovereignty of the islets had even wider consequences for Asia-Pacific economic and political co-operation, as Asia's two largest nations were not able to easily work together on other Asian regional co-operation initiatives.

Against this background of rising political and military tensions between China and Japan, there has been growing concern within Japanese political parties and the general public about China's rising military capabilities, whereas the total size of the Japanese military budget has been heavily constrained by ongoing government expenditure cuts. With Japan's long-term growth outlook for GDP growth of only around one per cent per year due to the impact of ageing demographics and the high levels of government debt as a share of GDP, this also heavily restricts Japan's budgetary ability to match China's defence spending budget growth.

While Japan has increased its military budget since 2013 in response to rising military tensions with China, its total defence budget reached USD 42 billion (4.98 trillion yen) in 2015, compared with China's defence budget of 140 billion in 2015. Between 2002 and 2012, the Japanese defence budget fell in nominal yen terms every year, from 4.96 trillion yen in 2002 to 4.71 trillion yen in 2012. In contrast, China's defence budget has risen by double digit annual increases during this same period, rising from USD 20 billion in 2002 to USD 140 billion by 2015. Therefore within a relatively short timeframe since 2002, the military balance of power in North Asia had shifted dramatically. In 2002 Japan's defence budget was twice the size of China's defence budget, but by 2015, China's defence budget had become 3.3 times larger than the Japanese defence budget when measured in USD terms.

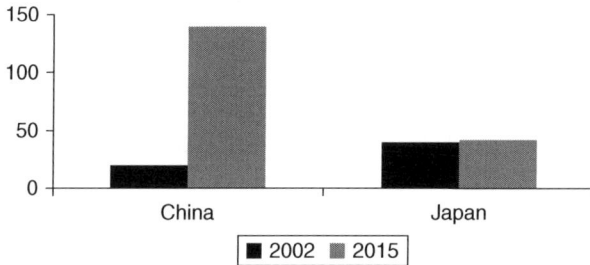

Figure 14.1   Defence budgets for China and Japan (nominal USD billion)
Source: National defence budget data.

Is conflict inevitable?

China is a rising superpower that is expected to become the world's largest economy within a decade. The fast-growing size of the Chinese economy has allowed the Chinese military budget to grow rapidly, providing the funding for modernization of the Chinese armed forces as well as rapid progress in developing advanced military technology.

With China increasingly seeking to project its military capabilities through the construction of aircraft carriers as well as new airfields built in areas of disputed sovereign territorial claims in the South China Sea, the risk of a military confrontation triggering an incident that escalates into open conflict is becoming a more probable scenario. Once such a conflict situation develops, there is a high degree of uncertainty about how the situation would evolve, and whether it would lead to an escalation of the conflict or whether it could be contained.

"The United States is deeply concerned about the pace and scope of land reclamation in the South China Sea, the prospect of further militarisation, as well as the potential for these activities to increase the risk of miscalculation or conflict among claimant states."

Speech by Dr Ashton Carter, US Secretary of Defense, "The United States and
Challenges of Asia-Pacific Security", IISS Shangri-La Dialogue,
Singapore, 30 May 2015.

As China's conventional military strength becomes increasingly overwhelming against any other single Asian state, the threat of an escalating arms race in the Asia-Pacific where military powers such as Japan or India attempt to counterbalance China's rising military dominance using advanced military technology for achieving air superiority and superior missile capabilities is also a significant risk.

There is also the possibility that the response by other Asian powers to China's increasing military dominance may eventually be to pursue a nuclear deterrence option. Until very recently, Japan's military capability was sufficiently large that Japan felt it provided an adequate deterrent to China. However with the rapid increase of in size and technological capability of the Chinese armed forces, Japan may eventually reach a point when a conventional response may no longer be considered to be a feasible option. While there are strong historical reasons why Japan would be extremely reluctant to pursue such a path, it cannot be entirely ruled out as a possible response.

The Korean peninsula

The Korean peninsula remains a key potential source of conflict, with large standing armies of both North Korea and South Korea facing off across the Demilitarized Zone. The South Korean military must remain in a continuous state of readiness to tackle the potential threat of a surprise North Korean military attack, particularly given the proximity of the DMZ to Seoul. North Korea has regularly undertaken hostile military acts that could have triggered escalation into war.

The sinking of the *Cheonan*, a South Korean corvette, in March 2010 with the loss of 46 South Korean naval personnel was one of the most serious provocations. An international inquiry of experts found that the *Cheonan* had been sunk by a North Korean torpedo, mostly probably fired by a small submarine. In November 2010, tensions between North and South Korea escalated further when North Korean artillery shelled Yeonpyeong island on the disputed maritime border between North and South Korea, causing severe damage to both civilian and military structures on the island as well as killing and injuring South Korean civilians. With North Korea also having nuclear weapons, the possibility of a conventional conflict escalating into a nuclear war also remains a real risk. Depending on the future actions of North Korea in terms of its nuclear weapons program, South Korea could also eventually decide that it needs to have a nuclear deterrence option to deter North Korea (CNN, "Under Threat South Koreans Mull Nuclear Weapons", 19 March 2013).

India's border wars

India and Pakistan have fought a number of conventional wars since their bitter partition at the time of independence in 1947. Ever since independence, large Indian and Pakistani armies have confronted each other along their borders. There have been three wars between India and Pakistan, in 1947, 1965 and 1971. Since the last war ended in 1971 when India inflicted a crushing defeat on Pakistan's armed forces, there have been ongoing skirmishes and artillery exchanges from time to time that have sometimes escalated to the brink of war. With Pakistan and India also being nuclear powers, there is also the threat of nuclear war on the Indian subcontinent if a conflict escalates out of control.

The Kargil conflict, which occurred in 1999, was essentially a limited border war, triggered when Pakistani military forces and insurgents crossed the Line of Control along the India-Pakistan border. This resulted in a major border conflict involving an estimated 30,000 Indian military personnel as well as the Indian Air Force to recapture the territory along the Line of Control. Over 1,000 soldiers were estimated to have been killed on both sides during a three-month border war.

Since then, border skirmishes continue to occur on a regular basis, with ongoing clashes occurring from July 2014 that continued into 2015. Exchanges of artillery fire became so intense that thousands of villagers living along the Indo-Pakistani border in Jammu and Kashmir had to evacuate their villages and seek safety in early 2015.

India also had a border war with China in 1962, over disputed territory along their common border. After border skirmishes in September of that year, China launched an offensive against India in October 1962, inflicting a heavy defeat on India's poorly prepared army in the mountainous border regions of Aksai Chin and the Northeast Frontier Agency. From the outset, the intent of Chairman Mao was to teach India a lesson rather than seize large tracts of new territory. After achieving their objectives, the Chinese army unilaterally withdrew from most of the territory it had occupied, although some areas of strategic value were retained.

When Chinese forces were driving back the Indian army and the extent of the Chinese military objectives were still unknown to India, the Indian government managed to secure US military support to help to defend India, with the US deploying an aircraft carrier towards India as well as mounting round the clock transportation of military supplies to the Indian army with the United States Air Force 40th Airlift Squadron, which was deployed to India and carried out airlifts of Indian troops and supplies to airstrips in the Himalayas. However these operations started shortly before the Chinese declared a ceasefire, so that the US military was never actually directly engaged in the actual fighting, although the 40th Airlift Squadron continued airlift operations in India for a year afterwards to help strengthen the Indian military's border defence.

Creating an Asia-Pacific framework for peace and cooperation

The East Asian economic miracle has brought hundreds of millions of Asians out of poverty since 1980, with sustained rapid economic growth and economic development in many Asian economies. Maintaining peace across much of East Asia was fundamental to this sustained economic progress.

Two major factors have played an important role in maintaining peace and stability in the Asia-Pacific during the last four decades. The first was the role of the United States military in the Asia-Pacific as a global superpower acting as regional peacekeeper. The supremacy of the US military was further boosted by the collapse of the Soviet Union after 1991. The second factor was China's decision to pursue economic development as a primary strategic objective after 1980, recognizing that its military required substantial modernization over a long period of time. Under Senior Leader Deng Xiaoping, China concentrated on economic development and deliberately avoided provocative confrontation on most of its territorial claims in the East China Sea and South China Sea. Deng's long term plan was to focus on economic development while avoiding confrontation, and as the size of the economy grew, that would allow the incremental modernization of the Chinese armed forces.

After decades of relative stability, the geopolitical status quo set by Deng Xiaoping has begun to erode. The US has continued to maintain a strong military presence in the Asia-Pacific with major military bases in Japan and South Korea to deter any potential aggression. Nevertheless the very heavy US military commitment to the Middle East theatre over the last two decades, combined with the need for fiscal austerity after the global financial crisis, have combined to constrain the US military presence in the Asia-Pacific despite political commitments to an "Asian pivot".

In parallel with these constraints on the US military resources in the Asia-Pacific, China has experienced very rapid growth during the last 25 years that has propelled its economy from a total GDP value of USD 400 billion in 1991 to USD 10.3 trillion by 2014. This has completely altered the funding of China's armed forces, as the massive expansion in the total size of China's GDP has allowed the annual defence budget to grow rapidly over the past 25 years. This has fundamentally transformed the capabilities of China's armed forces as new military technology and modernization programmes have made China a military superpower.

This transformation of China's military capabilities may be gradually altering China's long-standing commitment to the single-minded pursuit of economic development while keeping its military might in the background, as Senior Leader Deng had advocated. Due to the tremendous changes in the capabilities of the Chinese armed forces, there may be a gradual policy shift taking place in Beijing to allow the greater use of China's military might as an instrument of foreign policy. The era of China's voluntary strategic restraint may already have ended.

China's economic policy in building stronger trade and investment ties with other Asia-Pacific nations has been extremely successful in binding other Asian nations closer to China and building better economic relations. On the other hand, China's increasingly aggressive military posture in handling its territorial disputes in the South China Sea and East China Sea appears to be working in completely the opposite direction to its economic policy, by making many Asia-Pacific nations increasingly fearful of China's territorial ambitions and of the future regional implications of its rising military capabilities.

Constructing a new security architecture in the Asia-Pacific

After more than a decade of futile efforts aimed at the creation of a regional forum for dialogue that would maintain peace and stability in the Asia-Pacific, it would appear that such a regional forum will no longer have a meaningful role to play in prevention of conflict in the near-term. It is also increasingly clear that China is not supportive of the efforts of other Asian countries to create such a regional framework for conflict prevention and resolution. A number of ASEAN countries had attempted to create such a forum under the auspices of ASEAN+Eight Defence Ministerial dialogues but China has stymied such efforts with its insistence that any conflicts should be resolved through bilateral negotiations rather than in multilateral forums.

While it is never too late to pursue the establishment of such a regional forum for working towards regional peace and stability, it is definitely too late to rely on such a forum to deal with the mounting crises in the South China Sea and East China Sea.

If regional tensions continue to escalate in the South China Sea and East China Sea, this could potentially create sufficient political momentum to trigger the formation of a closer military alliance of Asia-Pacific nations centred on the US to counterbalance China's military expansionism in the Asia-Pacific. This could be one possible strategic development that might evolve to prevent a near-term crisis in the Asia-Pacific, as a military solution that would counterbalance China's rising military power. The creation of a military coalition might be used by a grouping of Asia-Pacific nations to prevent such a crisis.

The prototype for this type of military coalition has already been well developed in Europe. The establishment of a permanent military force in the Asia-Pacific could be similar in structure to the North Atlantic Treaty Organisation (NATO), which acted as a Western European deterrent to the potential military power of the Soviet Union during the Cold War. (Though having spent some time on one of these NATO bases during the Cold War, I was never very convinced that there would have been much deterrence to a surprise attack on a Sunday morning after the wild excesses of a Saturday night. Then again the other side would probably also have been nursing serious hangovers from overdoses of vodka.)

In the event that such an Asia-Pacific security alliance is formed, it would necessarily have to be built around the US military at its very core. The framework for this US presence in the Asia-Pacific already exists, with major US military bases in Japan and South Korea, as well as other US bases on US territory in the Pacific. Therefore the backbone for an Asian military alliance structure is already in place. Other major Asia-Pacific nations that wished to join would most probably have to make clear military commitments to this new alliance, including being willing to permanently deploy military units that would be under the direct command of the Asian military alliance.

The US, Australia and Japan have already been taking steps to boost trilateral military co-operation. US Defense Secretary Ash Carter stated in 2015 that the US is working together with Japan and Australia to boost security co-operation in Southeast Asia with the US developing plans for a Southeast Asia maritime security initiative.

In the event that a more formal alliance structure were to develop, the first group of members of a new Asian military alliance, in addition to the US, would probably be those nations that are already trying to establish closer bilateral military ties with the US, including Philippines and Vietnam. It is likely that other ASEAN nations may also wish to join such a defensive military alliance, as it would certainly provide a tremendous boost to their own national security to be part of such a grouping.

Member countries of an Asia-Pacific alliance would probably be required to ante up credible force capabilities to be part of such an organization, such as leading edge fighter aircraft squadrons and modern naval ships to contribute meaningful capability to an Asian military alliance, in addition to ground forces capabilities. The macroeconomic circumstances of both the Philippines and Vietnam have improved considerably over the last five years, making such defence spending commitments increasingly realistic.

Member countries would likely agree at the outset what types of force contributions would be required from each of the member countries. Whatever the required contributions, members of such a security alliance may consider this to be a relatively low cost insurance policy for peace and stability in their region. The creation of a formal new military alliance may increasingly become a strategic imperative, since loose bilateral arrangements involving closer defence co-operation without formal treaty obligations provide little or no deterrence value and also do not create any kind of effective counterbalance to the large shifts in the regional military balance of power that are taking place in the Asia-Pacific.

Clearly creating such a military alliance will involve large costs, which will be difficult to finance for governments facing high government debt to GDP ratios and under tremendous pressure to reduce government debt. However the relative costs of creating such an organization to preserve the peace in the Asia-Pacific would need to be weighed up against the tremendous costs of a regional war. Seen in this context, the cost of an Asian military alliance would be a relatively low cost insurance policy for the future peace and security of the Asia-Pacific region.

In parallel with efforts to create such a military alliance in the Asia-Pacific, one of the greatest challenges for the Asia-Pacific region over the next two decades and beyond will be to find a framework for peaceful prevention and resolution of conflicts, so that the Asia-Pacific powers do not have to resort to military force as an instrument of diplomacy and statecraft. European powers attempted to do so for centuries, with disastrous results that triggered many wars, including two World Wars and the loss of tens of millions of lives. If Asia stumbles into a major conflict, it could destroy many years of economic development and undo much of the progress towards greater economic co-operation that has been achieved over the last three decades.

India's role in a new Asian security architecture

Since its independence in 1947, India has always maintained its foreign policy stance of being a non-aligned nation that is neutral. At present, it is hard to envisage India shifting from its long-held stance of neutrality, particularly since it is trying to build strong political and economic relations with China. However the geopolitical landscape is changing dramatically and it is not inevitable that India would maintain this posture in the medium to long-term.

India's long-standing reliance on Russian defence technology and equipment has served India well for many decades, but changing global alliances are also creating potential problems for India in this long-standing partnership. While Russia remains a strong strategic partner for India in defence equipment and technology, the problem that India faces is that Russia has been forced to undertake a pivot in foreign policy towards China due to the Ukraine crisis. With the US and EU placing sanctions on Russia, the political and economic pivot by Russia towards China may also extend more significantly towards defence technology in future. Therefore for reasons unrelated to bilateral Indo-Russian relations, India may eventually have to significantly diversify its military equipment and technology supply towards the US.

At the same time as Russia is pivoting towards China, China is also embarking on a major initiative to develop closer economic ties with Pakistan, with a planned investment of USD 46 billion in Pakistan's infrastructure that will include a USD 10 billion investment in transport infrastructure to create an advanced transportation corridor from China to the Indian Ocean port of Gwadar in Pakistan.

China is already a key military ally of Pakistan, providing advanced fighter jets as well as missile technology to Pakistan. China already has contracts to supply 110 JF-17 fighter jets to Pakistan, with the Pakistani Air Force eventually planning to have a total of 250 JF-17s. A deal is also being negotiated for China to supply eight conventional submarines to Pakistan, which could eventually carry nuclear missiles to enhance Pakistan's nuclear weapons capability.

This changing geopolitical landscape could eventually create the momentum for India to also become part of an Asian military alliance arrangement, since it would significantly enhance India's own security, as well as providing a potentially very large boost to the regional capability of such an Asian military alliance. Since the 1960s, India has always been able to count on Russian support in the event of a military crisis. However with Russia now increasingly locked in to a strengthening bilateral partnership with China, India may eventually wake up to the cold reality that it no longer has a superpower ally in the evolving geopolitical landscape. Moreover, if its main military rivals possess the same military technology, Indian armed forces would lack the edge of superior technology in a conflict.

Should such a scenario develop where India was willing to join an Asia-Pacific military coalition, the Indian navy and air force could offer significant capabilities towards any regional military co-operation initiative to stabilize the Indian Ocean. India has one aircraft carrier acquired from Russia that has been in service since mid-2014, with two Indian-built Vikrant-class carriers to be constructed over the next eight years. The first Vikrant-class carrier is due to enter service in 2018, with the second expected to be in service by 2023. Four stealth guided missile destroyers are also to be built over the next decade, in addition to two more Kolkata-class destroyers. Six French-designed submarines are to be built in India over the next five years, with another tender for six more submarines currently underway. This substantial Indian investment in building its naval capability means that India would be able to make a significant contribution to protecting shipping lanes in the Indian Ocean and helping to maintain regional stability.

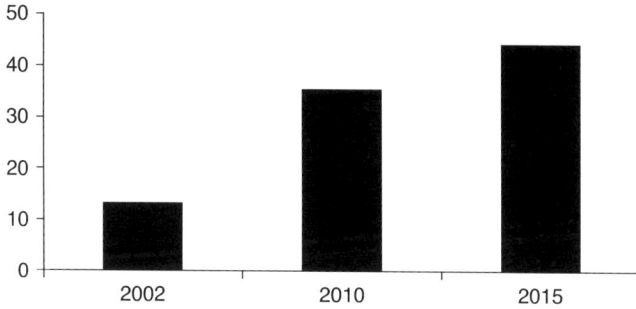

Figure 14.2   Indian defence budget, 2002–15 (USD billion)
Source: Indian Budget statistics.

Since the BJP victory in the 2014 general elections in India, defence spending has received significant increases in the BJP budgets. Even more importantly, the BJP government has accelerated tender processes and decision-making for new military equipment, with a flurry of new defence orders being approved by the government. There is a strong commitment from the BJP government to modernizing the Indian armed forces, as well as to giving much greater priority to the development of India's domestic defence industry, particularly to developing the capabilities of private sector Indian firms.

India's defence relations with the US have also gradually thawed after having remained in the deep freeze for many years after US President Nixon backed Pakistan during the India-Pakistan War in 1971, including by supplying fighter jets to Pakistan and sending a US carrier fleet towards the Bay of Bengal to put pressure on India. These manoeuvres were thwarted by the Russian Navy, which created the foundations for decades of very close Indian defence ties with Russia.

Defence co-operation between India and the US was gradually rebuilt during the administration of President George W. Bush, and Prime Minister Modi's strong push for modernization of the Indian armed forces has also been reflected in improving defence ties with the US. India and the US renewed their bilateral Defence Framework Agreement in 2015 for a ten year term, with plans for enhanced co-operation on key areas of defence technology including for jet engines and aircraft carriers.

India has already made significant purchases of US military aircraft, including 12 Lockheed C-130J Super Hercules and eight Boeing P-8I Poseidon maritime surveillance patrol aircraft.

Several major new acquisitions have also been negotiated, including the purchase of 22 Boeing Apache attack helicopters and 15 Chinook helicopters.

However in the critical area of advanced fighter jet technology, India is still primarily dependent on Russian fighter jets. The highly capable Sukhoi SU-30MKI forms the backbone of the Indian Air Force, with a total of 272 having been ordered to date. India is also participating in a joint project with Russia to develop a fifth generation stealth fighter, the Sukhoi PAK-FA/T-50, which is expected to enter production by 2017. India has also ordered 41 MIG-29K fighters for the Indian Navy, with deliveries having commenced in 2009. Indian negotiations for the acquisition of 126 Dassault Rafale fighter jets from France after a tender process and extensive evaluation of various other advanced fighter jets were scaled back after very protracted negotiations. India finally decided during 2015 to only acquire 36 Rafale fighters. Therefore at present the Indian Air Force is expected to remain mainly reliant on Russian fighter jet technology.

Mechanisms for conflict prevention and resolution

The creation of the Association of Southeast Asian Nations (ASEAN) in 1967 was important for establishing a framework for regular dialogue amongst leaders of Southeast Asian nations. Since its establishment, ASEAN has helped to defuse considerable political and military tensions amongst its initial five member countries, namely Indonesia, Malaysia, Singapore, Philippines and Thailand. With another five Southeast Asian countries having subsequently joined ASEAN, the role of the organization in fostering peace and stability in Southeast Asia has continued to become stronger.

Prior to the establishment of ASEAN, military tensions in Southeast Asia had reached a fever pitch during the early 1960s. Years of suspicion and mistrust between Indonesia and Malaysia occurred during the period of *Konfrontasi*, when Indonesian President Sukarno attempted to undermine plans for the creation of Malaysia by using Indonesian paramilitary forces. There were fears that Indonesia and Malaysia might be on the brink of a war that could have also involved British and Australian troops in support of Malaysia. CIA and US Defense Department analysis prepared in 1964 clearly shows how severe the military confrontation in Southeast Asia had become.

Recent Indonesian paramilitary landings in Malaya are part of Sukarno's long-range campaign to break up Malaysia and oust the British from their military bases there. The mission of the 150 or so infiltrators includes sabotage and terrorism, guerilla recruitment and training, and the setting up of guerilla redoubts in Malaya's jungles and highlands. Such raids will almost certainly continue. In the long run, through repeated infiltrations of this sort, Sukarno hopes to build up a revolutionary potential sufficient to overthrow the moderate, pro-Western government of Tunku Abdul Rahman.

Special National Intelligence Estimate prepared by Central Intelligence Agency and the intelligence organisations of the Departments of State and Defense, and the NSA. SNIE 54/55–64, Washington DC, September 16th 1964. Foreign Relations of the United States, 1964–1968, Volume XXVI, Document 75, US Department of State.

The period of *Konfrontasi* resulted in years of border conflict on the Malaysia-Indonesia borders, as joint Malaysian and British military forces fought to defend Malaysia's borders from incursions by Indonesian forces. It was the ousting of Sukarno from power in 1967 after Major General Suharto led the Indonesian armed forces in quashing an attempted communist coup in Indonesia that eventually created a more favourable political climate for the creation of ASEAN.

Since its initial creation, ASEAN has continued to play an important role in building co-operation amongst its ten member states, and ASEAN leaders have often intervened to prevent bilateral disputes between ASEAN nations. Given the tremendous political and military confrontations in Southeast Asia prior to the creation of ASEAN, the ASEAN model has been a remarkable success at helping to maintain peace and stability in Southeast Asia.

However the ASEAN model for conflict prevention and resolution has not yet led to the successful creation of a wider Asian forum to pursue similar objectives for the whole Asia-Pacific region, despite efforts by some ASEAN leaders to create such a forum.

In October 2010, ASEAN did establish a forum for dialogue amongst ASEAN defence ministers together with regional partners, which is called the ASEAN Defence Ministers Plus with Eight Dialogue Partners Forum (ADMM+). The eight dialogue partners are Australia, China, India, Japan, New Zealand, South Korea, Russia and the US.

However, this forum has clearly not been able to play a useful role so far in defusing tensions in the South China Sea or East

China Sea. What the forum has been able to do more successfully is to create expert working groups that have helped to build
up regional co-operation at the senior officials level in a number
of areas. So far these regional co-operation working groups are
taking place in five areas: maritime security, counter-terrorism,
military medicine, peacekeeping operations and humanitarian
assistance and disaster relief.

ASEAN as a regional grouping has also been unsuccessful in
attempting to negotiate with China on a peaceful framework
for resolution of territorial disputes in the South China Sea. In
2002, the foreign ministers of ASEAN and China agreed upon
a Declaration on the Conduct of Parties in the South China Sea.
This declaration was signed by the ASEAN foreign ministers
as well as by Wang Yi, then Special Envoy and Vice Minister of
Foreign Affairs for the People's Republic of China. This Code of
Conduct included in Article Five of the Declaration that:

> *"The Parties undertake to exercise self-restraint in the conduct of
> activities that would complicate or escalate disputes and affect peace
> and stability including, among others, refraining from action of
> inhabiting on the presently uninhabited islands, reefs, shoals, cays
> and other features and to handle their differences in a constructive
> manner."*
>
> Article 5, 2002 Declaration on the Conduct of Parties in the South China Sea,
> ASEAN Summit, Phnom Penh, Cambodia.

This Code of Conduct has since proven to be about as effective
as a European peace treaty in the 1930s, with China frenetically
engaged during 2014–15 in building structures and airfields on
various shoals and reefs in the South China Sea, and other countries with territorial claims also building some structures in the
South China Sea, albeit not on a comparable scale to the Chinese
construction initiatives. At the ASEAN Foreign Ministers Meeting
in Kuala Lumpur in August 2015, Chinese Foreign Minister Wang
Yi was reported to have said that China was in the process of ending its construction of structures and artificial islands in the South
China Sea, although only time will tell whether this is a temporary halt of construction or a more long-lasting cessation (Wall
Street Journal, "China Says It Is Ending Island-Building Effort",
6 August 2015).

With little meaningful progress to date in creating an effective
regional forum for peaceful conflict prevention and resolution,

the focus of new mechanisms for confidence-building may need to shift towards a sharper focus on confidence-building measures and protocols for avoidance of escalation of military incidents.

A key priority would be the strengthening of high-level communications between military leaders of Asia-Pacific nations, to ensure that well-rehearsed protocols are in place for reacting to a military incident to prevent escalation and to negotiate a peaceful solution.

While high level political efforts still need to be pursued by Asian political leaders to create a high level political forum that will have a central focus on conflict prevention and resolution, it seems unrealistic to expect such a forum to be effective in the near term. However in the long-term such a forum could have a very positive role to play, as the successful track record of ASEAN has demonstrated since its creation in 1967.

While future wars in the Asia-Pacific are not inevitable, there will need to be considerable political efforts amongst regional leaders to create mechanisms to prevent such conflicts occurring. After decades of rapid economic development in many Asian economies due to peace and stability, Asia-Pacific leaders cannot afford to be complacent and must urgently put in place regional solutions to prevent the devastating scourge of war again afflicting Asia.

Conclusion

Conflict or Co-operation in Asia?

Future Asia

Since the 1960s, the Asia-Pacific region has seen tremendous economic progress. In the last decade, the importance of the Asia-Pacific region in the global economy has also increased rapidly. The Asia-Pacific region's share of world GDP has risen from 23.7 per cent in 2005 to 32.6 per cent by 2015, which represents a very large increase within just one decade.

Much of this recent increase in the Asia-Pacific's share of world GDP is attributable to the rapid economic growth of China. The economic ascendancy of China has been one of the key megatrends transforming the Asia-Pacific economic and geopolitical landscape. Since 1980, the economic reforms in China have lifted an estimated 750 million Chinese out of absolute poverty. Moreover, the wider transmission effects of China's rapid economic growth have been felt across the Asia-Pacific region through rapid growth in regional trade and investment flows.

With China having entered the group of upper middle income nations, rising domestic demand is increasingly becoming a powerful growth engine that is boosting the entire Asia-Pacific region. China has become the largest economy in Asia since 2009, when it became larger than Japan in terms of total GDP measured in nominal USD terms.

However it is not the only new growth engine in Asia. India and ASEAN are also important new growth engines for the Asia-Pacific region, with their combined GDP in 2015 already larger than Japanese GDP. Therefore over the next two decades, the further economic ascendancy of China, India and ASEAN will create strong growth in intra-Asian trade and investment flows. For the rest of the world, the Asian economic ascendancy will be a positive force, with Asian emerging market consumer spending increasingly becoming the new driving force for world consumer demand growth. This will be particularly important for other developing countries in Africa, the Middle East and Latin America, as rising

Asian consumer demand creates rapid growth in South-South trade and investment flows.

Until the 1990s, much of East Asia was heavily dependent on export-led growth to the key markets of Europe and the US. However domestic demand within the Asia-Pacific region will become an increasingly important driver of regional economic growth over the next two decades. While the US and EU will remain important export markets for Asia, the Asia-Pacific will increasingly be powered by four growth engines of its own: China, Japan, India and ASEAN.

Closer economic integration has played an important role in this process. The Asia-Pacific region has been at the forefront of global efforts to promote trade liberalization over the last two decades, with a large number of bilateral free trade agreements and multilateral trade agreements having been concluded within the last decade. The ten member countries of ASEAN have also pursued regional trade and investment integration through the ASEAN Free Trade Agreement implemented in 2010 and the planned ASEAN Economic Community initiative for closer economic integration among the ASEAN member states.

In the financial sector, the Chiang Mai Initiative has strengthened financial co-operation among the ASEAN +3 member governments. The process of closer co-operation among Asian countries in finance has been accelerated by China's recent initiative to create the AIIB and Silk Road Fund to provide infrastructure finance for Asian developing countries. China's One Belt One Road initiative also has the potential to catalyse economic development in an economic corridor extending from China through Central Asia and ASEAN to link up with the Middle East and Europe.

The benefits of rapid economic growth and continued trade liberalization in the Asia-Pacific region have been reflected in key human development indicators, as poverty rates and malnutrition have continued to decline. According to the Food and Agricultural Organisation of the United Nations, the Asia-Pacific region has achieved the UN Millennium Goal hunger target of reducing by half between 1990 and 2015 the number of people who suffer from hunger. According to the FAO estimates, the share of the total Asia-Pacific population who suffer from hunger has been reduced from 24 per cent in 1990 to 12 per cent in 2015. This means that the total number of people suffering from hunger has declined by 236 million people since 1990.

However Asia still has tremendous economic and social challenges to confront. Despite the tremendous progress in reducing poverty and malnourishment, an estimated 490 million people are still malnourished in Asia, mainly concentrated in the Indian subcontinent.

Asia also faces considerable challenges from a wide range of other economic and social pressures, including rising urbanization and the continued growth of megacities, which is putting increasing pressure on infrastructure. Many Asian developing countries still face large shortages of essential infrastructure such as public hospitals, schools and colleges, electricity and safe water.

If Asian nations continue to strengthen their economic co-operation through trade liberalization and increasing intra-regional flows of exports and investment, then the economies of the Asian region will increasingly be powered by the four Asian growth engines of China, Japan, India and ASEAN. However the Japanese growth engine will become increasingly feeble due to the impact of demographic ageing, whereas the Indian growth engine is expected to become a much stronger growth driver for the region. On Asia's current economic growth trajectory, the total GDP of the Asia would double over the next decade, rising from around USD 23 trillion in 2015 to around USD 50 trillion by 2025. This would also result in a doubling of per capita GDP by 2025, delivering substantial improvements in living standards across the Asian region.

However after decades of strengthening economic co-operation across much of Asia, there are new risks emerging of escalating geopolitical tensions which could threaten the future economic ascendancy of the Asia-Pacific region and derail regional co-operation. Disputed territorial claims in the South China Sea between China and several ASEAN nations have resulted in escalating tensions among these nations, with the construction of buildings and infrastructure on some of the reefs and cays in the Spratly Islands having heightened fears of some form of accidental military incident that could trigger an escalating chain-reaction of events. Since 2012, tensions have also escalated in the East China Sea between China and Japan over disputed sovereign claims to the Senkaku/Diaoyu islets.

These disputes have already resulted in economic disruption of trade and commerce in East Asia. Anti-Japanese protests in China resulted in boycotts of purchases of Japanese goods, resulting in a sharp slump in sales of key Japanese products, notably autos, in

China. Tourism travel between the two nations was also heavily impacted. While economic relations have gradually normalized, the 2012 protests did have a serious negative impact on bilateral trade. Meanwhile the entry of a Chinese oil-drilling rig into an area whose sovereignty is in dispute between China and Vietnam triggered widespread rioting in Vietnam targeting assets owned mainland Chinese companies.

The escalation of geopolitical tensions in East Asia has created increasing alarm amongst Asian political leaders. There are already signs of an emerging arms race in East Asia, as countries attempt to modernize their armed forces to create a credible deterrent to rival sovereign territorial claims.

In order to ensure future peace and stability in the Asia-Pacific that will allow further economic development and rising living standards throughout the region, the escalation in geopolitical tensions will need to be defused.

In order to find a pathway towards building foundations for peace and co-operation in Asia, it is important to recognize the remarkable achievements made in Western Europe after the end of the Second World War. The widespread destruction and loss of millions of lives as a result of the military ambitions of the Nazi regime in Germany could easily have resulted in ongoing bitterness and hatred amongst European nations. However the leaders of France and Germany at the time, President Charles de Gaulle and West German Chancellor Konrad Adenauer, made a historic act of reconciliation at Notre Dame Cathedral in Reims in 1962, as they attended Mass together at the cathedral, which had itself been a site of bitter wartime fighting, and signed the Franco-German Friendship Treaty. Successive French and German political leaders have continued to reinforce this bilateral relationship with many other symbolic acts to ensure that the ties remain strong.

After centuries of wars between European nations that culminated in the horrific loss of life in World War One and World War Two, a climate of peace and stability has endured in Western Europe since the end of the Second World War.

It is time for Asia to also set aside historic differences over the Second World War that still create political tensions between Northeast Asian nations, to build a similar strong political foundation for peace and stability in the Asia-Pacific.

The ten member states of ASEAN have been at the forefront of building such a spirit of co-operation, using the ASEAN forums and conferences to strengthen political and economic ties. While there have been political differences and even border clashes between ASEAN member nations, the ASEAN grouping has become an important underpinning for political and economic co-operation in Southeast Asia.

In the last three decades, the economic co-operation among Asian nations has continued to strengthen, with a broadening network of free trade agreements among Asian countries as well as strong investment flows between Asian nations. Overall, Asia has been very successful at building regional economic co-operation and trade liberalization. The economic and financial architecture to support this regional co-operation is continuing to develop, with the establishment of the Chiang Mai Initiative in 2000 and the most recent steps led by China to establish a new development finance architecture for Asia with the creation of the AIIB.

The size of the Asian regional economy is set to double over the next decade, with per capita GDP levels also projected double over this timeframe. Such rapid growth will bring considerable further economic progress and economic development for many Asian developing countries, with the potential to lift hundreds of millions of Asians out of poverty.

However, a new security architecture needs to be built in Asia in order to ensure that the substantial economic achievements that many Asian nations have made over the last half century are not swept away by escalating geopolitical tensions that create a climate of fear and mistrust among Asian nations. If this is not done, the rapid modernization of Asian military forces that is currently underway could escalate, with risks increasing of accidental confrontations or military incidents that could escalate in unpredictable ways.

Therefore Asian political leaders will need to give a high priority to building a new security architecture for Asia that will create a framework of peace and co-operation in the Asia-Pacific region. The process of creating regional dialogue has already been underway through the ASEAN Defence Ministers Plus Eight Dialogue Partners forum (ADMM+) which was established in 2010 and the ASEAN Regional Forum (ARF).

However recent geopolitical developments since 2011 have made it apparent that these dialogue processes need to be reinforced further. This will require a strong political commitment by Asia-Pacific leaders for the creation of such a high-level dialogue process. If a strong infrastructure for high-level regional dialogue is built up for conflict prevention and resolution, this will help to better manage the geopolitical risks in the Asia-Pacific region.

If Asian governments can successfully build a new regional political architecture with a regular high-level political dialogue process to underpin regional peace and co-operation, it will help to ensure that Asia's economic development can continue without being disrupted by regional geopolitical tensions and potential conflicts.

In such a climate of regional peace and co-operation, the long-term prospects for the Asia-Pacific region remain favourable, with regional economic growth driven by the continued rise of China, India and ASEAN as key growth engines. The continued economic ascendancy of Asia has the potential to deliver substantial gains in living standards for the populations of Asia's low-income countries, creating a large Asian middle class that will boost the size of Asian consumer markets as well as lifting hundreds of millions of Asians out of poverty.

Bibliography

Addison, T. and Nino-Zarazua, M., "Redefining Poverty in China and India", *WIDER Angle Newsletter*. [United Nations University, UNU-WIDER] (Helsinki, January 2012)

Airbus, "Airbus in China", www.airbus.com

Airbus, "Worldwide Presence: Airbus in China", *Airbus.com*.

Associated Press, "Maine Lobster is Booming in China". (17 February 2015)

Bangkok Post, "New PTT Chief Will Have Work Cut Out Say Experts". (28 May 2015)

Bank of Japan, *"Outlook for Economic Activity and Prices"*. (Tokyo, 30 April 2014)

Bayly, C.A and Harper, T.N., *Forgotten Wars: The End of Britain's Asian Empire*. [Penguin] (London, 2008)

Bernanke, B., "Japanese Monetary Policy: A Case of Self-Induced Paralysis?", in Mikitani, R. and Posen, A., (eds), *Japan's Financial Crisis and Its Parallels to US Experience*, Special Report 13, Chapter 7. [Institute of International Economics] (Washington D.C., 2000)

Biswas, R., *Future Asia: The New Gold Rush in the East*. [Palgrave Macmillan] (London 2013)

Biswas, R., "Combating Organised Crime", in *Commonwealth Public Administration Reform 2004*, Part Two: Democracy and Security, Commonwealth Secretariat. [The Stationery Office] (London, 2004)

Blake, R., *Jardine Matheson: Traders of the Far East*. [Weidenfeld & Nicolson] (London, 1999)

Blood, P., ed. *Pakistan: A Country Study*. [GPO for the Library of Congress] (Washington, D.C., 1994)

Boeing. *Current Market Outlook 2014–2033*. [Boeing] (Seattle, 2014)

CDKN (Climate and Development Knowledge Network), *The IPCC's Fifth Assessment Report: What's in It for South Asia?* [Overseas Development Institute] (London, 2014)

Clapper, J.R., *Worldwide Threat Assessment of the US Intelligence Community*, Statement for the Record, US Senate Armed Services Committee. (Washington D.C., 11 February 2014)

Clinton, B., *My Life*. [Hutchinson] (New York, 2004)

Clutterbuck, R., *The Long, Long War: The Emergency in Malaya 1948–60*. [Cassel] (London, 1966)

CNN-IBN, *Statement of Accused David Coleman Headley*. Transcript, National Investigation Agency, Government of India. (30 May 2011)

Cohan, W.D., *The Last Tycoons*. [Penguin Books] (London, 2008)

Dekle, R. and Kletzer, K., *Deposit Insurance, Regulatory Forbearance and Economic Growth: Implications for the Japanese Banking Crisis*, Working Paper 2004–26. [Federal Reserve Bank of San Francisco] (San Francisco, 2004)

Dikotter, F., *Mao's Great Famine*. [Bloomsbury] (London, 2010)

Enright, M J., Hoffmann W. J., *China into the Future: Making Sense of the World's Dynamic Economy*. [Wiley] (Singapore, 2008)

European Commission, "China: Fighting the Consequences of Very Loose Monetary Policies" in *European Economic Forecast Spring 2010*, European Economy Vol. 2. [Directorate-General for Economic and Financial Affairs] (Brussels, 2010)

European Commission, *Impact Assessment Report on EU-Japan Trade Relations*, Commission Staff Working Document. [European Commission] (Brussels, 18 July 2012)

FAO (Food and Agricultural Organisation of the United Nations), *Regional Overview of Food Insecurity: Towards a Food Secure Asia and the Pacific*. [FAO] (Bangkok, 2015)

Farrell, B.P., *The Defense and Fall of Singapore 1940–42*. [Tempus Publishing] (Stroud, 2005)

Ferguson, N., *Civilization: The West and the Rest*. [Allen Lane] (London, 2011)

Feyzioglu, T., Skaarup, M. and Syed, M., "Addressing Korea's Long-term Fiscal Challenges", *IMF Working Paper*, WP/08/27. [IMF] (Washington D.C., 2008)

Financial Express (Dhaka), "3.5 Million Live in Dhaka Slums". (25 February 2013)

Galbraith, J.K., *A Short History of Financial Euphoria*. [Penguin] (New York, 1993)

Ganapathy, N. and Lian, K.F., "Policing Minority Street Corner Gangs in Singapore: A View from the Street", *Policing and Society*, Vol. 12, No. 2. [Routledge] (2002)

Geithner, T.F., *Stress Test: Reflections on Financial Crises*. [Random House] (London, 2014)

Giegerich, B., *Europe and Global Security*. [Routledge] (Oxon, 2010)

Greenspan, A., *The Age of Turbulence: Adventures in a New World*. [Penguin] (New York, 2007)

Griffith-Jones, S., "A BRICS Development Bank: A Dream Coming True?", *UNCTAD Discussion Paper*, No. 215. [UNCTAD] (Geneva, March 2014)

Hall, J.W., *Japan: From Prehistory to Modern Times*. [Tuttle Publishing] (Germany, 1968)

Hart, A.F. and Jones, B.D., "How Do Rising Powers Rise?", *Survival: Global Politics and Strategy*, Vol. 52 No.6. [IISS] (December 2010–January 2011)

Hill, P., "Heisei Yakuza: Burst Bubble and Botaiho", *Social Science Japan Journal*, Vol. 6, No. 1. (April 2003)

Hindustan Times, "MCD Test Finds Bacteria in Delhi's Drinking Water". (25 March 2011)

Hobsbawm, E.J., *Industry and Empire*. [Pelican Books] (Great Britain, 1968)

Holslag, J., *Trapped Giant: China's Military Rise*. IISS. [Routledge] (Oxon, 2010)

Howard, J., *Lazarus Rising*. [Harper Collins] (Australia, 2010)

Hughes, J., *The End of Sukarno. A Coup That Misfired: A Purge That Ran Wild*. [Archipelago Press] (New York, 1967)

Huq, S. and Alam, M., "Flood Management and Vulnerability of Dhaka City", in Kreimer, A., Arnold and Carlin, A., (eds), *Building Safer Cities: The Future of Disaster Risk*, Disaster Risk Management Series No. 3, Chapter 9. [World Bank Disaster Management Facility] (Washington D.C., 2003)

Huawei Investment and Holding Co. Ltd, 2014 Annual Report

IMF, "Where Are We Headed? Perspectives on Potential Output", *IMF World Economic Outlook*. [IMF] (Washington D.C., April 2015)

IMF, *Republic of Korea, 2013 Article IV Consultation, Staff Report and Statement of the Executive Director,* Press Release and Statement by the Executive Director. [IMF] (Washington D.C., April 2014)

IMF, "People's Republic of China 2011 Article IV Consultation", *IMF Country Report,* No. 11/192. [IMF] (Washington D.C., July 2011)

IMF, Global Financial Stability Report: Navigating Monetary Policy Challenges and Managing Risks, [IMF] (Washington D.C., April 2015)

Indonesia: The First 50 Years, 1945–1995. [Archipelago Press] (New York, 1995)

Jalan, B., *India's Politics: A View from the Back Bench.* [Penguin & Viking] (New Delhi, 2007)

James, L..., *Raj: The Making of British India.* [Abacus] (London, 1998)

Jordan, D.P., *Napoleon and the Revolution.* [Palgrave Macmillan] (London, 2012)

Kissinger, H., *On China.* [Penguin Press] (New York, 2011)

Kissinger, H., *Power Shifts.* Survival, Vol. 52, No. 6, December 2010 – January 2011, International Institute for Strategic Studies [Routledge Journals] (London, 2011)

Krugman, P., *The Return of Depression Economics and the Crisis of 2008.* [W.W. Norton] (New York, 2009)

Lee, K.Y., *From Third World to First: The Singapore Story: 1965–2000.* [Times Media Private] (Singapore, 2000)

LVMH Group, "LVMH 2014 Annual Report"

Lyman R., *Slim, Master of War: Burma and the Birth of Modern Warfare.* [Robinson] (London, 2004)

Magnus, G., *Uprising: Will Emerging Markets Shape or Shake the World Economy?* [Wiley] (Chichester, 2011)

Mahbubani K., *The New Asian Hemisphere.* [Public Affairs], (New York, 2008)

Mahbubani, K., *The Great Convergence: Asia, The West, and the Logic of One World.* [Public Affairs] (New York, 2013)

Masuda, H., Discuss Japan , *The Death of Regional Cities.* No. 18, Japan Foreign Policy Forum, 20th January 2014 [Ministry of Foreign Affairs of Japan], (Tokyo, 2014)

Mikitani, R. and Posen, A., (eds), *Japan's Financial Crisis and Its Parallels to US Experience.* Special Report 13. [Institute of International Economics] (Washington D.C., 2000)

Moller, J.O., *How Asia Can Shape the World: From the Era of Plenty to the Era of Scarcities.* [ISEAS Publishing] (Singapore, 2011)

Moody's Investors Service, Credit Analysis, *"IBRD (World Bank)".* (31 January 2014)

Moscow Times, "Russian Central Bank Increases Capital Flight Estimate by USD 38 Billion". (10 November 2014)

Myint, H., *Economic Theory and the Underdeveloped Countries.* [Oxford] (London 1971)

Nakaso, H., "The Financial Crisis in Japan during the 1990s: How the Bank of Japan Responded and Lessons Learned", *BIS Papers,* No. 6. [Bank for International Settlements] (Basel, October 2001)

National Institute of Population and Social Security Research, *Population Projection for Japan 2011–2060.* . [National Institute of Population and Social Security Research] (Tokyo, January 2012)

OCBC Bank, Annual Report 2014

OECD, "Growth Prospects and Fiscal Requirements Over the Long Term", *OECD Economic Outlook*, Chapter Four, Vol. 2014/1. [OECD] (Paris, 2014)

Office of the Director of National Intelligence, "Global Water Security", *Intelligence Community Assessment*, ICA 2012–08. [Defense Intelligence Agency] (Washington, D.C., February 2012)

Office of the Director of National Intelligence, *National Intelligence Strategy of the United States of America*. [DNI] (Washington, D.C., 2014)

Olinto, P., Beegle K., Sobrado, C., Uematsu, H., "The State of the Poor: Where are the Poor, Where is Extreme Poverty Harder to End, and What is the Current Profile of the World's Poor?", *Economic Premise*, No. 125. [World Bank] (Washington D.C., October 2013)

Overtveldt J.V., *Bernanke's Test: Ben Bernanke, Alan Greenspan and the Drama of the Central Banker*. [Agate] (Chicago, 2009)

Pangestu, M. and Habir, M., "The Boom, Bust and Restructuring of Indonesian Banks", *IMF Working Paper*, WP/02/66. [IMF] (Washington, D.C., 2002)

Pargal, S. and Banerjee, S.G., "More Power to India: The Challenge of Distribution", *Directions in Development*. [World Bank] (Washington, D.C., 2014)

Poston, D.L., Alnuaimi, W.S.K. and Li, Z., "The Muslim Minority Nationalities of China: Towards Separatism or Assimilation?", poster presented at the Population Association of America Annual Meeting. [Princeton University] (Princeton, 2010)

Prestowitz, C., *Three Billion New Capitalists: The Great Shift of Wealth and Power to the East*. [Basic Books] (New York, 2005)

Prime Minister's Office, Republic of Singapore, *A Sustainable Population for a Dynamic Singapore: Population White Paper*. [National Population and Talent Division, Prime Minister's Office] (Singapore, 2013)

Reinhart, C.M. and Rogoff, K.S., *This Time is Different: Eight Centuries of Financial Folly*. [Princeton University Press] (Princeton, 2009)

Reuters News, "Suspected Uighurs Rescued from Thai Trafficking Camp". (14 March 2014)

Reuters News, "Global Forex Reserves Poised to Record First Quarterly Drop since 2008/09". (17 December 2014)

Roach, S.S., *The Next Asia: Opportunities and Challenges For a New Globalization*. [Wiley] (New Jersey, 2009)

Rogers, J., *Investment Biker: Around the World with Jim Rogers*. [Wiley] (Chichester, 2000)

Rostow W.W., *The Stages of Economic Growth: A Non-Communist Manifesto*. [Cambridge University Press] (London, 1960)

Sachs, J. andBono, *The End of Poverty: How We Can Make It Happen in Our Lifetime*. [Penguin] (London, New York, 2005)

Sanyal, S., *The Indian Renaissance: India's Rise After a Thousand Years of Decline*. [Penguin & Viking] (New Delhi, 2008)

Scott-Clark, C. and Levy, A., *The Siege*. [Penguin] (London, 2014)

Seymour, W., *British Special Forces*. [Grafton Books] (London 1986)

Smith, C., *Singapore Burning: Heroism and Surrender in World War II*. [Penguin] (London, 2005)

Soros, G., *The Crash of 2008 and What It Means*. [Perseus Books Group] (New York, 2008)

Soros, G., *The New Paradigm for Financial Markets*. [Public Affairs] (New York, 2008)

Standard and Poor's Rating Services, Ratings Direct, "International Bank for Reconstruction and Development". [McGraw Hill Financial] (New York, April 2014)

Taleb, N. N., *Fooled by Randomness: The Hidden Role of Chance in Life and in the Markets*. [Penguin] (London, 2004)

Tariq, A., *The Nehrus and the Gandhis*. [Picador] (London, 1985)

Thant, Myint-U, *Where China Meets India: Burma and the New Crossroads of Asia*. [Faber and Faber] (London, 2011)

Thompson, J., *Ready for Anything: The Parachute Regiment at War*. [Fontana] (London, 1990)

Times of India, "Delhi Water Crisis Grows as Haryana Cuts Supply". (14 June 2012)

Transparency International, *Corruption Perceptions Index 2014*. [Transparency International] (Berlin, 2014)

United Nations Department of Economic and Social Affairs, *World Urbanisation Prospects, the 2014 Revision*, Methodology Working Paper No. ESA/P/WP.238. [United Nations Department of Economic and Social Affairs, Population Division] (New York, 2014)

UNDP (United Nations Development Program), "Sustaining Human Progress: Reducing Vulnerabilities and Building Resilience", *Human Development Report 2014*. [United Nations] (New York, 2014)

UNODC (United Nations Office on Drugs and Crime), *Transnational Organised Crime in East Asia and the Pacific: A Threat Assessment*. [UNODC] (Bangkok, April 2013)

UNWTO (United Nations World Tourism Organization), "China the New Number One Tourism Source Market in the World", Press Release 13020. [UN World Tourism Organization] (Madrid, 4 April 2013).

US Department of Defense, *Annual Report to Congress: Military and Security Developments Involving the People's Republic of China 2012*. [Office of the Secretary of Defense] (Washington, D.C., May 2012)

US Department of Defense, *Annual Report to Congress: Military and Security Developments Involving the People's Republic of China 2014*. [Office of the Secretary of Defense] (Washington, D.C., April 2014)

US Department of Justice, Office of Public Affairs, "David Coleman Headley Sentenced to 35 Years in Prison for Role in India and Denmark Terror Plots", Press Release. [USDOJ] (Washington, D.C., 24 January 2013)

Vogel, E., *Japan as Number One*. [Harvard University Press] (Cambridge, MA, 1979)

Von Tunzelmann, A., *Indian Summer: The Secret History of the End of An Empire*. [Pocket Books] (London, 2007)

Wall Street Journal, "Chinese Steel Consumption Falls". (29 January 2015)

Warren, A., *Singapore 1942: Britain's Greatest Defeat*. [Talisman] (London, 2002)

Webster, D., *The Burma Road*. [Pan Books] (New York, 2003)

Welsh, F., *A History of Hong Kong*. [Harper-Collins] (London, 1994)

Williams, R., Rassenfosse, G., Jensen, P. and Marginson, S., *U21 Ranking of Higher Education Systems 2013*. [Melbourne Institute of Applied Economic and Social Research, University of Melbourne] (Melbourne, 2013)

World Bank, "Poverty Overview". [World Bank] (Washington D.C., 6 April 2015)

World Bank News, "The National Ganga River Basin Project". [World Bank] (Washington D.C., 23 March 2015)

World Bank Press Release, "India: Green Growth is Necessary and Affordable for India, Says New World Bank Report". [World Bank] (Washington D.C., 17 July 2013)

WHO (World Health Organization), "Ambient (Outdoor) Air Pollution in Cities Database". [WHO] (Geneva, May 2014)

WHO (World Health Organization), "Air Quality Deteriorating in Many of the World's Cities", Press Release. [WHO] (Geneva, 7 May 2014)

Xi, Jinping, *The Governance of China*. [Foreign Languages Press] (Beijing, 2014)

Yoong, L.Y., *ASEAN Matters*. [World Scientific Publishing Co.] (Singapore, 2011)

Index

Printed and bound in the United States of America